PLEASURES EVERMORE

The Life-Changing Power of Enjoying God

SAM STORMS

NAVPRESS

BRINGING TRUTH TO LIFE

P.O. Box 35001, Colorado Springs, Colorado 80935

OUR GUARANTEE TO YOU

We believe so strongly in the message of our books that we are making this quality guarantee to you. If for any reason you are disappointed with the content of this book, return the title page to us with your name and address and we will refund to you the list price of the book. To help us serve you better, please briefly describe why you were disappointed. Mail your refund request to: NavPress, P.O. Box 35002, Colorado Springs, CO 80935.

The Navigators is an international Christian organization. Our mission is to reach, disciple, and equip people to know Christ and to make Him known through successive generations. We envision multitudes of diverse people in the United States and every other nation who have a passionate love for Christ, live a lifestyle of sharing Christ's love, and multiply spiritual laborers among those without Christ.

NavPress is the publishing ministry of The Navigators. NavPress publications help believers learn biblical truth and apply what they learn to their lives and ministries. Our mission is to stimulate spiritual formation among our readers.

© 2000 by Sam Storms
All rights reserved. No part of this publication may be reproduced in any form without written permission from NavPress, P.O. Box 35001, Colorado Springs, CO 80935. www.navpress.com

ISBN 1-57683-188-4

Cover photo by Hans Stand/Tony Stone Images
Cover design by Dan Jamison
Creative Team: Steve Webb, David Owen, Terry Behimer

Some of the anecdotal illustrations in this book are true to life and are included with the permission of the persons involved. All other illustrations are composites of real situations, and any resemblance to people living or dead is coincidental.

Unless otherwise identified, all Scripture quotations in this publication are taken from the *New American Standard Bible* (NASB), © The Lockman Foundation 1960, 1962, 1963, 1968, 1971, 1972, 1973, 1975, 1977; Other versions used include: *HOLY BIBLE: NEW INTERNATIONAL VERSION* ® (NIV®). Copyright © 1973, 1978, 1984 by International Bible Society. Used by permission of Zondervan Publishing House. All rights reserved. the *Revised Standard Version Bible* (RSV), copyright 1946, 1952, 1971, by the Division of Christian Education of the National Council of the Churches of Christ in the USA, used by permission, all rights reserved.

Printed in the United States of America

1 2 3 4 5 6 7 8 9 10 / 03 02 01 00

CIP Data applied for

Lovingly dedicated to
Melanie and Joanna
(Psalm 127:3-5)
and
Ann
(Proverbs 31:10)

Contents

Foreword

By Dr. Larry Crabb

Oscar Wilde was sentenced to prison for committing, as the old English court put it, "acts of gross indecency."

Wilde was an avowed aestheticist, one who lived to indulge his passion for beauty. Rules were justifiably broken if they interfered with the experience of pleasure. That was his philosophy. Wherever he found beauty, wherever he discovered an opportunity to bring a sense of pleasure into his life, he indulged himself.

For Wilde, those opportunities included the company of young men. Victorian law referred to the homosexual activity he enjoyed with those men as "gross indecencies." Those who stood against him in court raised high the banner of morality, a morality that properly declared violations of lawful decency as wrong. The choice facing citizens in that culture was either to pursue pleasure where you found it or to abandon the pursuit of pleasure in favor of doing what was right.

It never seemed to occur to advocates of either view that doing right and pursuing pleasure might not be incompatible. Many of us still think there is a choice to be made between these supposed contradictions.

The conservative church has long stood on the side of the do-righters and condemned those who long to experience pleasure as sensualists given over to their base nature.

"Hedonists!" we sneer. "Pleasure-seeking, narcissistic selfists who care nothing for the holy law of God and live only for immediate feel-good sensations."

As I think about Oscar Wilde's dilemma and the typical response of the Christian world, I find myself wondering what Jonathan Edwards might have said had he been asked to testify at Wilde's trial. Would he have begun by holding his Bible high, opening to Paul's letter to the Romans, and censorially quoting, "God gave them over to shameful lusts. They abandoned natural relations with women and were inflamed with lust for one another?"

Would he have walked over to the defendant and, again quoting Paul, have declared, "Men committed indecent acts with other men and received in themselves the due penalty of their perversion?"

I think so. After all, these are words inspired by God. Homosexual activity *is* a gross indecency. Edwards believed the Bible. He believed that God's standards are moral absolutes and that all violations are sin.

But I don't think he would have stopped there. I don't think he would have then returned to his seat in the courtroom, enjoying the approving nods of the pharisees whose self-righteousness by then would have been strengthened by the belief that *they* were not guilty of any gross indecency. I envision Edwards turning to the judge and saying, "If it please the court, I must say more."

And then, to the irate bewilderment of the prosecutors, I think he might have said something like this: "Although I believe Oscar Wilde's behavior is morally wrong and grossly indecent, I do *not* quarrel with his desire to pursue pleasure. I quarrel with his understanding of where pleasure is to be found.

"Real pleasure, the only kind that satisfies the human soul and, at the same time, transforms a man into a marvelously decent person, is the sheer pleasure of living for the glory of God. It's what each of us was designed to do. As the eagle finds pleasure in soaring through the heights, so a person finds pleasure in knowing God and doing God's will. There is no choice to be made between the pursuit of true pleasure and obedience to a holy God. They are one path. Oscar Wilde's greatest sin is unbelief. He does not believe there are pleasures evermore at the right hand of God."

Perhaps more than ever, we need to hear the wisdom of Jonathan Edwards. In our postmodern world, we have even more sharply separated the choice to become whole through authentic living from the choice to buckle under imposed rules. Too many Christians struggle against *sinful* passions (which we should do) by running away from *all* passions (which we shouldn't do). We're like children who grudgingly eat our spinach of obedience, hoping someday we'll receive a cookie.

But the battle to *resist* pleasure and instead do what's right isn't the core battle Christianity introduces into our lives. The core battle is to believe that the Eternal Community of God is a party that we all long to attend and to discover and freely indulge our deepest passions for their kind of fun.

Sam Storms stands on the shoulders of John Piper who stands on the shoulders of Jonathan Edwards who, perhaps more than most theologians, stands on the shoulders of the writers of Scripture who declare that God's command to be holy is His invitation to a party.

Sam goes so far as to say that the only hope for experiencing meaningful victory over sin is to live for a greater pleasure. There are pleasures in sin for a season. But they turn sour, always, eventually. There are true pleasures in holiness for a lifetime. They never turn sour.

We are invited in this book to become Christian hedonists, aesthetics who yield ourselves fully to the pursuit of the pleasure available in the beauty of God, in all that He is, in all that He does, and in all that He commands.

If Sam's thoughtful, disarmingly simple, and powerfully biblical presentation of the Christian life had been understood by Oscar Wilde, he would have remained a passionate lover of beauty and all its pleasures by repenting of homosexuality and becoming an ardent follower of Jesus Christ.

If we digest the message of this book, we will find ourselves standing in the company of pleasure seekers who have discovered that godly living is the friend, not the enemy, of all true pleasure.

This volume belongs on the shelf of every counselor who longs to lead people into freedom and joy, of every pastor who desires to persuade his people that satisfaction and holiness are not alternatives between which we must choose, of every person who cannot escape the fervent wish to be profoundly happy and who suspects that happiness is somehow tied to living for God's glory.

I read Sam's words as God's invitation to come to His party, where everyone learns that goodness and joy belong together. To party animals everywhere, I say, leave the pigpen behind, become party *humans,* and prepare yourselves for the greatest party ever held.

This book will help. It will help a lot.

Acknowledgments

Aside from that day in 1960 when I trusted Jesus Christ as my Lord and Savior, the most important thing I ever did in life, at least in terms of my spiritual development, was to read, in 1986, *Desiring God* by John Piper. Reading that book awakened in me the stunning realization that I am a hedonist. It revealed to me, for the first time, what no sermon I had heard or movie I had watched or book I had read had been able to reveal. I discovered, much to my soul's delight, that I am in the core of my being a hedonist. I am driven by the pursuit of pleasure.

But because of what had occurred in my heart twenty-six years earlier, I am not merely a hedonist—I am a Christian hedonist. You may not know this, but if you are born again, so are you. Better still, so is God!

"I beg your pardon! God is a hedonist?"

He most certainly is. Although it wouldn't be appropriate to say that God is a "Christian," His desire for pleasure is the only thing that accounts for there being "Christians." What this means, in a nutshell, is that the aim of God in all He does is His delight in my delight in Him. If nothing else, I hope this statement drives you to read Piper's book. In fact, if you can only read one book, let it be his rather than mine.

This book is not primarily an exposition or defense of Christian Hedonism. Rather, it is an attempt to cast a vision for the pursuit of holiness based on the biblical foundation of Christian Hedonism. If Christian Hedonism is a valid concept, as I believe it is, what implications does this carry for our struggle with sin and our deep longing to be conformed to the image of Christ Jesus? This book is an attempt to answer that question.

John Piper wrote in his book *Future Grace* (Multnomah) a chapter entitled "The Debt I Owe to Jonathan Edwards." I should write a chapter entitled "The Debt I Owe to Them Both!" Whereas I don't want either of them held accountable for mistakes in my thinking, the fact is that I am deeply indebted to Edwards and Piper for what you are about to read. Of course, all of us believe that ultimately this viewpoint comes from God via the Holy Scriptures. Whether that be true remains for you to judge.

You will hear much about Jonathan Edwards in the pages that follow. I regard it as an indescribable privilege (and pleasure!) to stand on the theological shoulders of this man whom I regard as the greatest thinker since the apostle Paul. My initial exposure to Edwards came in 1973 during my first semester of seminary studies. I undertook an independent readings course in the theology of Edwards and began, but by no means ended, with what most scholars regard as his most important and complex work, *The Freedom of the Will*. I eventually wrote my master's thesis (1977) on that volume and my doctoral dissertation (1984) on his treatment of Original Sin (subsequently published by University Press of America).

Simply put, if I am but a faint echo of Edwards and Piper, so long as the echo is accurate, I will regard what I have done as a success. I could hardly ask for more of you than that you turn to Edwards and Piper after reading my book and drink of the river from which this small spring has emerged.

There are others whose contribution is of a different sort. I want to thank the entire pastoral team of Metro Christian Fellowship in

Kansas City for their constant support and encouragement, but most of all for their relentless passion for Jesus. Thanks to all of you for your love and friendship.

I want to express my deep appreciation to my editor, Steve Webb, for his excellent work in making this a better book. Thanks, Steve, for believing in this project and devoting your time and energy to making it happen!

A special word of thanks goes to several women who have exercised an extraordinary measure of influence in my life: First and foremost my mother, Tsianina Storms, my sister, Betty Jane Cawley, and my niece, Kristen Trantham, without whose prayers I wouldn't have made it this far. What a blessing to have been raised in a home with such godly women. I love you.

I also thank my mother-in-law, Betty Mount, whose love and affirmation have meant so much to me. And I am deeply grateful for Nancy Heche and Abigail Tinnerello whose courage and perseverance in the midst of indescribable testing has encouraged me beyond words. Your friendship means more to me than you will ever know.

Finally, thanks to the three to whom this book is dedicated: Ann, Melanie, and Joanna. Talk about pleasure!

CHAPTER ONE

Falling in Love

THE KEY TO HOLINESS IS FALLING IN LOVE.

I got married in the summer of 1972. My wife, Ann, is still with me twenty-eight years later. Although we had a beautiful wedding, our honeymoon was necessarily brief. Only three days. We both returned to work in Norman, Oklahoma, where we were preparing for our senior year at the University of Oklahoma. She worked evenings in the emergency room of a local hospital. I was headwaiter at a steak restaurant in town. My routine on Friday night was simple. After work, we employees would count our tip money, drive to the restaurant owner's home, and play poker till dawn. It never crossed my mind to tell Ann about this routine. After all, I was only twenty-one. About midnight on one of those Fridays, I called her to let her know that I would be home "soon." I assumed she would go to bed, just happy that I was considerate enough to call at all. Remember that I was only twenty-one. What I didn't count on was her taking me literally. To me, "soon" meant "after the Friday night poker game." You know, somewhere around 5:00 or 6:00 A.M. I figured I'd slip into the apartment and into bed without her waking up. If she did, the news that I'd won would be enough to overcome any anger she might feel. But, to her, "soon" meant fifteen minutes, thirty at the outside. It's amazing how literal newly wed women can be. Oh well.

At 4:00 A.M., I tiptoed in as quietly as I could. I was feeling fairly proud of myself for leaving my buddies as early as I did. I had told them, "I just got married, guys. I've got a responsibility to my wife, you know." Feeling gallant, I crept into the living room of our apartment only to run headlong into my bride of three weeks. Tears were streaming down her face, which was very red. "Where have you been?" she shouted in disbelief. "I've been driving all over town since 2:00 A.M. trying to find you. You promised you'd be home 'soon' (there's that word again). I hate you! I hate you!" The words hurt more than her fists, which by now were pounding against my chest.

I never played poker again. It was an easy decision. I didn't care that the guys at work snickered under their breath. Their snide, cutting remarks fell on deaf ears. Their demands that I give them a chance to win their money back had no effect. Nothing could convince me to play again. Not the prospect of winning. Not the avoidance of mockery. Nothing. I quit gambling. Why?

I can think of a lot of reasons, none of which is exactly the right one. I could have said No to gambling because we were relatively poor and the chances of losing were as high as winning. We really couldn't afford for me to lose the tips from the best paying night of the week. But that didn't factor into my decision.

I'd also heard that gambling could become an addiction. Some said it was more powerful and harder to break than dependence on drugs. I probably believed them, but I was not fazed by either this or the potential for getting too deeply involved with the wrong kind of people. There were, after all, some pretty unsavory characters who started showing up to join the game. But I never gave them a second thought. I knew that gambling was illegal. I considered myself a fairly "moral" person. But rationalizing your way around the law comes easily when you're twenty-one. So why did I quit?

I quit because I loved my wife. I quit because I had found in her a thrill and a joy that the biggest, richest pot in the world couldn't rival. Winning was a rush. I'd be lying if I didn't admit that gambling was exciting. But being with Ann was better! Being in her presence was incomparably superior. The joy I felt in feeling her delight in me and my delight in her was worth any sacrifice I might have to make. As appealing as gambling might be (even when I won), it couldn't hold a candle to Ann. The allure of her countenance. The warmth of her embrace. The sound of her voice. My heart was captivated. My mind was entranced. Being with her and she with me! Gambling didn't stand a chance. Ann was a royal flush and won hands down. In the final analysis, I found the strength to quit gambling because I had fallen in love.

That's what this book is all about. It's not like a mystery novel. You don't have to wait till the final chapter to find out if it was the butler who killed Professor Plum with a candlestick. I'm revealing the plot up front. The key to holiness is falling in love . . . with Jesus.

KNOWING HOW VERSUS KNOWING WHAT

Few Christians wrestle or struggle to know what God wants them to do. When it comes to questions of right and wrong, good and evil, what is sin and what isn't, most Christians know their moral obligation. Even those with but a cursory knowledge of the Bible are aware that they're not supposed to drink to excess. They know that God prohibits stealing. They know that He wants them to be generous with their money and possessions. They know what it is that pleases God.

We could also expand this to a corporate level. We know what God wants of us as a church, as the body of Christ. We know He wants us to touch the poor and to evangelize the lost and to provide for the study of His Word and times for worship.

But knowing *what* isn't the problem. Our problem is in knowing *how*. Certainly there are grey areas on which the Bible does not speak and where moral ambiguity exists. But, aside from that, our principal struggle is how. How do I give generously when my heart is held captive to greed and materialism? What, if anything, can sever the root of joy in money and release my soul from a sinful reliance on what I mistakenly believe money can do for me? How do I love irritating people when I can't stand the sight of them? How do I walk in sexual purity when my flesh rages with lust and sinful passion? How do I serve in children's ministry when I don't want to be bothered? How do I resist when tempted to lie, especially when being less than truthful will win a promotion or enhance my reputation?

The apostle Paul articulated a frustration we all share when he said, "that which I am doing, I do not understand; for I am not practicing what I would like to do, but I am doing the very thing I hate. . . . For the good that I wish, I do not do; but I practice the very evil that I do not wish" (Romans 7:15,19). We know what Paul means. There are times when we feel like spiritual schizophrenics, as if we lived in two minds, desperately wanting one thing while doing yet another. The bewilderment can be overwhelming.

But worse than the confusion is the crippling weight of guilt as we repeat over and again the same sinful mistakes. Before long, we're convinced that living even a moderately successful Christian life is hopeless. Frustration gives way to despair. "Will it ever change? Will I ever change?" This agonizing cry is what leads me to focus on the internal spiritual drive, the energy, if you will, that enables us to do what we know all too well God wants us to do. My focus is on how we as Christians might find the strength to refuse what our flesh finds so appealing.

Not only do I live among and minister to people who are crying for change, I am one of those people. All of us ache for change. We are desperate to be different. Life as it is will never suffice for those who long to walk as Jesus walked and talk as Jesus talked. We agonize to displace from our hearts the tyrannous reign of sin, to dislodge from our souls the crippling grip of lust and anger and jealousy and petty rivalry and pride. Yet we feel so helpless—and eventually hopeless. Must we resign ourselves to the monotony of failure, hanging on by our spiritual fingernails until Jesus returns and delivers us from the mess we've made of our lives? Or can something be done now?

A SUPERIOR PLEASURE

I've already said it once: the key to holiness is falling in love. My agenda in this book is to explain what that means and why it works. However, if I'm not careful, I run the risk of losing some of you before you escape chapter one. Love is a slippery term. Sometimes it gets a bit mushy and loses its punch. So I want to be clear about what I mean.

I don't believe (as I once did) that the power to turn from "the passing pleasures of sin" (Hebrews 11:25) is the result of a religious Just-Say-No campaign. I'm not mocking well-meant efforts to motivate people to choose righteousness. We must educate ourselves to identify sinful behavior and beliefs. No less important is exhorting one another to flee youthful lusts. But, let's be honest. Drawing up a list of proscribed activities, gritting our moral teeth, clenching our legal fists, and together shouting "No!" at sin has minimal long-term impact. If that's the extent of our enabling, sin will win in the end. Appeals to shame, threats of divine reprisal, as well as the tactics of fear, won't do it. I'm all for saying No to sin. But if we just say No, that is to say, if volitional restraint is the most that we bring to bear against temptation, our chances of more than a fleeting victory are slim. So what's the answer?

You may remember the award-winning epic film *Ben Hur*. There are numerous reasons why it won the Oscar for best picture, not least of which was a spectacular chariot race. But one scene stands out in my mind. It came early in the movie. Massala, childhood friend of Judah Ben Hur (played by Charlton Heston) and newly appointed commander of the Roman troops in Jerusalem, is speaking with the man he is replacing. The latter is clearly weary from waging a relentless battle with the Jewish people. "Religion is everywhere," he bemoans. "And now there is word of a coming deliverer, the 'Messiah,' they call him." Massala isn't impressed. His solution is simple: crush the leaders, weed out all religious seditionists. "It may seem easy to you," comes the reply. "But how do you fight an idea?" After a moment's pause, Massala, though cruel, wisely responds: "You ask me, 'How do you fight an idea?' I'll tell you: with another idea!"

Here's my point. How do you fight the pleasure of sin? I'll tell you: with another pleasure. Holiness is not attained, at least not in any lasting, life-changing way, merely through prohibitions, threats, fear, or shame-based appeals. Holiness is attained by believing in, trusting, banking on, resting in, savoring, and cherishing God's promise of a superior happiness that comes only by falling in love with Jesus. The power that the pleasures of sin exert on the human soul will ultimately be overcome only by the superior power of the pleasures of knowing and being known, loving and being loved by God in Christ. Or again, the only way to conquer one pleasure is with another, superior, more pleasing pleasure!

A dear friend is dealing with a family member who has turned her back on the Lord. The family member is living a life of open and defiant sin and evidently loving every minute of it. We met recently to determine the best way to approach the problem. "What do I say to her?" she asked. "How do I get through?" My response was immediate and pointed: "It won't happen by indicting her with a superior morality but by inviting her to a superior joy!"

Make no mistake about it, my friend does have a far superior morality. It is infinitely better. It is biblical. I told her: "Your moral principles are right and hers are wrong. Period. But telling her that will probably get you nowhere. In fact, she will become more entrenched in her lifestyle and will dig in her heels. In all likelihood, the only thing she will think is: 'Oh, you just want me to be miserable. You're probably jealous of my success. You and God want me to forsake all these pleasures and the happiness I've found so I can live like a monk and punish my body and suppress my desires and walk around with some sour, austere look on my face.' No matter how well you say it, she will probably interpret you as the enemy of her pleasure and happiness. You will invariably be portrayed as advocating a stiff, stoical, boring life."

I continued: "Instead, look at her wealth and drugs and sexual promiscuity and self-absorbed lifestyle and fancy clothes and whatever else it is that she is convinced is essential to her happiness and say: 'You've got to be kidding. I can't believe you've settled for so little. I can't believe that you would deprive yourself this way. What pathetic little pleasures you have. My goodness, you have no idea what you're missing!'"

My point was simply that the way to get someone to do what is right is not by telling him or her, "Don't do what is wrong." The reason for this is that "wrong," to his or her way of thinking, is enticing and pleasing and fun and a lot more enjoyable than "right." The answer is to give him or her a taste of the superior sweetness of God, of the surpassing peace of Christ, of the satisfying pleasure of intimacy with the Holy Spirit. C. S. Lewis put it this way:

> If we consider the unblushing promises of reward and the staggering nature of the rewards promised in the Gospels, it would seem that Our Lord finds our desires not too strong, but too weak. We are half-hearted creatures, fooling about with drink and sex and ambition when infinite joy is offered [to] us, like an ignorant child who wants to go on making mud pies in a slum because he cannot imagine what is meant by the offer of a holiday at the sea. We are far too easily pleased.[1]

If all we eat for lunch is rancid ground beef, in time we will learn to ignore its odor and will adjust to its taste. We will even learn to tolerate the physical nausea it provokes. We are a hungry people who will settle for whatever brings immediate satisfaction to the cravings of our stomachs. But once we are fed with filet mignon, saying No to spoiled hamburger will come quite easily. The point is this: *There is no way to triumph over sin long-term unless we develop a distaste for it because of a superior satisfaction in God. The only way to find sin distasteful is to eat and savor the sweetness of all that God is for us in Jesus.* The solution isn't to stop eating. The answer isn't found in ignoring our hunger pangs. The key is ingesting the joys of Jesus and the grace, mercy, kindness, love, forgiveness, power, and peace that He alone can bring to the famished soul.

TRIED AND FOUND WANTING

I'm convinced that the traditional "religious" approach to dissuading people from sinning is seriously flawed. For centuries our strategy has been negative in thrust. I don't mean it's evil. Rather, it focuses primarily on either prohibitions or threats.

We often begin by creating a list of proscribed activities, people, places, and events. After we've exhausted those mentioned in the Bible, we throw in a few of our own making. You know what I mean. All of us have a private list of taboos, dont's, and off-limit issues that we believe are the mark of true spirituality. It doesn't matter if the Bible is silent on these issues. We've "heard from God" and can't believe that anyone else wouldn't recognize and accept our image of what it means to be godly.

I'm baffled continually at how easily Christian people treat as moral law those things that God has neither forbidden nor required. Some feel an irresistible urge to speak loudly whenever the Bible is silent. They find the ethical stipulations of Scripture inadequate for living the Christian life and feel compelled to supplement the Word of God with countless little do's and dont's that they are persuaded are essential to winning God's favor and blessing.

Holiness is then measured by how successful we are in saying No to our list of personal prohibitions. Being a Christian becomes an issue of restraint. We define our identity in Christ in terms of what we don't do. We judge the spiritual status and maturity of others based on how diligent they are to withdraw from the same list of prohibited activities that we do. Love for God is measured by our commitment to separate from the unsavory and avoid the unacceptable. The result, notes Jeff Imbach, is this:

Life becomes proscribed by all the things we should avoid and prescribed by all the things we must be careful to do. We get so busy trying to demonstrate our spiritual correctness that we lose the art of living out of our souls. We downsize our souls to achieve a safer bottom line of religious acceptability. We are left to live between the rock of crisp correct religious doctrines and rules, and the hard place of duty-bound activity as supposed proof of our spiritual fervor.[2]

THE FAILURE OF FEAR

When we see others falling into temptation or on the verge of crossing a forbidden boundary line, we quickly (and sanctimoniously) remind them that where they're heading is off-limits, out-of-bounds, taboo. If our warning falls on deaf ears and a stubborn heart, we reinforce our stance with threats based on the inevitable prospect of either shame or fear. It might sound something like this:

If you do that you will betray your wife (or husband). You will embarrass your kids. Do you want to be exposed in front of your entire family? Think about how horrible and ashamed you'll feel.

Or,

Don't do that anymore or the people at church will find out. The leaders will have to be told and you'll be publicly disciplined. You might even get excommunicated. Whatever ministry you once had will be over forever.

Or,

What will your neighbors think? No one will want to associate with you anymore. You'll never be invited to a backyard barbecue. Once they hear about what you've been doing, they'll tell their kids they can't play with your kids ever again. Is that what you want?

Or,

If your boss finds out, you might get fired. Doesn't the possibility of losing your income scare you enough to get you to stop? You've worked so hard to get where you are on the corporate ladder and now you're willing to risk it all for a little sin! I can't believe it. You've earned the respect of your coworkers. They look up to you. And now you're just going to throw it all away.

Or,

Are you crazy? That kind of behavior is a sure-fire way to catch a disease. People die from that, you know. And even if you live, your wife (husband) will certainly divorce you. Your kids will be humiliated. So will you. So, stop!

What's important to remember is that every one of these warnings is valid! Sinful behavior does carry serious consequences, sometimes worse than what I've listed above. You may have already felt the sting of embarrassment, of getting caught, of public humiliation, of divine discipline, of lost wages, of squandered opportunities. You know what it is to feel the crippling power of shame and guilt. You've been deeply wounded by people you once regarded as friends who now never seem to be around. So, make no mistake. Nothing that I've said or will say is meant to minimize the debilitating effects of sin and disobedience.

But, in the long run, how effective in your fight against sin are prohibitions, threats, and warnings? Do they really work? *Do you find yourself more and more conformed to the image of Jesus as a result of their impact on your behavior?* When you warn or threaten others who are being tempted, do they report back to you that they are sinning significantly less? Are they experiencing noticeable deliverance from bondage to sin and perversion? I doubt it.

Not long ago I received a letter from a lady whose pastor had decided to abandon his wife and children for a high school sweetheart with whom he had reconnected at his twenty-year reunion. Everyone was devastated. His wife and children were inconsolable. The church felt deeply betrayed. The lady who wrote the letter, other church members, personal friends, and family members sat with the pastor pleading with him to reconsider. Didn't he realize what this would do to the church? Didn't he care what effect it would have on his kids? Doesn't he know how the gospel will be vilified in the marketplace once word of this spreads in the community? They asked him how he would ever face his parents and in-laws? Every question, every appeal, every warning had considerable truth and weight behind it. But it was to no avail. In the end, the allure of the immediate pleasure of sin was more powerful than the threat of its long-term consequences. He left his wife and family, and the rest, as they say, is history.

If the primary thing keeping you from sinning is the fear of getting caught or the prospect of shame or of being exposed as immoral, you don't stand much of a chance. Oh, these might work for a while. You might find enough strength to resist for the time being. But the relentless assault of temptation will eventually wear you down and the power of resistance will gradually erode until you give in, tired, frustrated, bitter, angry with God, doubting if a life of obedience will ever bring the satisfaction your soul so deeply craves.

Once again, I'm not suggesting that there is no place for warnings or threats or prohibitions. The Bible is full of them. They are there for our welfare. They are there to be heeded. But, in the final analysis, something more is needed to energize our hearts to recognize their truth and find joy in obedience to the direction in which they point us.[3]

Let me speak for a moment to the men reading this book. Most of you, no, all of you, at one time or another have found yourself sitting alone either at home or in a hotel room while on a business trip, fighting the urge to find sexual satisfaction in the absence of your wife. All it would take is a brief trip to the video store, perhaps that one on the other side of town where no one knows you. All it would take is pushing a few buttons on the remote control device in your hotel room. So easy. So safe. Complete anonymity. The words appear on the TV screen, with the obvious intent of making a sale: "No record is kept of which movie you order." When faced with that kind of temptation, all the threats and warnings in the world suddenly lose their punch. Merely knowing it is wrong doesn't seem to work when you're lonely and vulnerable and bored. Rationalization comes so easily. The potential for getting caught is minimal, perhaps even non-existent. Before you can catch your breath, it's done. Why?

THE REASON WE SIN

The ease of sinning stems from the reason why we sin. Few people I've talked to can explain why they sin. They're clueless. They just do it! But why? Let me begin by telling you why not. People don't sin because they feel morally obligated to do so. No one sins from a sense of duty. Not one of you reading this book got up this morning and said, "Okay, let's see. I need to commit four sins before breakfast. I was supposed to commit ten sins before midnight yesterday, but I fell asleep. So maybe after getting the kids off to school I'll have time to squeeze a couple more in before lunch. My quota for sinning today is twenty-three, so I'll have to speed it up a bit this afternoon. Maybe I'll turn on a soap-opera and find a little incentive there." No, people don't sin because they feel they have to.

We sin because we enjoy the pleasure it brings. We sin because it feels good. We sin because it brings a thrill to our bodies, fleeting satisfaction to our souls and excitement to the banality and boredom of our everyday lives. In a passage of Scripture we'll look at later, the author of Hebrews refers to the "passing pleasures of sin" (Hebrews 11:25). We sin because we believe the lie that the pleasure

it brings, though passing, is more satisfying than the pleasure obedience brings. Thus the power of temptation is the false promise that
sin will make me happier than God can. As John Piper has said, "Sin
is what you do when your heart is not satisfied with God."[4] The fight
against sin is, therefore, the fight to stay satisfied with God.

Temptation to sin really isn't that hard to understand. Its appeal
is actually quite simple. Sin comes to us, taps us on the shoulder
or tugs at our shirttail and whispers in our ear: "You deserve better
than what God has provided. He's holding out on you. You deserve
to feel good about yourself. I'll affirm you in a way no one else can.
Why live in misery any longer? Come to me. I'll give you a sense
of power you've never known before. I'll expand your influence.
I'll fill your heart with a sense of accomplishment. I'll nourish your
soul. You've never had a physical rush like the one I've got in store
for you. Obeying God is boring. It's a pain. He's always telling you
to do stuff that's difficult and burdensome and inconvenient or order-
ing you to forsake the few things that really bring you happiness.
Come on. You've only got one life. Obedience is ugly. My way is
fun. My way feels good."

We succumb; we give in; we say Yes to sin because we believe
its promise of more pleasure than God gives. This leads me to the
simple conclusion that the only way for us to successfully resist
sin is by maximizing our pleasure in God. The key to victory over
sin is satisfaction with all that God is for us in Jesus. Or again, the
only way to fight the seductive power of one pleasure is with a
greater pleasure, a more pleasing pleasure, the pleasure that
comes from falling in love with Jesus. Says Piper,

> Faith stands or falls on the truth that the future with God is
> more satisfying than the one promised by sin. Where this
> truth is embraced and God is cherished above all, the power
> of sin is broken. . . . Sin has power through promising a
> false future. In temptation sin comes to us and says: "The
> future with God on his narrow way is hard and unhappy; but

the way I promise is pleasant and satisfying." The power of
sin is in the power of this lie.[5]

Dallas Willard says much the same thing but in slightly different terms. It is our "failure to attain a deeply satisfying life," says
Willard, that makes sinful actions seem good. Willard amplifies his
point thus:

> Our success in overcoming temptation will be easier if we
> are basically happy in our lives. To cut off the joys and plea-
> sures associated with our bodily and social existence as
> "unspiritual" can actually have the effect of weakening us in
> our efforts to do what is right. It makes it impossible for us
> to see and draw strength from the goodness of rightness.[6]

Willard's statement that success in overcoming temptation
comes from being "happy" in our lives might strike you as odd,
perhaps even unspiritual and self-indulgent. But foundational to
everything I will say is my belief that happiness is the very
reason God created the universe. Indeed, it is for happiness that
we exist. I'll have much more to say about this in the next chapter (and throughout the book). I simply ask now that you not too
quickly dismiss this as "humanistic" mumbo-jumbo. One of my
goals is to demonstrate that it is both thoroughly biblical and at the
very heart of personal holiness.

Perhaps your first reaction to what I have said is to contend that
the reason why God created the universe is to glorify Himself, and
that is our ultimate reason for existence as well. And I would agree.
What I will argue for in chapter two is something the Puritan pastor
and theologian of the First Great Awakening, Jonathan Edwards
(1703-1758), so eloquently articulated centuries ago:

> One truly glorifies God precisely by rejoicing and delighting
> in the manifold display of who God is and what He does.

Merely understanding the perfections of God cannot be the
end for which God created us as beings who think and feel.
Neither can the highest aim of creation be the declaring of
God's glory to others, for, as Edwards says, "the declaring
[of] God's glory is good for nothing otherwise than to raise
joy in ourselves and others at what is declared."[7]

The aim of God in creation and redemption is therefore the
delight He Himself enjoys in seeing His creatures delight in Him.
The "glorifying of God," contends Edwards, "is nothing but rejoicing in the manifestations of Him."[8] Or, to put it in words that
anticipate the next chapter, God is most glorified in us when we
are most happy and delighted and satisfied in Him. And it is this
happiness in Him that alone will, at the end of the day, win our
hearts for holiness and wean us from sin. Pleasure in God is the
power for purity.

WHO'S MORE HOLY?

Recently our church hosted a conference for church leaders. In
attendance were men and women from virtually every part of the
United States and several foreign countries. I scanned the regis-
tration list and took note not only of the geographical distribution
but especially of the denominational breakdown. I was stunned.
There were Baptist (Southern and otherwise), Presbyterian,
Lutheran, Methodist, Vineyard, Assembly of God, Foursquare,
independent Bible church, independent charismatic, Disciples of
Christ, Episcopalian, Nazarene, and Mennonite Brethren, just to
mention a few!

There were Calvinists present with us, Arminians, premillenni-
alists, amillennialists, pretribs and posttribs, dispensationalists and
covenant theologians, and probably quite a few who refuse to bear
any such theological labels. As I considered this representative
group across the broad spectrum of the body of Christ, as I mingled

among them and became acquainted with many of them, I found a question turning over and over in my mind. "Is any particular denominational group more holy than all the others? Are Calvinists godlier than Arminians? Do Baptists sin less than Presbyterians? As a rule, do people in the Vineyard seek God with greater fervency than those in independent charismatic churches? Was there any group present at our conference which, because of its heritage or theology, stands out as spiritually superior or morally more mature than all the others? Knowing these people as I do, having traveled as widely as I have, having seen these people in their "natural religious habitat," if you will, I can honestly answer that question with a resounding "No!"

The amazing thing is that each of these groups has its own set of distinct theological convictions (and what I am saying should not be taken as minimizing the importance of biblical and theological accuracy). Each denomination has its own unique list of proscribed activities. Nazarenes don't do some things that Baptists do. Baptists don't do some things Presbyterians do. Presbyterians don't do some things Anglicans do. And on and on and on. But I have yet to note or see or hear of one group being distinctly and undeniably more holy than the others.

In my library, I have several books that are devoted to discussing the nature of the Christian life and, in particular, how we might best achieve holiness. In one of the books, representatives from five different theological traditions debate each other on how best to be holy. The Reformed, Lutheran, Wesleyan, Pentecostal, and Contemplative traditions are all well-defined and defended. In another book, based much on the same format, the Keswick and Dispensational viewpoints join the battle.

Here's my point. I seriously doubt that any one of the authors of these books is significantly more righteous than any of the others. I seriously doubt that the theological traditions or denominational persuasions they represent are characterized by noticeably less scandalous sin than any other. So what does make a difference? Is there no way at all to increase and deepen and expand the transformation of our hearts? Is there anything that will effectively energize the human heart in its war with sin? Just how do we grow in grace and the power to say No to the world, the flesh, and the Devil?

I'm convinced that we have only one of two options. Either we can devote ourselves and our time and our energy to demonstrating the ugliness and futility of sin and the world, hoping that such will embolden our hearts to say No to it as unworthy of our affection, or we can demonstrate the beauty and splendor of all that God is for us in Jesus and become happily and joyfully enticed by a rival affection.

I favor the latter. Both my biblical convictions and my personal experience persuade me that I can talk all I want about how ugly sin is, but I will never enjoy lasting victory over it until my heart is captivated by a comparatively superior pleasure. To put it simply:

> The only way to liberate the heart from servitude to the passing pleasures of sin is by cultivating a passion for the joy and delight of beholding the beauty of God in the face of Jesus. What breaks the power of sin is faith in the promise that the pleasures of sin are temporary and toxic but at God's right hand are pleasures evermore. (see Psalm 16:11)

Holiness does not come merely by creating a list of moral taboos and then exerting our willpower to resist them. "Just Say No" alone doesn't work. Of course, we must say No. Please don't misunderstand me. But lasting, meaningful victory will come only if there is something more enticing to which we can say Yes! If we try to fight sin merely with prohibitions and threats, we will fail.

The decision to say No to sin must itself be energized by the assurance of delight in an alternative "Yes". We must fight sin with a massive promise of superior happiness. We must swallow up the flicker of sin's pleasure in the forest fire of holy satisfaction. The only thing that will ultimately break the power of sin is passion for

Behold His beauty

Jesus. The only thing that will guard me from being entrapped by sin is being entranced by Jesus. In other words, the key to holiness is falling in love!

A PREVIEW OF COMING ATTRACTIONS

This perspective on the Christian life is grounded in certain assumptions about human nature and what I believe is our God-given impulse for pleasure. In what follows I will argue not only for the reality of our passion for pleasure but for the rightness of it. I'm going to suggest, to the surprise of many, that everything we do, we do for the pleasure it brings. Far from denigrating the glory of God, pursuing pleasure is the only way we can truly honor Him. What I hope to explain in the next two chapters is that my thesis on living a holy life is the inescapable fruit of a much larger vision concerning the nature of Christianity itself. There are certain truths that must be understood about what motivates us in our behavior and what truly glorifies God if any of my book's thesis is going to make sense.

But this perspective on the pursuit of holiness is no less grounded in certain assumptions about the divine nature — that is, about who God is and what motivates Him in His behavior. Perhaps even more to your surprise will be my suggestion in chapter four that everything God does He does for the pleasure it brings, and that knowing this is absolutely foundational to our success in our struggle with sin. So stay tuned.

CHAPTER TWO

THE POWER OF PLEASURE

I WAS IN MY CAR LISTENING TO CHRISTIAN RADIO WHEN ONE of America's most famous Bible teachers said something that forced me to pull off to the side of the road. Normally, I find myself in agreement with what he says, and I've even enjoyed several books that he's written. But this time he said something that struck me as profoundly unbiblical. The surprising thing is that when most of you hear what he said, you will probably say, "Well, what's wrong with that? It sure sounds biblical to me." Here is my paraphrase of his comment:

> The greatest single insight I've ever had in studying Scripture, the single most important principle I ever discovered is this: The goal or purpose of the Christian is to glorify God, not to be happy.

> I can already hear most of you saying, "Sam, don't tell me you disagree with that!" Sorry, but I do. In fact, let me be even bolder and put it this way: The greatest single insight I've ever had in studying Scripture, the single most important principle I ever discovered is this: the goal or purpose of the Christian is precisely the pursuit of happiness—in God. The reason for this is that there is no greater way to glorify God than to find in Him the happiness that my soul so desperately craves.

I understand where this Bible teacher was coming from. All of us are sickened at the arrogant, egotistical pursuit of pleasure that ignores God and looks on others as little more than stepping-stones for personal advancement. Our world is pathologically self-centered. People think only of themselves. They demand their "rights" and are quick to file a lawsuit against anyone who stands in their way. Satisfying oneself at any cost is the dominant philosophy of our day. Seeking pleasure for its own sake is our national pastime. Philosophers have called this perspective on life *hedonism.*

So when this Bible teacher said what he did, he probably evoked a chorus of "Amen!" from countless thousands of Christians in their cars and kitchens who happened to be listening to his message. Many might even say to themselves or others, "We've got to stop thinking about our own happiness for once and focus on the glory of God!" I certainly agree that God's glory must be our preeminent focus. But I don't believe it is to be done at the expense of human happiness. In fact, I'm convinced it can't be done apart from human happiness. That is why I embrace a philosophy of life called Christian Hedonism. That probably sounds like a contradiction in terms, the intellectual equivalent of "fried ice." How can one be a Christian and a hedonist at the same time? A Christian is one who seeks God's glory above everything else, and a hedonist is one who seeks pleasure above everything else. So how can you mix fire and gasoline and come up with anything other than a heretical explosion? So what exactly is Christian Hedonism?

ENJOYING GOD

In the mid-1970s, while in theological seminary, I was interim pastor of a small Presbyterian church in Dallas, Texas. It thus became necessary for me, a former Southern Baptist, to learn more about the heritage of the denomination in which I was ministering. Those of you who were raised Presbyterian are undoubtedly familiar with what is known as the Shorter Catechism. Its first question reads: "What is the chief end of man?" The appropriate answer is: "The chief end of man is to glorify God and to enjoy Him forever."

All of us, whether Southern Baptist or Presbyterian or Vineyard, agree on the priority of glorifying God. No matter what our background may be, we unite in affirming with the apostle Paul that whether we eat or drink or whatever we do, we do it "all to the glory of God" (1 Corinthians 10:31). But I strongly suspect that when it comes to how we might best glorify God, differences of opinion arise. Christian Hedonism insists that the truth is revealed with the change of one word in the Shorter Catechism. Simply put, the principal way in which we glorify God is *by* enjoying Him forever. God is most greatly extolled when we find our eternal happiness in Him.

Some of you may still be uncomfortable with my use of the word *happiness,* so a brief explanation is in order concerning its importance. The simple fact is that everyone does everything in order to be happy. You should never be ashamed of your desire to be happy. It is as natural as hunger. Perhaps the primary obstacle people have in accepting the concept of Christian Hedonism is their belief that to the degree that they seek their own happiness they diminish the virtue or value of an act. They have this distorted idea that the only way an act is virtuous is if we compel ourselves to do it, contrary to our desire not to do it. We tend to measure the worth of an act by the depth of pain and sacrifice we endure to perform it. Doing something because we enjoy doing it seems to empty the deed of its moral worth. Christian Hedonism contends that nothing could be further from the truth. Blaise Pascal expressed this central tenet of Christian Hedonism as follows:

All men seek happiness. This is without exception. Whatever different means they employ, they all tend to this end. The cause of some going to war, and of others avoiding it, is the same desire in both, attended with different views. The will never takes the least step but to this object. This is the motive of every action of every man, even of those who hang themselves.[1]

I know what you're thinking: "But doesn't someone commit suicide because he or she is unhappy?" Yes, but suicidal people choose to end their life precisely because they are convinced (wrongly, of course, but no less convinced) that death will bring them more happiness than life ever could. Or perhaps it would be better to say that they believe death will deliver them from the miseries of life. In either case, they kill themselves because they no longer want to be miserable and depressed. Believing that living can no longer bring them the happiness they so desperately desire, they take their own lives.

HAPPINESS: A UNIVERSAL HUNGER

Although what I'm describing may sound unfamiliar, even unspiritual, to some of you, Christian Hedonism has a rich heritage in the church. Perhaps no one understood it as clearly or expressed it as vividly as did Jonathan Edwards. The soul of every man, said Edwards, "necessarily craves happiness. This is a universal appetite of human nature, that is alike in the good and the bad."[2] Two words in that statement jump out at me: *necessarily* and *universal*. In other words, when it comes to happiness, *everybody* must seek it.

This desire for happiness is "insuperable, . . . never can be changed, . . . never can be overcome, or in any way abated. Young and old love happiness alike, and good and bad, wise and unwise."[3] Certainly people have different notions of what constitutes happiness, and will pursue it according to their particular appetites, but this in no way alters the fact that its presence is universal among mankind.

Edwards was only eighteen years old when he preached a sermon entitled "Christian Happiness," in which he for the first, but by no means last, time affirmed the inescapable yearning for happiness among both the righteous and wicked:

They certainly are the wisest men that do those things that make most for their happiness, and this in effect is acknowledged by all men in the world, for there is no man upon the earth who isn't earnestly seeking after happiness, and it appears abundantly by the variety of ways they so vigorously seek it; they will twist and turn every way, ply all instruments, to make themselves happy men. Some will wander all over the face of the earth to find it: they will seek it in the waters and dry land, under the waters and in the bowels of the earth, and although the true way to happiness lies right before them and they might easily step into it and walk in it and be brought into as great a happiness as they desire, and greater than they can conceive of, yet they will not enter into it. They try all the false paths; they will spend and be spent, labor all their lives' time, endanger their lives, will pass over mountains and valleys, go through fire and water, seeking for happiness amongst vanities, and are always disappointed, never find what they seek for; but yet like fools and madmen they violently rush forward, still in the same ways. But the righteous are not so; these only, have the wisdom to find the right paths to happiness.[4]

It is this ruthless determination among the wicked to find happiness in whatever sinful or perverse experience imaginable that hardens the believing heart against its own impulse for pleasure. Not wanting to be classed among those who reject Jesus, many Christians have wrongly assumed the problem is in their passion and have taken whatever steps they believe will effectively suppress and stifle its expression. But the righteous, says Edwards, ought to differ from the lost in choosing "the right paths to happiness," not in seeking to rid themselves of the desire itself. The problem isn't in the passion; it's in the paths.

Painful Choices

People struggle with what I've just said because it strikes them as experientially misguided. I can imagine someone asking, "How can you say I want happiness and joy and satisfaction when I'm always making decisions that I know are painful and sacrificial?" The answer is that we always choose what we think will ultimately maximize personal happiness and minimize personal misery. If you make a decision that is immediately painful and uncomfortable and unsettling, I assure you it is because you believe that such a choice will generate more pleasure than not in the long term. In other words, you gladly forgo present pleasures if you believe the long-term benefits outweigh whatever short-term discomfort you might experience or sacrifice you might make. Likewise, you will ignore long-term consequences if you believe the immediate pleasures of a decision are worth the risk.

You may deny yourself the pleasures of a banana split now because you believe the joy of weight loss later is worth it. Your desire for a long-term satisfaction (the joy of a slimmer waistline) is stronger than the appeal of ice cream now. You weigh (pardon the pun) competing pleasures. Your will is energized based on your belief that one pleasure (whether immediate or long-term) is better than others. But in every case you choose and act with a view to increasing joy and avoiding pain.

Satan isn't responsible for this. God is. God made you this way so that you would choose Him and His soul-satisfying pleasures in lieu of those that pass with the using and ultimately leave you empty and miserable. The alternative to resisting the passing pleasures of sin isn't religious misery but relishing the permanent pleasures of God. More on this later.

To Prize God Is to Praise God

Now back to the original point, which is that the chief way in which Christians can glorify God is to seek the enjoyment and happiness that only He can provide. Simply put, *pleasure is the measure of our treasure.*[5]

This isn't just a cute phrase. It calls for a little explanation. Let's start with a question: "How do you measure or assess the value of something you cherish? How do you determine the worth of a prize?" Is it not by the depth of pleasure you derive from it? Is it not by the intensity and quality of your delight in what it is? Is it not by how excited and enthralled and thrilled you are in the manifold display of its attributes, characteristics, and properties? In other words, your satisfaction in what the treasure is and does for you is the standard or gauge by which its glory (worth and value) is revealed. Hence, your pleasure is the measure of the treasure. Or again, the treasure, which is God, is most glorified in and by you when your pleasure in Him is maximal and optimal.

Let me illustrate what I mean. My ministry has required that on occasion I travel, often overseas. When my two daughters were younger, they did not adjust well to my absence, which is to say they were not as happy as when I was at home. Upon my return, they would drop everything they were doing and rush madly to the door to greet their dad. It mattered little whether it was Mr. Rogers on TV or a visiting friend; when I came home all they could think about was running to their dad who alone at that moment could satisfy the longings of their heart.

How do you suppose I reacted to such treatment? Of course, I was honored by their need of me. They treasured who I am, the measure of which was their degree of pleasure in my presence. I was honored as a father when they found in me and in me alone the fulfillment of their hearts' desire. At that moment, no one else in the world could do for them what I could do. My success as a father was magnified when their happiness was so totally dependent on who I am and what I can do for them.

The last thing I would ever consider doing was rebuke them for being self-centered. As they ran to me, hoping to be embraced and loved and kissed, I didn't call a halt to their pursuit and say, "How evil of you to be so consumed with the fulfillment of your personal pleasure that you would treat me this way." On the contrary, I was honored and, if I may say so, glorified by their need of me. They were telling me in those moments that I was more important to them than anything else in the world: more important than TV, than friends, than toys, than food. Their enjoyment of me honored, magnified, and drew attention to me.

When we come to God our heavenly Father and find in His arms the only comfort that truly comforts, He is honored. When we come to Him and find in Him the satisfaction of beholding the most beautiful being in the universe, He is exalted. When we come to Him and find the forgiveness and blessedness that alone bring lasting peace to our souls, He is extolled. When we come to God for the joy that being in His presence produces, He gets all the praise for being the One who alone is the source of our happiness.

DUTY OR DELIGHT?

This raises a related and important question that each of us needs to wrestle with: Is your pursuit of God's glory motivated by a sense of duty or delight? Let me explain what I mean by going back to my earlier illustration. Envision again my daughters running up to me and leaping into my arms, smiling, hugging, kissing, clinging to me as if they would never let go. Now imagine if I asked them: "Hey, girls, why are you doing this?" What do you think might be their answer? Let's suppose they said, rather matter-of-factly: "Mom told us to. She said we had to do it as dutiful children. She set us down before you arrived home and reminded us of all the things you've provided: a house, a car, clothes, toys, food. She said we are indebted to you and that it is our duty to respond to you this way upon your return."

How do you think that would make me feel? How would that

reflect on me as a father or just as a person? Am I honored by their fidelity to fulfill their duty? I may be moderately pleased that they are obedient, but I don't think I would feel cherished and valued and enjoyed. I might even feel used.

Or consider another example. In May of 2000 my wife and I will celebrate our twenty-eighth wedding anniversary. Let's suppose that I choose to send her two dozen roses. When I arrive home after work she greets me at the door with tears of joy streaming down her face and says, "Oh, Sam, they're the most beautiful roses I've ever seen. Thank you! I love you!" At that, I raise my hand to restrain her exuberance and say, "Think nothing of it. It is my duty as a husband." I don't know about you, but I seriously doubt that my anniversary is going to be much of a celebration! John Piper put it this way:

> Dutiful roses are a contradiction in terms. If I am not moved by a spontaneous affection for her as a person, the roses do not honor her. In fact they belittle her. They are a very thin covering for the fact that she does not have the worth or beauty in my eyes to kindle affection. All I can muster is a calculated expression of marital duty.[6]

Here's my point: *Duty discharged without delight dishonors God*. Is duty important? It most certainly is. We have a responsibility to obey God's commands and to fulfill His will. But if our motivation in doing so is merely duty and not also the delight that is the fruit and reward of obedience, God is not honored.

If later in the evening of our anniversary I take my wife out to a nice restaurant, she may at some point ask again, "Why are you doing this?" My earlier explanation for why I sent her roses has made her understandably suspicious. This time, however, I trust that my honest and heartfelt answer would be, "I've brought you here tonight because nothing in the world makes me happier than to be with you. I find in your presence and company the greatest joy of my life. I asked myself, 'What could I do tonight that would make me happier than I've ever been?' The answer was obvious: dinner with you." Now that glorifies and honors my wife!

What I hope will become evident as we proceed, and as we examine several important biblical texts, is that such is preeminently true in our relationship with God. By enjoying Him and who He is and all the blessings that He provides, we glorify His goodness, His sufficiency, His power, and everything else about God that brings us the delight we desire.

PLEASURES EVERMORE

Perhaps looking at one text will help us understand this. In Psalm 16:11 David says this about why he hungers and yearns for God: "Thou wilt make known to me the path of life; In Thy presence is fullness of joy; In Thy right hand there are pleasures evermore." This is not merely a statement of fact. It is an incentive to pursue God. We come to Him and seek after Him with all our heart (compare Jeremiah 29:13) because in His presence our joy is made full. No one else can do this. Getting drunk can't do it. Illicit sex can't do it. No human relationship can do it. Money can't buy it. Only being with God can bring us all the joy we could ever hope to find.

Think about what David is saying. God is offering us a joy that infinitely transcends all other joys combined in the power and potential to satisfy, thrill, fill, and fulfill. He is talking about spiritual ecstasy, incomparable ecstasy, unparalleled ecstasy, and unfathomable ecstasy. And it is all to be found in only one place: in God's presence, at His right hand.

There is an unspoken premise apart from which this statement in Psalm 16:11 makes no sense. There is a principle that one must assume to be true if this verse is to have any significance for us. It is this: Human beings desire optimum joy and unending pleasure— and it is good that they do! We must come to grips with the fact that the Bible unashamedly appeals to our desire for pleasure and happiness. And it does so because God built into us an undeniable, unrelenting, inescapable hunger for joy and satisfaction and delight.

God built us to be fascinated, to be intrigued, to be exhilarated, to be stunned. Our desire for these experiences will never let up. There are no breaks, no rest, no sabbatical. This is no surface, fleeting diversion, but a basic, foundational, instinctive orientation of the human soul. Fighting it is like trying to hold your breath. You can only hold out for about forty-five seconds.

You can no more escape from your desire for eternal pleasure than you can cease to be human, nor should you try. Let me be even bolder and say that your responsibility as a Christian is to be as happy as you possibly can. In fact, it is impossible for you to be too zealous for happiness or inordinately committed to the pursuit of pleasure. Your pursuit may be misdirected, as is the case when you prefer the passing pleasures of sin to the excellencies of God. But it can't be too strong. God's creative design was that your ravenous appetite for pleasure find fulfillment in Him, for nothing more wonderfully reveals His glory than the joy the creature has in its Creator. As Piper says, "the bottom line of happiness is that we are granted to see the infinite beauty of God and make much of Him forever."[7]

One of the worst injustices the church has perpetrated against its members is proclaiming a message of the evil of desire. God created us with a longing to be thrilled, hungry for the joy of being fascinated. Yet we have told people to stop wanting and to stop yearning; we've urged them to ignore, suppress, or anesthetize their desire for happiness. And, if such teachings should fail, we have worked hard to make them feel the sting of guilt and shame. All this will do is drive passion underground, so to speak, only to have it erupt at some moment of weakness when temptation offers a fleeting fulfillment.

The idea that holiness is antithetical to pleasure, that the pursuit of purity entails a suppression of one's desire for enjoyment, is a serious distortion of Christian truth. We are told to crucify the desire for pleasure—to kill it, numb it, and renounce it. If that isn't enough, we are told to try casting it out as if it were a demon or to simply pretend that it just doesn't exist. The tragic result is that, for generations, Christians have lived in condemnation and self-contempt, not for sin, but merely for wanting, desiring, and yearning.

WHY BOO RADLEY WOULDN'T SHOW HIMSELF

I recently reread (simply for the pleasure of it) *To Kill a Mockingbird*, Harper Lee's classic portrait of post-Depression life in the Deep South. Many are familiar with the story, if not from the book, then perhaps from the film adaptation starring Gregory Peck as Atticus Finch, lawyer, widower, and father of two children, Jem and Scout. At the heart of the story was a reclusive figure known as Boo Radley, whose reluctance to "come out" from the confines of his home not only perplexed the children but became fuel for countless fears and late-night tales.

> "Miss Maudie," said Scout one evening, "do you think Boo Radley's still alive?"
>
> "His name's Arthur and he's alive," she said. She was rocking slowly in her big oak chair. "Do you smell my mimosa? It's like angels' breath this evening."
>
> "Yessum. How do you know?"
>
> "Know what, child?"
>
> "That B—— Mr. Arthur's still alive?"
>
> "What a morbid question. But I suppose it's a morbid subject. I know he's alive, Jean Louise, because I haven't seen him carried out yet."
>
> "Maybe he died and they stuffed him up the chimney."
>
> "Where did you get such a notion?"
>
> "That's what Jem said he thought they did. . . ."
>
> "Arthur Radley just stays in the house, that's all," said Miss Maudie. "Wouldn't you stay in the house if you didn't want to come out?"
>
> "Yessum, but I'd wanta come out. Why doesn't he?"

Miss Maudie's eyes narrowed. "You know that story as well as I do."

"I never heard why, though. Nobody ever told me why."

Miss Maudie settled her bridgework. "You know old Mr. Radley was a foot-washing Baptist ——"

"That's what you are, ain't it?"

"My shell's not that hard, child. I'm just a Baptist."

"Don't you believe in foot-washing?"

"We do. At home in the bathtub."

"But we can't have communion with you all ——"

Apparently deciding that it was easier to define primitive baptism than closed communion, Miss Maudie said: "Footwashers believe anything that's pleasure is a sin. Did you know some of 'em came out of the woods one Saturday and passed by this place and told me me and my flowers were going to hell?"

"Your flowers, too?"

"Yes, ma'am. They'd burn right with me. They thought I spent too much time in God's outdoors and not enough time inside the house reading the Bible."[8]

I doubt if any "footwashing Baptists" will read this book, but like Mr. Radley, some of you *"believe anything that's pleasure is a sin."* Perhaps I'm overstating the case, but you get the idea. Many of you learned early on not to acknowledge the presence of your desires. Allowing them to surface brought a stinging rebuke or acute embarrassment for having botched it. In a manner of speaking, you've "stayed in the house." To venture outside, to allow yourself to feel the pleasures of life, "is a sin." Or at least, might well lead to one.

Many of you may think that to be passionate, to honestly engage one's feelings, is symptomatic of spiritual weakness. If you do find the courage to admit the reality of those inner yearnings, either your own experience or other people's—often those in a position of authority—teaches you to distrust them.

The problem is that ignoring our passions doesn't make them go away. We can suppress them deep within or lock them away in a safe corner of our heart or silence their voice with reminders of past sins, but like a submerged beach ball they will eventually, often at the most inopportune moments, resurface.

In the meantime, we replace our passions with performance. Doing well what others want from us substitutes for honestly embracing our heart's desire. If we do find the courage to tell someone of our yearning for happiness and our impulse to experience deep, lasting pleasure, we often hear only a disdainful scorn for yielding to the "flesh" and are stigmatized as being selfish and sub-spiritual. But not even that will make our desire disappear. For it is God who continues to call us to Himself, to a relationship in which passion can freely and fully exhaust itself in the arms of a Lover who will never leave us or forsake us (Hebrews 13:5). God is the consummate Romantic. He woos and sings and beckons and flirts with the human soul. He longs to draw us to Himself, to the joy of that intimacy He alone is capable of providing.

Authors Brent Curtis and John Eldredge do a superb job of identifying the fears we face in following our passions. They challenge us to acknowledge and embrace the reality of what God has put within. Instead of denying our desire for pleasure and intimacy, instead of indulging in sensuality, we must celebrate how God has made us and find satisfaction in His presence. The sacred romance, they explain,

> calls to us every moment of our lives. It whispers to us on the wind, invites us through the laughter of good friends, reaches out to us through the touch of someone we love. We've heard it in our favorite music, sensed it at the birth of our first child, been drawn to it while watching the shimmer of a sunset on the ocean. It is even present in times of great personal suffering—the illness of a child, the loss of a marriage, the death of a friend. Something calls to us

through experiences like these and rouses an inconsolable longing deep within our heart, wakening in us a yearning for intimacy, beauty, and adventure. This longing is the most powerful part of any human personality. It fuels our search for meaning, for wholeness, for a sense of being truly alive. However we may describe this deep desire, it is the most important thing about us, our heart of hearts, the passion of our life. And the voice that calls to us in this place is none other than the voice of God.[9]

It is Buddhism, not Christianity, that condemns desire. One of the four "noble truths" of Buddhist philosophy is that the cause of suffering is desire. When your desire is not satisfied, you suffer. The way to put an end to suffering, therefore, is to snuff out desire. Instead of increasing satisfaction, work at decreasing desire. Reduce your longings to a minimum and the pain of dissatisfaction will disappear. Such a view is decidedly nonChristian.

"Demonic" Wisdom

The Screwtape Letters by C. S. Lewis is a Christian classic. Screwtape is a seasoned veteran of spiritual warfare who mentors a younger demon named Wormwood. In one exchange, the elder demon gives this advice to his student:

Never forget that when we are dealing with any pleasure in its healthy and normal and satisfying form we are, in a sense, on the Enemy's ground. I know we have won many a soul through pleasure. All the same, it is His invention, not ours. He made the pleasures; all our research so far has not enabled us to produce one. All we can do is to encourage the humans to take the pleasures which our Enemy [God] has produced, at times, or ways, or in degrees, which He has forbidden . . . An ever-increasing craving for an ever-diminishing pleasure is the formula . . . To get the man's soul and give Him nothing in return—that is what really gladdens our Father's [Satan's] heart.[10]

Sometimes Lewis can be hard to decipher, so let me interpret this for you. The demon Screwtape knows intuitively what we humans endeavor to deny, namely, that God, not the Devil, is responsible for "healthy," "normal," "satisfying" pleasures. "It is His invention," notes Screwtape, "not ours." What, then, can the Enemy do to destroy us? Not create desire. God already did that. Rather, he must direct our hearts to find satisfaction for it in divinely forbidden ways.

Listen again to Screwtape's demonic, but perceptive, formula to ruining our souls: "an ever-increasing craving for an ever-diminishing pleasure." What is the problem here? It isn't that humans experience "cravings" that increase and intensify, but that these cravings fix themselves parasitically on pleasures that always diminish and ultimately disappoint. So what's the solution? Pleasures that never end! Pleasures evermore! Don't crucify the craving. Don't demonize it. Don't suppress it and let it fester in shame and self-contempt. Thank God for it and let it lead you to the "river of His delights."

You can't escape your passion for pleasure. It will haunt you in the night. It will whisper to you in the day. You will feel its impulse in all you do and think and say. The problem is not that we desire. The problem is that we desire sin rather than God. The problem is that we have been duped by the Devil. We have believed what is perhaps the most pernicious lie ever told, namely, that the pleasures and delights of the world, the flesh, and the Devil are more enjoyable and satisfying than who God is for us in Jesus.

Listen to the psalmist and tell me if he believed that the desire for pleasure is evil: "Oh, taste and see that the LORD is good!" (Psalm 34:8). Savor the Lord's goodness! Taste His grace! His mercy and kindness are sweet to the soul. In a word, God is delicious!

An amazing thing about this exhortation in Psalm 34:8 is yet another exhortation that follows immediately in 34:9. No sooner has he invited us to enjoy God than he calls upon us to fear Him! Without so much as a moment's pause, with evidently little if any concern for contradiction or confusion, David says, "O fear the LORD, you His saints" (34:9). That's right. The self-same God whom we are to "taste" we are also to "fear"! No greater mistake could be made in reading this book than thinking that I have replaced reverential fear with mindless frivolity. Unfortunately, many have lived and worshipped as if joy and fear were mutually exclusive. They invariably wind up fixating upon one to the exclusion of the other.

Perhaps the best, and yet most tragic, example of what happens when familiarity breeds flippancy is the incident involving Moses' nephews and Aaron's sons, Nadab and Abihu, as described in Leviticus 10:1-3. Nadab and Abihu were the two eldest of Aaron's four sons (Exodus 6:23). They had accompanied Moses and Aaron up Mount Sinai (Exodus 24:1) and, along with their two younger brothers, Eleazar and Ithamar, had been ordained as priests (Leviticus 8:30). Undoubtedly, Aaron must have experienced tremendous pride as he watched his sons follow him in ministry.

But scarcely had the heavenly fire descended in mercy to consume the sacrifice (9:24) when it again descended, this time in wrath, to consume those who made the sacrifice (10:1-3)! They are said to have offered up "strange fire" (10:1). What made it strange? Incense was produced from a mix of aromatic spices, which vaporized when put into a censer containing glowing lumps of charcoal. Leviticus 16:12 says these coals had to be taken from the altar. Had Nadab and Abihu taken them from somewhere else? Perhaps. All that is said, all that matters, is that they sought to offer strange fire "which the Lord had not commanded them" (10:1).

They arrogantly presumed upon their relationship with God and their position as priests, thinking that it gave them the freedom to approach God on their terms rather than His. God invites us to draw near, but on His terms, according to conditions He has established, in conformity with the pattern set forth in Holy

Scripture. It is dangerous, perhaps even lethal, to think that anything goes when it comes to drawing near to God.

With that crucial warning in mind, let us again heed the psalmist's exhortation to "delight" ourselves "in the LORD" (37:4). This is not optional. It is a command. We are not told merely to "delight" ourselves, for that would be secular hedonism. We are told to "delight" ourselves "in the LORD"! Yet once more we read that "they [that is, you] drink their fill of the abundance of Thy house; and Thou dost give them to drink of the river of Thy delights" (36:8).

The problem on planet Earth is not that people hedonistically pursue pleasure. The problem is that they rebelliously and foolishly refuse to find it in the one place where it may be genuinely and eternally found—in God's presence (see Psalm 16:11). Do you hear God speaking in this verse, issuing each of us an incredible invitation? The psalmist is telling us that the enjoyment of God is the supreme pleasure for which we were created.

We were made to enjoy Him. Our minds were shaped and fashioned to think about God, to reflect and meditate on His majesty and beauty and to experience the intellectual thrill of theological discovery. Our emotions were made to feel His power, love, and longing for us. Our wills were made to choose His will and ways; our spirits were formed to experience the ecstasy of communion with Him; our bodies were fashioned to be the temple where He Himself would delight to dwell!

BEWARE OF BOREDOM!

This explains why one of the most serious threats to the human spirit is boredom. Boredom is the breeding ground for wickedness. Bored people are easy targets of the flesh and the Devil. It is like putting a bull's-eye on your chest with a sign: "Tempt me. I'm easy!" Why? Because boredom is contrary to the natural, God-given impulse for fascination, excitement, pleasure, and exhilaration. There are only three possible reactions to boredom:

- You wither and die emotionally.
- You wither and die physically (suicide).
- You madly rush to whatever extreme and extravagant thrill you can find to replace your misery with pleasure, whether it be pornography, adultery, drugs, or fantasies of fame and power.

This is why people are so prone to an addictive lifestyle. Many people who fall into sinful addictions are people who were once terminally bored. The reason why addictions are so powerful is that they tap into that place in our hearts that was made for transcendent communion and spiritual romance. These addictive habits either dull and deaden our yearnings for a satisfaction we fear we'll never find or they provide an alternative counterfeit fulfillment that we think will bring long-term happiness, counterfeits like cocaine, overeating, illicit affairs, busyness, efficiency, image, or obsession with physical beauty. They all find their power in the inescapable yearning of the human heart to be fascinated and pleased and enthralled. Our hearts will invariably lead us either to the fleeting pleasures of addiction or to God.

WORLDS OF FUN

On my way to the airport not long ago I passed Worlds of Fun, a popular amusement park here in Kansas City. Hundreds of people—hot, sweating, irritable people—were standing in line to ride the newest roller-coaster rage, The Mamba! It was a stifling ninety-five degrees with an oppressively high humidity rate. But they were undeterred. The TV and radio ads for the ride have been enticing. It rises 205 feet in the air. It races seventy-five miles per hour down a narrow rail—"Better living through gravity!" I asked myself why relatively sane people would stand in line for hours in scorching heat for the opportunity to take a two-minute ride on the Mamba? And if that weren't enough, they paid for it, too! Why? Because the human heart was made for excitement. The human heart was built by God to be entertained. Neither animals nor plants react this way. There wasn't a single dog standing in line. No aardvarks, polar bears, or toucans. You don't find zucchini or broccoli or a kumquat making great physical and emotional sacrifice to experience this two-minute assault on the senses. Only those made in God's image seek for such thrills.

You may not find much excitement in the Mamba, but you desire a thrill no less than do those who paid to stand in line. And that's okay. Don't be ashamed. Don't run from it. Don't hide it. Rather, *glut yourself in God*. Immerse yourself in His blessings. Bathe yourself in His presence. Posture yourself to hear His voice and see His face and hear His word and taste His goodness and feel His presence. Embrace the reality of your passion for pleasure and satiate yourself in all that God is for you in Jesus.

HEDONISTS STILL SUFFER

None of this is to suggest that life will not be hard. I am not at all saying that enjoying God or finding satisfaction in Him guarantees worldly ease and physical comfort. Often, precisely the opposite is true. Someone once said that joy is not necessarily the absence of suffering, it is the presence of God. Christian Hedonism is, in my opinion, the only perspective that can successfully sustain the human soul when all of life seems to disintegrate.

Paul said it best when he spoke of the decay of our outer man, which occurs simultaneously with the renewal of our inner man (2 Corinthians 4:16). We spiritually feast upon God while often experiencing a physical famine. Our bodies may corrupt but our spirits soar with joy inexpressible and full of glory. "For momentary, light affliction," explains Paul, "is producing for us an eternal weight of glory far beyond all comparison" (2 Corinthians 4:17). "A good man is a happy man," said Edwards, "whatever his outward circumstances are."[11]

After I preached on Christian Hedonism, a man wrote me a letter of approval in which he said that "sometimes we must accept temporal pain and suffering in order to maximize our joy in eternity. I regard this as an investment with a wildly maximized rate of return." I couldn't agree more! The key is in the purpose statement: It is in order to maximize eternal joy that we often must willingly embrace temporal discomfort. No one better exemplified this than Jesus "who for the joy set before Him endured the cross, despising the shame, and has sat down at the right hand of the throne of God" (Hebrews 12:2).

The world is hell-bent on finding pleasure. That is why hedonism is the dominant philosophy in every age. But according to *Christian* Hedonism, pleasure can ultimately be found only in God. The pleasures of this world last only for a moment. They quickly thrill us and then just as quickly dissipate and disappoint. But the pleasure of being in God's presence and doing God's will and receiving God's blessings lasts forever and ever!

BEHOLDING HIS BEAUTY

There is perhaps no better way to enjoy God than to behold His beauty. We do this when we internalize, as it were, the objective statements of Scripture concerning the wonders of who God is and what He does. When we take the glorious truths of God and meditate on them, muse on them, soak our souls in them, so to speak, we become infatuated with the exquisite beauty of God.

This is clearly what David had in mind in Psalm 27:4, where he wrote, "One thing I have asked from the LORD, that I shall seek; that I may dwell in the house of the Lord all the days of my life, to behold the beauty of the LORD, and to meditate in His temple."

Beauty isn't a word we normally include in our vocabulary about God. We prefer words like sovereign, gracious, merciful, and the "omni" or "all" words: omniscient, omnipotent, and omnipresent. But I want us to think about God in terms of *beauty*.

In my doctoral studies I took several courses in what is called aesthetics, which is the philosophy of beauty. The frustrating thing about these aesthetics courses was that no one seemed to agree on what constitutes beauty. I came away from that time convinced of one thing: *God alone is beautiful in an absolute and unqualified sense.*

In God alone are perfect proportion, harmony, unity, and diversity in delicate balance, stunning brilliance, and integrity. God is beautiful! If we were able to think of God as a painting, we would say that there are no random brush strokes, no clashes of colors. God is aesthetically exquisite. In God there is absolute resolution, integration, the utter absence of even one discordant element.

God has, as it were, placed Himself on display in the art gallery of the universe. He beckons His people, you and me, to stand in awe as we behold the symmetry of His attributes, the harmony of His deeds, the glory of His goodness, the overwhelming and unfathomable grandeur of His greatness; in a word, *His beauty*. God is infinitely splendid and invites us to come and bask in His beauty that we might enjoy Him to the fullest.

In view of David's painful and distressing circumstances, one might have expected him to long for rest and bodily comfort, peace, three square meals a day, or perhaps a permanent and safe home away from his enemies. But for David there is a higher aspiration and desire in his heart. Note that in verse 4 the future tense is combined with the past tense to express an ardent longing which extends out of the past and into the future and therefore runs through his whole life. What is the essence of his desire? To dwell, to behold, to meditate. And who or what is the focus of this passion? God in all His uncreated beauty, His indescribable splendor, His glorious majesty, His unfathomable, ultimately incomprehensible grandeur.

Is this true of us? Can it be true of us? We aren't kings like David. We can't avail ourselves of courtiers and servants to do our every bidding, releasing us from the drudgery of daily life so that we might have the leisure time to bask in God's presence.

We have to go to work eight hours a day and raise kids and mow grass and pay bills. No matter. As Augustine once said, "God thirsts to be thirsted after," no less by you and me than by David (see Jeremiah 29:13).

David's desire, *our* desire, is to dwell in the presence of God, to behold God, to meditate upon the beauty and splendor of God, to bask in the invigorating light and glory of everything that makes God an object of our affection and delight and adoration. This is the culmination of our heart's desire. This is what we were made for, to enjoy God and the greatness of who He is and will be in Himself and for us.

"But," you say, "I feel so pushy when I press in to God. It seems so presumptuous of me. Are you sure He wants me to?" What do you want, an engraved invitation? It's okay if you do, for verse 8 gives you precisely that! "When Thou didst say, 'Seek My face,' my heart said to Thee, 'Thy face, O LORD, I shall seek.'" God "invites" us to seek His face, to dwell, to behold and to meditate upon His beauty. How does that affect you? This is God's desire: "Seek My face"! Some of you aren't accustomed to receiving an invitation to anything. You rarely get invited to lunch after church or to the birthday party or to the wedding or to share your opinion on an important topic. But this is the greatest invitation to the greatest experience of all! Note well: what God wants most isn't more church members, more programs, bigger offerings, more influence in the community, the respect of men in high places, bigger and better and more and more things. He wants you and me to seek His face!

The results of this passionate pursuit of God are staggering. Not only is beholding the beauty of the Lord indescribably enjoyable, it is profoundly transforming. That is because, says Piper, *"beholding is a way of becoming."*[12] The apostle Paul put it this way in 2 Corinthians 3:18: "We all, with unveiled face beholding the glory of the Lord, are being transformed into the same image from glory to glory. . . ." The point is that we become like that which we behold. We will never be transformed into the likeness of God or be conformed to the image of Christ Jesus until we learn how to behold His beauty. To see Him is to be like Him. As David beheld the beauty of the Lord, as he meditated on the glorious perfections and passions of God's character, he became more like God. More than that, he fell ever more in love with God.

HOLY DISSATISFACTION

Do you want to glorify God in all that you are, do, and say? Then begin to enjoy Him! Our God is an inexhaustible reservoir of infinitely satisfying spiritual delights. God will never lack for what will fascinate and intrigue and enthrall you. You will never devote yourself to understanding God and one day say: "Well, that's all there is." No. There is always more! But neither will you ever say: "Well, that's enough." Why? Because God satisfies in a way that always creates deeper dissatisfaction.

When you drink water to quench your thirst, there comes a point when water ceases to be appealing to you. Although you were desperately thirsty, there comes a point when you say "Enough!" There comes a point when you can't take anymore; you're filled; you're satiated. It would actually be painful to take more. You're on the verge of regurgitating. All of us revel in the physical joy of satisfying our hunger with food. But once full, food loses its appeal. Even those who stood repeatedly in line to ride the Mamba time and time again eventually had enough. They went home.

But God is the only being in the universe who, when received, when spiritually ingested, has the infinite capacity both to fill and satisfy without leading you to say, "Stop! Enough!" God is Himself passionate about touching His people. He loves to fill them, to thrill them, to bring them delight and joy and excitement and peace and purpose, even in the midst of painful trials and confusing tragedies. God enjoys bringing us virtually to the point of saturation where we think we've seen it all, heard it all, tasted it all, felt it all. Yet, precisely when we say, "Enough's enough; it's time to move on to something new and fresh and more exciting," He shows us something never before seen, something unexpected; a fresh taste, a new sound, something about Him yet more glorious and thrilling than we could ever have imagined.

How do we overcome our enjoyment of sin? With our enjoyment of God! We minimize our delight in the pleasures of the flesh by maximizing our delight in the pleasures of our Creator. Oh, taste and see that the Lord is good!

CHAPTER THREE

When Serving God Is Sinful

A PROPER UNDERSTANDING OF THE CHARACTER OF GOD IS crucial to the vision of holiness that I am proposing in this book. Without wanting to sound cynical, I'm convinced that many Christians have a horribly distorted and warped view of God, particularly in two areas. First, although they might not put it in precisely these terms, their lives reflect the fact that they view God as needful of their service and what they can do for Him. They often live in fear that if they don't give enough to God, whether what they give is obedience or money or time, He will suffer loss and perhaps lash out in anger. They envision God as a stern taskmaster who takes greatest delight in placing on his people unbearable demands, all the while cracking the whip of discipline when they fail to add to His depleted glory. I want to address that misconception in this chapter, and take up yet another in the chapter that follows.

Is God Needy?

The biblical fact of the matter is that, ultimately speaking, God has no need of us. I know this cuts deeply into our sense of self-importance, but look closely at what the apostle Paul said to the Athenian philosophers: "Neither is He served by human hands as though He needed anything, since He Himself gives to all life and breath and all things" (Acts 17:25). In another text Paul extols God precisely because "from Him and through Him and to Him are all things" (Romans 11:36). If God already owns everything and is in Himself perfectly complete, what do we think we could possibly add to His already immeasurably sufficient being? The truth is that *the God of the Bible is the kind of God whose greatest delight comes not from making demands but from meeting needs.*

Yet, tragically, many Christians exhaust themselves in trying to shore up what they think are deficiencies in God. Their approach to the Christian life is to give to God what they evidently think He lacks. But God is most honored not when we strive to bolster what we mistakenly think is His diminishing supply, but when we come to Him humbly to receive from His mercy and goodness what only He can provide. Contrary to what some have said about Christian Hedonism, that in all its talk of seeking pleasure and happiness it is man-centered, it is, rather, profoundly theocentric. Here's how.

BELITTLING GOD

I know this sounds strange, but there is a way of "serving God" that belittles Him, insults Him, and thus robs Him of glory. We must beware of serving Him in a way that implies a deficiency on His part or asserts our indispensability to Him. God is not in need of our service or help. We are in need of His. His purpose in the earth is not sustained by our energy. Rather, we are sustained and strengthened by His. We have nothing of value that is not already His by right.

It was Jesus Himself who said, "For even the Son of Man did not come to be served, but to serve, and to give His life a ransom for many" (Mark 10:45, Matthew 20:28). Here Jesus makes a claim that is nowhere to be found on the lips of any other religious leader or teacher. Jesus is not just another moral philosopher or religious zealot with a set of rules who is trying to drum up a following of men and women who will wait on Him hand and foot. Jesus says to His followers, "I didn't come to the earth so that you could serve Me! I came so that I might serve you."

Look once again at the passage in Acts that I noted earlier: "The God who made the world and all things in it, since He is Lord of heaven and earth, does not dwell in temples made with hands; *neither is He served by human hands, as though He needed anything, since He Himself gives to all life and breath and all things*" (Acts 17:24-25, emphasis added). A few verses later Paul declares that in God "we live and move and exist" (17:28). We breathe on borrowed air! All our movements, indeed, our very being are the fruit of divine mercy. Anyone who tries to serve God as if He were needy is merely giving God what He had already given to him or her. As Piper points out: "So no one can bribe God or coerce Him in any way. Whatever you or I or anyone or any circumstance offers to God, it is only the reflex of something He has already given or already done. The source of all things cannot be enriched or tempted with angelic or human service."[1]

The fact that God cannot be served is not good news to those who are determined to maintain an aura of self-sufficiency and independence. If you are convinced (I should say "deluded") that you can bargain with God for acceptance and reward, Paul's statement in Acts 17:24-25 will come as a surprise. If you are among those who think they can do or give or supply something for God that will place Him in their debt, this principle will be painfully unsettling to your soul. But if you are weak and desperate and feel spiritually impotent to do anything apart from the grace that God supplies, you will celebrate Paul's declaration. Nowhere is this truth seen more clearly than when it comes to our use of money.

GIVING IS FROM GOD

Consider the description of the spiritual dynamics involved when David undertook what may have been the largest building program in history. In 1 Chronicles 29:6-20 we read of the wealth that was raised for the construction of the temple. From a purely human perspective it would appear that David and the Israelites are to be congratulated for giving so generously to the work of the Lord. But we must look beyond what can be seen and discern the hand of God at work.

It's truly a remarkable story. "With all my ability" (29:2) and "in my delight" (29:3), says David, "I give to the house of my God" (29:3). The people likewise "offered willingly" (29:6) and "with a whole heart" (29:9) to supply the resources necessary for this massive undertaking. Again, "in the integrity" of his heart David "willingly" (29:17) offered all these things. No one gave under compulsion or out of fear or guilt. They rejoiced in the freedom and opportunity to participate.

But there is more to this story than meets the eye. Behind the scenes of David's prayer with its glad, willing, happy human endeavor is the hand of an all-sufficient God who overflows in abundance to His people.

We first see this abundance in the fact that David immediately blesses God (verse 10). His response to this tremendous influx of earthly wealth and riches is to bless God, not men or women! This blessing takes the form of a dozen affirmations concerning who God is and what He does, all of which are revealed in the willingness of His people to give so much to the building of the temple.

Let me skip down through the list to the sixth of the twelve declarations concerning God. In verse 11 David states that "everything that is in the heavens and the earth" belongs to God. This is why giving is all about God: He already owns everything! He owns your clothes and your car and your bank account and your body and your house and your books and your jewelry and your television set(s)— He owns it all. He owns your mind and your emotions and your spirit and your eyes and your ears and your hair and your blood and your toenails. He has graciously and freely given us these things to use and enjoy for His glory, and He may take them back anytime He wishes. We are trustees or stewards of what God possesses. He also owns every dime (or sheckel) that we might willingly and joyfully choose to give to Him.

The ninth of these twelve declarations is no less stunning in its ramifications. In verse 12, David says of God that "both riches and honor come from Thee." God is no usurper of things that are not rightfully His. From a purely human point of view, the money and wealth given for the building of the temple seem to come from the work and energy and savings and investments of the people. Perhaps some of them had profited from shrewd business transactions. Perhaps a few had turned an incredible profit on the sale of some land. But no matter, David says that all riches come from God! Whatever anyone worked for, earned, invested, sold and then gave, they first got it from God.

Again in verse 12, David asserts that it lies in God's hand "to make great and to strengthen everyone." Whatever energy or accomplishments may be traceable to the people that accounted for what and why they gave, all of it ultimately came from God. Power, influence, ingenuity, success, commitment, whatever it might be, are the result of the gracious and kind operation of a benevolent and giving God working in and through His people for their welfare and His own glory.

The eleventh thing David says comes in the form of a question: "But who am I and who are my people that we should be able to offer as generously as this?" (verse 14). This is David's way of saying that God is the one who enables us to do what we do not deserve help to do. Who are we, asks David, that we should receive the help of God that would mobilize us to produce this wealth and then stir our hearts to give it away? We are sinners. We deserve nothing but judgment.

Perhaps the most instructive thing David says comes next in verse 14: "For all things come from Thee, and from Thy hand we have given Thee." He doesn't say, "To Thy hand," as if it originated with us and ended with you. Rather, it is "From Thy hand." In other words, whatever they gave they first received. He says much the same thing in verse 16: "O LORD our God, all this abundance that we have provided to build Thee a house for Thy holy name, it is from Thy hand, and all is Thine." We do not offer to God what He lacks. In giving, we do not add to His resources or increase the balance of His bank account. How can you increase the wealth of someone who already owns it all? Our giving is but a reflex of God's giving.

Twelfth, and finally, David prays that God would "preserve this forever in the intentions of the heart of Thy people, and direct their heart to Thee, and give to my son Solomon a perfect heart to keep Thy commandments" (verse 18). God's enabling in this matter is not simply that He makes it possible for us to work hard, not simply that He bestows riches on whomever He pleases, but that He actually gives us the willingness to give! Yes, the people did the giving (verse 9). They gave willingly, of their own accord, and with joy. It was genuine giving, freely chosen, joyfully engaged. They made decisions. Real decisions. Sacrificial decisions. Decisions that made a difference. Decisions without which the temple would not have been built. But mysteriously, in ways that you and I will never fully understand, beneath and behind these choices was the gracious, enabling work of God.

What all this means is that our God is a God of infinite, immeasurable wealth. He owns everything that is. He does not stand in need of gifts or offerings or contributions as if He were poor and helpless and dependent. We are the poor, the helpless, the dependent ones. God is always the giver. We are always the getters! We simply must understand this if we are to progress in growth in our Christian lives and in our pursuit of holiness.

FROM CHRONICLES TO CORINTH

Let's take a leap of several centuries from 1 Chronicles to 2 Corinthians and note that the service of God on behalf of His people doesn't diminish with time (or with the change of testaments).

Paul's passionate appeal in 2 Corinthians 8–9 to give generously grew out of the poverty of the church in Jerusalem (see 1 Corinthians 16:1-4; Romans 15:25-27). The reasons for this crisis are numerous: in addition to overpopulation, there was social and economic ostracism, disinheritance following conversion, disruption of family ties, persecution, and the lingering effects of the famine of A.D. 46 (compare Acts 11:27-30). Paul's efforts to raise money to help the saints in Jerusalem were obviously justified. This was a concrete expression of his resolve as stated in Galatians 2:10: "They only asked us to remember the poor—the very thing I also was eager to do." By pointing to the example of sacrificial giving set by the Macedonians (that is, the Christians in Philippi, Thessalonica, and Berea), Paul hopes to stimulate the Corinthians to complete their efforts at contributing to their poverty-stricken brethren in Jerusalem (compare 2 Corinthians 8:10-11).

Yes, Paul appeals to what believers in Macedonia had done. But like David in 1 Chronicles, he is quick to acknowledge that what they did in serving their brethren is the fruit of what God had done in serving them! If the Macedonians "gave themselves to the Lord" in this ministry (verse 5), it is because God had first "given his grace" (verse 1) to them. Whatever achievement on their part is praised, it is ultimately attributed to the prior activity of divine grace. Here we see the harmony between the antecedent presence of divine grace and the moral accountability of human decisions. In verse 3 Paul says they gave "of their own accord," while in verse 1 their willingness is traced to a gift of God: grace. The same principle is found in verses 16-17 where Paul says God put "earnestness" in Titus's heart, who in turn, "of his own accord," went to the Corinthians.

They didn't give because God had prospered them financially. He hadn't! Financial blessing didn't lead to joy. Rather, joy led to a financial blessing (for the saints in Jerusalem). Their joy, therefore, was not in money, but in God and the experience of His grace. Piper explains:

> How did such countercultural and counter-natural behavior come about? How were the Christians freed from the natural

love of money and comfort? Part of the answer in verse 2 is that their abundance of joy overflowed. Joy in something else had severed the root of joy in money. They had been freed by joy to give to the poor. But where did this powerful, unearthly joy come from? The answer is that it came from the grace of God. . . . What the Corinthians [as well as you and I] are supposed to learn from this story is that the same grace that was given in Macedonia is available now in Corinth [and in whatever city you live, in whatever church you call home].[2]

Don't miss the spiritual dynamic at work here: grace comes down, joy rises up, generosity flows out. It is because of divine grace that they experienced joy, and it is because they experienced such joy in grace that they gave so generously.

As they looked at their ability to give, they no doubt took into consideration both their present situation and their future needs and obligations. Having done so, they then showed total disregard for both! This is not because they were foolish. Undoubtedly they knew the consequences for themselves and willingly embraced them. In all likelihood, they first determined what they could reasonably give and then went above and beyond that amount. They were able to take this approach because grace was operative in their hearts. God was serving them so that they could gladly serve others! That alone can account for this remarkable demonstration of love and earnestness on their part.

And again, this in no way diminishes the moral value of what was done, for Paul insists that they gave not because they felt compelled or coerced but of their own accord—that is, freely and voluntarily (2 Corinthians 8:3). They didn't give out of greed (thinking that by giving they would eventually get back more in return), guilt, fear, in response to an apostolic command, or any such reason. In fact, Paul refused to ask them for money for the collection, knowing full well their financial condition. They were forced to urgently plead, indeed, beg Paul for the opportunity to participate in this ministry! Amazing!

Most people beg to get money; the Macedonians beg to give money! Here's how Piper explains the situation:

> When poverty-stricken Macedonians beg Paul for the privilege of giving money to other poor saints, we may assume that this is what they want to do, not just ought to do, or have to do, but really long to do. It is their joy—an extension of their joy in God. To be sure, they are "denying themselves" whatever pleasures or comforts they could have from the money they give away, but the joy of extending God's grace to others is a far better reward than anything money could buy. The Macedonians have discovered the labor of Christian Hedonism: love! It is the overflow of joy in God which gladly meets the needs of others.[3]

Paul puts all this in perspective in 2 Corinthians 9 with two statements that are relevant to our discussion. First, he declares that "God loves a cheerful giver" (verse 7). But, if God loves a cheerful giver, He is displeased when people give but don't do it gladly, even if their giving is generous. Piper says, "When people don't find pleasure (Paul's word is 'cheer!') in their acts of service, God doesn't find pleasure in them."[4] Does that mean if we don't have joy we shouldn't give at all? No, because, as Piper goes on to say, "though joyless love is not our aim, nevertheless it is better to do a joyless duty than not to do it, provided there is a spirit of repentance for the deadness of our heart."[5]

Then note also the promise of abundance in verses 8-11, a passage that has been sorely abused by many who advocate a crass form of prosperity gospel. In effect, God says to those who gladly and generously give: "Okay, I see that you're going to take this seriously. Good. You mean business. Well, so do I. I'm going to make a promise to you. As long as you are willing to give [a willingness that, as we saw in both 1 Chronicles and 2 Corinthians 8, flows first from God's antecedent activity of gracious enablement], I will never leave you without the resources to do it. I will never let you give yourself into poverty. That's a promise."

Clearly, God promises to supply abundantly those who give generously. Paul wants the Corinthians to be free from the fear that generous giving will leave them impoverished. But for what purpose or with what goal in mind does God cause the generous Christian steward to abound? Why does God promise financial abundance to those who cheerfully and freely give to others?

Before I answer that, did you notice Paul's unapologetic use of universals in 2 Corinthians 9:8? He says, "God is able to make all grace abound to you, that always having all sufficiency in everything, you may have an abundance for every good deed." One would almost think that Paul is trying to make a point!

So, why does God promise financial abundance to you if you are cheerful and free in your giving? God promises to continue serving you financially in order that "you may have an abundance for *every good deed*" (9:8). Again, it is in order that He might "multiply your *seed for sowing*" (9:10, emphasis added). Finally, it is in order that you might be enriched in everything "*for all liberality*" (9:11, emphasis added). Paul is claiming that God will never stir your heart to give and then fail to supply you with resources to do so. But the idea that we should give so that God will then enrich us personally with a view to increasing our comfort and convenience and purchasing power is foreign to Paul's teaching. Personal wealth is here viewed, not as an end in itself, but as a means to a yet higher goal—generosity to those in need.

We should also note in verse 9 that Paul envisions God's faithfulness in giving to us so that we might give to others as an expression of His righteousness. In other words, the truth of the promise to us in verse 8 is a matter of divine integrity: If God were not to serve us by amply supplying what we need to engage in the good deed of giving, His reputation as righteous would be impugned. God's name is on the line. That is why we may confidently know that He will never fail to fulfill the assertions of verse 8.

Finally, verses 12-13 remove any vestiges of doubt as to whether this entire scenario is the result of God's serving His people. There Paul says that this ministry of giving evokes gratitude to God, for all giving has its source in His grace (verse 12). Then again in verse 13, as they contemplate your giving, says Paul, they will be prompted to glorify God, something that makes sense only if it is God who is ultimately serving us by supplying the resources to give.

IF GOD WERE HUNGRY

In a passage that virtually drips with divine sarcasm, God slaps our arrogance in the face when He says, "If I were hungry, I would not tell you; for the world is Mine, and all it contains. . . . And call upon Me in the day of trouble; I shall rescue you, and you will honor Me" (Psalm 50:12,15). When we come to God for rescue and deliverance and help in our time of need, everyone wins. We get rescued and God gets honored! Piper reminds us of some facts Christians should remember: "The gospel is not a Help Wanted ad. Neither is the call to Christian service. On the contrary, the gospel commands us to give up and hang out a Help Wanted sign."[6] Recruits who want to help Him out do not glorify Him. Our God is so completely full and self-sufficient and so overflowing in power and life and joy that He glorifies Himself by serving us. That is why becoming a Christian is so humbling: it is our admission that we need God's help, not an offer to help Him. One of the reasons so many Christians continue to experience so much failure is that they think of holiness as if it meant "revving up" their own moral and volitional engines and giving God a lift.

My challenge to you is that you lay down your preconceived notions about God and what most pleases Him and consider the fact no one "has first given to Him that it might be paid back to Him again. For from Him and through Him and to Him are all things. To Him be the glory forever. Amen" (Romans 11:35-36). There is no better illustration of this magnificent truth than in the following illustration by John Piper. Reading and pondering it carefully will pay rich rewards:

> God has no needs that I [or anyone else] could ever be required to satisfy. God has no deficiencies that I might be required to supply. He is complete in himself. He is overflowing with happiness in the fellowship of the Trinity. The upshot of this is that God is a mountain spring, not a watering trough. A mountain spring is self-replenishing. It constantly overflows and supplies others. But a watering trough needs to be filled with a pump or bucket brigade. So if you want to glorify the worth of a watering trough you work hard to keep it full and useful. But if you want to glorify the worth of a spring you do it by getting down on your hands and knees and drinking to your heart's satisfaction, until you have the refreshment and strength to go back down in the valley and tell people what you've found. You do not glorify a mountain spring by dutifully hauling water up the path from the river below and dumping it in the spring. What we have seen is that God is like a mountain spring, not a watering trough. And since that is the way God is, we are not surprised to learn from Scripture—and our faith is strengthened to hold fast— that the way to please God is to come to him to get and not to give, to drink and not to water. He is most glorified in us when we are most satisfied in him.

My hope as a desperate sinner, who lives in a Death Valley desert of unrighteousness, hangs on this biblical truth: that God is the kind of God who will be pleased with the one thing I have to offer—my thirst. That is why the sovereign freedom and self-sufficiency of God are so precious to me. They are the foundation of my hope that God is delighted, not by the resourcefulness of bucket brigades but by the bending down of broken sinners to drink at the fountain of grace.

In other words, this unspeakably good news for helpless sinners—that God delights not when we offer him our strength but when we wait for his—this good news that I need to hear so badly again and again, is based firmly on a vision of God as sovereign, self-sufficient and free.[7]

GOD THE SERVANT

Again, I know how odd this will sound, but it should be carefully considered: God is our servant in the sense that He uses all His divine resources to help us and strengthen us and support us and provide our needs as we obey His command to serve others. In one of His parables, Jesus said, "Be dressed in readiness, and keep your lamps alight. And be like men who are waiting for their master when he returns from the wedding feast, so that they may immediately open the door to him when he comes and knocks. Blessed are those slaves whom the master shall find on the alert when he comes; truly I say to you, that he will gird himself to serve, and have them recline at table, and will come up and wait on them" (Luke 12:35-37). Here we see that the "master" insists on serving even in the age to come when He will gloriously appear "with his mighty angels in flaming fire" (2 Thessalonians 1:7). Why? Because the very heart of His glory is the fullness of grace that overflows in kindness to needy people.

Consider this stunning declaration from the prophecy of Isaiah: "From of old they have not heard nor perceived by ear, neither has the eye seen a God besides Thee, *who acts in behalf of the one who waits for Him*" (Isaiah 64:4, emphasis added). The good news is that this God who acts and works on our behalf *never tires, becomes weary, or sleeps!* God never says, "Whoahh, give Me a break. I've been up for days and I'm tuckered out. I need a rest." According to Psalm 121:3, God never sleeps: "He who keeps thee will not slumber." Why? Because "the Everlasting God, the LORD, the creator of the ends of the earth does not become weary or tired" (Isaiah 40:28). He never sleeps because He's never tired. After all, how could a Being whose power is limitless suffer exhaustion?

The fact that He isn't tired isn't because He doesn't work. On the contrary, God works all the time. He governs the nations (see Revelation 15:3) and upholds the universe in existence each moment (see Hebrews 1:3) and continually feeds the animals of the earth (see Matthew 10:29; Psalm 104:21). As 2 Chronicles 16:9 tells us, God is constantly "on the prowl" looking for ways to work for those who put their hope in Him. He wants more work because it means more opportunities for Him to demonstrate His power and wisdom and love and mercy. To think that we might have resources to relieve Him or resupply His depleted energy is to besmirch His infinitely self-sufficient character. If God has need of something to do anything, He simply speaks it into existence out of nothing!

This is what sets apart the God of Israel from all the so-called "gods" of the ancient world. All other "gods" expected the people to act on their behalf. But God delights most in acting on our behalf: "For the eyes of the LORD move to and fro throughout the earth that He may strongly support those whose heart is completely His" (2 Chronicles 16:9). In our misguided zeal, we say: "Oh, God, what can I do for you?" To which God replies: "No, no. You've got it backwards. The question is, 'What can I do for you? You don't strongly support me. I'm God! I strongly support you.'" We must never forget that God is always the Giver and we the recipients.

Again, we read, "Behold as the eyes of servants look to the hand of their master, as the eyes of a maid to the hand of her mistress; so our eyes look to the LORD our God, until He shall be gracious to us" (Psalm 123:2). And still again, Jesus declares, "I am the vine, you are the branches; he who abides in Me, and I in him, he bears much fruit; for apart from Me you can do nothing" (John 15:5). In 1 Peter we find, "Whoever serves, let him do so as by the strength that God supplies, so that in all things God may be glorified through

Jesus Christ" (4:11). Peter's point is that our service to others is produced by God's service to us. Consider also the following:

> For I will not presume to speak of anything except what Christ has accomplished through me, resulting in the obedience of the Gentiles by word and deed. (Romans 15:18; compare 2 Timothy 4:17)

> Now the God of peace . . . equip you in every good thing to do His will, working in us that which is pleasing in His sight, through Jesus Christ, to whom be the glory forever and ever. Amen. (Hebrews 13:20-21)

THE ANTECEDENT GOD

There are countless texts that make this point but none more forcefully than Philippians 2:12-13.[8] Paul encourages the Philippian believers (and us) to "work out your salvation with fear and trembling." Had he stopped at that, my vision for how to live a holy life would have to be recast in an entirely different mold. But he continues with the reassuring promise, "for it is God who is at work in you, both to will and to work for His good pleasure." Here Paul asserts the urgency of responsible human behavior based on the promise of *prior divine activity*. To put it simply: *God is always previous!*

Paul unashamedly declares that the antecedent presence of God's enabling power is the foundation on which you and I actively and obediently do the things that are pleasing in His sight. He assures us that our efforts, if undertaken in the strength that the Spirit supplies, will not prove vain. We have genuine hope for working out our salvation in all its varied dimensions because God is already at work in us to stir, stimulate, and sustain our volitional response. As I have written elsewhere, "each impulse and act of the human heart may be traced to the prior operation of divine power without in any way diminishing its moral value. The urgent call for responsible human 'doing' follows and flows out of the assurance of a divine 'done.'"[9] No one knows exactly how God does it, but J. I. Packer reminds us that

> the Holy Spirit's ordinary way of working in us is through the working of our own minds and wills. He moves us to act by causing us to see reasons for moving ourselves to act. Thus our conscious, rational selfhood, so far from being annihilated, is strengthened, and in reverent, resolute obedience we work out our salvation, knowing that God is at work in us to make us " . . . both . . . will and . . . work for His good pleasure."[10]

Here, then, in my paraphrase is what Paul is saying: "Serve, knowing that it is God who is serving you by enabling you to serve Him and others."

Biblical texts such as this are what lead me to conclude that the radical call to self-sacrificing discipleship and holiness of life is not fundamentally a call to serve Jesus. It is a call to be served by Jesus so that we may then serve others. Many mistakenly think of God as if He were an insecure bully who likes to flex His heavenly muscles by putting down those who are weaker than He is. But God loves to show off His greatness and glory by being an inexhaustible source of strength to build up weak people like you and me.[11] We honor God, not by pretending to give Him what we arrogantly think He needs, but by praying for and posturing ourselves to receive all that He is and has obtained for us in Jesus. Why? Because the very heart of God's glory is the fullness and abundance of grace that overflows in kindness to needy people like you and me. God will gladly receive from us only that which reveals our dependence and His all-sufficiency.

People have often read Psalm 119 and come away utterly confused. They simply cannot fathom how David is able to speak of the "law" and "precepts" and "requirements" and "rules" of God with a smile on his face. What pleasure can possibly be found in a seemingly endless list of "do's and dont's"? That's an easy question to answer once you realize that nowhere does the goodness and generosity and grace of God shine forth with greater brilliance than in His commands. Edwards explains:

> What could the most merciful being have done more for our encouragement? All that He desires of us is that we would not be miserable, that we would not follow those courses which of themselves would end in misery, and that we would be happy.[12]

Whoa! Stop! Did you hear that? Read it again. All that God desires of us is that "we would not be miserable . . . and that we should be happy." Does that sound like the God you've been "serving" these many years? It should. Now, let's pick up with Edwards as he explains how God goes about fulfilling this great desire:

> God, having a great desire to speak after the manner of man, that we should not be miserable but happy, has the mercy and goodness that He forwards us to it, to command us to do those things that will make us so. Should we not think Him a prince of extraordinary clemency, He a master of extraordinary goodness, He a father of great tenderness, who never commanded anything of His subjects, His servants, or His children, but what was for their good and advantage? But God is such a king, such a lord, such a father to us.[13]

Every syllable of every statute, every clause of every commandment that ever proceeded from the mouth of God was divinely designed to bring those who would obey into the greatest imaginable happiness of heart. Don't swallow God's law like castor oil. For when you understand His intent, it will be like honey on your lips and sweetness to your soul.

OUR DUTY TO OBEY

How, then, do we properly "serve" God? There is no escaping the fact that in some sense of the term we are God's "servants." Paul called himself a "bond-servant" of Christ Jesus (Romans 1:1) and exhorted the church in Rome to "serve the Lord" (Romans 12:11). We must begin by defining what it means to be God's "servants" without belittling Him as needful of us.

First of all, we are rightly called God's "servants" or "bond-slaves" because He owns us: we "have been bought with a price" (1 Corinthians 6:20), the blood of Christ. We belong to Him. Jonathan Edwards gave expression to this truth in an entry to his personal diary, dated Saturday, January 12, 1723:

> I have this day solemnly renewed my baptismal covenant and self-dedication, which I renewed when I was received into the communion of the church. I have been before God; and have given myself, all that I am and have to God, so that I am not in any respect my own: I can challenge no right in myself, I can challenge no right in this understanding, this will, these affections that are in me; neither have I any right to this body, or any of its members: no right to this tongue, these hands, nor feet: no right to these senses, these eyes, these ears, this smell or taste. I have given myself clear away, and have not retained any thing as my own. I have been to God this morning, and told Him that I gave myself wholly to Him. I have given every power to Him; so that for the future I will challenge no right in myself, in any respect.[14]

Clearly, by "giving" himself in this way to God, Edwards refers both to a recognition on his part of God's absolute ownership of all he is and his willing submission to God's prior claim on the whole of his life.

Second, we are rightly called God's "servants" insofar as we submit to His authority and acknowledge His right to tell us to do whatever He pleases. But we have mistakenly interpreted God's commands as directives for how we are to serve Him, when in fact they are God's way of defining how He wants to serve us. Whenever the Scriptures call for my obedience I immediately turn to the Son of God who has promised to carry my burden and infuse me with His power to do His will. Jesus does not need my help. He commands my obedience and then amazingly offers His help. That is why obedience is not hard (see Deuteronomy 30:11; Matthew 11:28-30 [contrast Matthew 23:4]; 1 John 5:3). Christ's "yoke" is easy and His "burden" is light because whatever God requires, He provides! The God who commands is the God who mobilizes all His inexhaustible resources and divine energy on behalf of those who wait on Him.

The radical call to commitment and obedience to everything commanded in Scripture is not something we do for Him, but things He enables us to do for others. The reason we may confidently sacrifice ourselves in the service of others is because Jesus will sacrifice Himself in serving us. He has promised to serve me by sustaining my will as I risk loving those who may not love back. There is nothing to which He calls me that He does not gladly and with unwavering consistency promise to provide that I may fulfill.

To use another metaphor, God is like a doctor and you are the patient. The patient doesn't go to the doctor with a prescription in hand or a diagnosis in mind. He goes to the doctor because the latter alone knows the problem and can prescribe a remedy. The patient magnifies the doctor when he goes for relief from pain. The patient does not elevate himself above the doctor by seeking his aid. The doctor's glory is revealed in serving his patient and using all his knowledge and resources to relieve his discomfort or heal his disease. Likewise, God is most honored when we seek from Him the healing and restoration and joy and fulfillment that He delights in providing for us. We are the patients in need of help. God is the physician who provides a cure. Piper says, "Patients do not serve their physicians. They trust them for good prescriptions. The Sermon on the Mount and the Ten Commandments are the Doctor's prescribed health regimen, not the Employer's job description."[15] Thus we honor God most when we trust Him to serve us as a physician serves his patients.

To so honor God relates directly to our motivation in worship, something I'll address more fully in a later chapter. For years I used to view worship as a time during which I would give of myself to God. But worship is primarily a craving for God. Worship is me declaring to the world that God is my all in all, that He alone can quench the thirst of my soul and satisfy the hunger of my heart.

David had this in mind when he compared his yearning for God with the vivid imagery of a deer in a desert land, panting for life-giving water: "As the deer pants for the water brooks, so my soul pants for Thee, O God. My soul thirsts for God, for the living God" (Psalm 42:1-2). The focus in this word-picture is not the deer, but the water. It is on the cool, refreshing, sustaining properties of the desert stream that all eyes are fixed. The deer brings nothing to the brooks but its desperation and its thirst. This is how we must come to God when we worship: desperate, thirsty, hungry, yearning, and dependent. Here is what you are:

- You are the thirsty deer and God is the overflowing spring.
- You are the lost sheep and God is the good shepherd.
- You are the bankrupt beggar and God is the generous philanthropist.

Who, in each of these relationships, gets the glory? To sum up: *The heart of all that God helps us do in His service of us is to maximize our satisfaction in Him.* God is committed (that's His grace) to do in service for us everything we need to find maximum pleasure and delight and satisfaction of soul (that's our joy) in His Son.

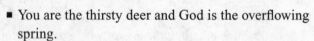

THE TWO MOST POWERFUL PASSIONS IN THE WORLD

In a fascinating little phrase, John Piper unites for us the two most powerful forces in the universe, namely, *God's passion to be glorified* and *your passion to be satisfied*: "God is most glorified in us when we are most satisfied in Him."[16]

The glorious good news is that, contrary to what the church has been told for centuries, these are not mutually exclusive passions. The glory of God and the gladness of your heart go together like love and marriage, like a horse and carriage!

If that is the case, then *my principal motivation in life must be to increase my pleasure in God*. In fact, my prayer every day is "Oh, God, mobilize all your power on my behalf to maximize my pleasure and delight in You." Don't misunderstand what I'm suggesting. I'm not saying that pleasure is put above God, nor that pleasure is God. I'm saying that our pleasure must be in God. The pleasure or satisfaction we seek is God Himself. God is not a tool for finding pleasure. God is not the shovel, so to speak, with which we dig for buried jewels. God is Himself that treasure. The Christian's pursuit of happiness is consummated when we find in God our all in all. He and He alone is our exceeding great reward. He is not a means to a higher end. He is the end.

So, let me say it again: *God is most glorified in us when we are most satisfied in Him*. Therefore, it is incumbent on us to do everything we can to increase, expand, and intensify our pleasure and happiness in God.

This vision for the Christian life is not one of passivity or quietism. It is activity in the strength that God supplies. Turn away from sin, say No to sin; believe, bank on, and rest in God's promise that what He offers you in Christ is infinitely sweeter and more satisfying. Don't wait passively for God to drag you kicking and screaming into a godly life. Rather, do and say this: (1) "I trust God's promise" (that the pleasures He offers are superior to the passing pleasures of sin). (2) "I choose God's path" (I will say No to sin and run from it). And (3) "I rely on God's power" (to energize me in the pursuit of Him and His ways).

Summing Up

Before closing this chapter, perhaps a brief summary of where we've been might help. Piper has articulated the five convictions on which this approach to the pursuit of holiness is built.

1. The longing to be happy is a universal human experience, and it is good, not sinful.
2. We should never try to deny or resist our longing to be happy, as though it were a bad impulse. Instead we should seek to intensify this longing and nourish it with whatever will provide the deepest and most enduring satisfaction.
3. The deepest and most enduring happiness is found only in God. Not from God, but in God.
4. The happiness we find in God reaches its consummation when it is shared with others in the manifold ways of love.
5. To the extent we try to abandon the pursuit of our own pleasure, we fail to honor God and love people. Or, to put it positively: the pursuit of pleasure is a necessary part of all worship and virtue. That is, the chief end of man is to glorify God by enjoying Him forever.[17]

CHAPTER FOUR

GOD'S PASSION FOR GOD

THE KEY TO HOLINESS, ONCE AGAIN, IS FALLING IN LOVE WITH Jesus. By "falling in love" I don't mean mindless mush. I have in mind having in one's mind a passionate delight in the infinite excellencies of God in Christ. Falling in love with Jesus means having your heart and mind entranced, bedazzled, and captivated by the superlative beauty and sweetness of the Son of God.

This experience begins at conversion, for the essence of being born again, says Edwards, "is to give the heart a Divine taste or sense; to cause it to have a relish of the loveliness and sweetness of the supreme excellency of the Divine nature."[1] This is no static deposit, however, but a living seed that comes to full flower and blossoms throughout the course of one's life in Christ. It is a live coal, if you will, on which the Holy Spirit deigns to blow and bring to white-hot intensity. This new taste for the sweetness of the Savior, developed and cultivated, is the only thing that turns sin sour in our souls. That's why falling in love with Jesus is the key to holiness.

Another way of putting it is that our fight for happiness in God must fuel our fight against sin. Delight in God will alone dislodge sin from our hearts. Delight in God is therefore the aim of all our thoughts and efforts and appetites. Long term, this alone will undermine our delight in sin. In other words, this book focuses on the preeminent passion of our hearts, namely, joy in God. If this passion for God does not consume us, sin will. What I now want to suggest is that our glad-hearted passion for God is exceeded only by God's glad-hearted passion for God, and that the latter is foundational to the former. Let me put it in the form of a question.

What is the preeminent passion in God's heart? What is God's greatest pleasure? How does the happiness of God manifest itself? In what does God take supreme delight? I want to suggest that *the preeminent passion in God's heart is His own glory*. God is at the center of His own affections. The supreme love of God's life is God. God is preeminently committed to the fame of His name. God is Himself the end for which God created the world. Better still, God's immediate goal in all He does is His own glory.

God relentlessly and unceasingly creates, rules, orders, directs, speaks, judges, saves, destroys, and delivers in order to make known who He is and to secure from the whole of the universe the praise, honor, and glory of which He and He alone is ultimately and infinitely worthy.

We have already seen that, according to the Westminster Confession of Faith, "the chief end of man is to glorify God and enjoy Him forever." Foundational to this is something else I learned from Edwards and Piper: "The chief end of *God* is to glorify *God* and to enjoy *Himself* forever." Apart from this decidedly theocentric view of the universe, all our efforts at holiness, be they ever so much in the grace of God, will be seriously deficient.

Two objections are often voiced to this assertion. First, this sounds terribly selfish and egocentric. And second, if God loves Himself preeminently, how can He love me at all? How can we say that God is for us and that He desires our happiness if He is primarily for Himself and His own glory? I want to argue that it is precisely because God loves Himself that He loves you. I want to argue that it is precisely in seeking His own happiness that He seeks yours. Let me prove my thesis from the Bible with a little help from Jonathan Edwards.[2]

WHY?

I was greatly helped in understanding this principle by something J. I. Packer wrote in his book *Hot Tub Religion*. Packer says, "The only answer that the Bible gives to questions that begin: 'Why did God . . . ?' is: 'For his own glory.'"[3] Everything God does is for His own glory. Everything God permits is for His own glory. Everything God pursues is for His own glory. When God acts it is for the sake of His name. And all this graciously redounds to our happy benefit. To put it more directly, *the aim of God in creation and redemption is His delight in our delight in Him!*

I want to demonstrate this by citing a number of important biblical texts. Resist the temptation to skip over them. I encourage you to read and meditate on each of them and the comments I have made.

GOD: "THE FIRST AND THE LAST," THE ALPHA AND OMEGA

1. Isaiah 44:6: "Thus says the LORD, the King of Israel and his Redeemer, the LORD of hosts: 'I am the first and I am the last, and there is no God besides Me.'"
2. Isaiah 48:12: "I am He, I am the first, I am also the last."
3. Revelation 1:8: "'I am the Alpha and the Omega,' says the Lord God, 'who is and who was and who is to come, the Almighty'" (see also Revelation 1:17; 21:6; 22:13).
4. Colossians 1:16: "For in Him all things were created . . . all things have been created by Him and for Him."
5. Hebrews 2:10: "For it was fitting for Him, for whom are all things, and through whom are all things. . . . "

GOD'S GLORY: THE ULTIMATE END OF ALL HE DOES

The term "glory" refers to the visible splendor or moral beauty of God's manifold perfections. The "glory" of God is the exhibition of His inherent excellence; it is the external manifestation of His internal majesty. To "glorify God" is to declare, draw attention to, or publicly announce and advertise His glory. Piper explains that

> another term which can signify much the same thing is "the name of God." When Scripture speaks of doing something "for God's name's sake" it means virtually the same as doing it "for his glory." The "name" of God is not merely his label, but a reference to his character. The term "glory" simply makes more explicit that the character of God is indeed magnificent and excellent. This is implicit in the term "name" when it refers to God.[4]

Again, there are numerous passages that support this assertion:

1. Romans 11:36: "For from Him and through Him and to Him are all things. To Him be the glory forever. Amen."

According to Edwards, "the way in which all things are to God, is in being for His glory."[5] As for Paul's doxological declaration at the end of the verse, "he expresses a joyful consent to God's excellent design in all to glorify Himself, in saying, 'to Him be glory forever'; as much as to say, as all things are so wonderfully ordered for His glory, so let Him have the glory of all, forevermore."[6]

2. Isaiah 43:6-7: "I will say to the north, 'Give them up!' And to the south, 'Do not hold them back.' Bring My sons from afar, and My daughters from the ends of the earth, everyone who is called by My name, and whom I have created for My glory, whom I have formed, even whom I have made."

In these places, writes Edwards, "we see that the glory of God is spoken of as the end of God's saints, the end for which

He makes them, that is, either gives them being, or gives them a being as saints, or both. It is said that God has 'made' and 'formed' them to be His sons and daughters, for His own glory: that they are trees of His planting, the work of His hands, as trees of righteousness that He might be glorified."7

Also, this text does not mean that God seeks His own glory as merely a means to the achieving of a yet more ultimate end, namely, the happiness of His people. Rather, in these texts, the promises of happiness for God's people (for example, in verses 1-2 and 4-7) are so that God may be glorified.

3. Isaiah 60:21: "Then all your people will be righteous; they will possess the land forever, the branch of My planting, the work of My hands, that I may be glorified."

Again, after noting that verses 19-20 speak of the blessings of God's people, Edwards points out that "all the preceding promises are plainly mentioned as so many parts or constituents of the great and exceeding happiness of God's people[,] and God's glory is mentioned rather as God's end, or the sum of His design in this happiness, than this happiness as the end of this glory."8

4. Isaiah 61:3: "To grant those who mourn in Zion, giving them a garland instead of ashes, the oil of gladness instead of mourning, the mantle of praise instead of a spirit of fainting. So they will be called oaks of righteousness, the planting of the LORD, that He may be glorified."

Edwards writes that "the work of God promised to be effected is plainly an accomplishment of the joy, gladness and happiness of God's people, instead of their mourning and sorrow; and the end in which the work issues, or that in which God's design in this work is obtained and summed up, is His glory. This proves . . . that God's glory is the end of the creation."[9]

Some other texts that identify the end or goal of God's activity as His own glory include the following:

1. Ephesians 1:5-6: "He predestined us to adoption as sons through Jesus Christ to Himself, according to the kind intention of His will, to the praise of the glory of his grace, which He freely bestowed on us in the Beloved."
2. Second Thessalonians 1:9-12: "And these will pay the penalty of eternal destruction, away from the presence of the Lord and from the glory of His power, when He comes to be glorified in His saints on that day, and to be marveled at among all who have believed—for our testimony to you was believed. To this end also we pray for you always that our God may count you worthy of your calling, and fulfill every desire for goodness and the work of faith with power; in order that the name of our Lord Jesus may be glorified in you, and you in Him, according to the grace of our God and the Lord Jesus Christ" (see also Isaiah 44:23; 49:3; John 17:10).

THE PURPOSE OF HUMAN MORAL CHARACTER AND ACHIEVEMENT

Numerous Scripture passages tell us that ultimately human moral character and achievement are designed for God's glory:

1. Matthew 5:16: "Let your light shine before men in such a way that they may see your good works, and glorify your Father who is in heaven."
2. Philippians 1:10-11: " . . . so that you may approve the things that are excellent, in order to be sincere and blameless until the day of Christ; having been filled with the fruit of righteousness which comes through Jesus Christ, to the glory and praise of God."
3. John 15:8: "By this is My Father glorified, that you bear much fruit, and so prove to be My disciples."
4. Romans 15:5-6: "Now may the God who gives perseverance and encouragement grant you to be of the same mind with one another according to Christ Jesus; that with one accord you may with one voice glorify the God and Father of our Lord Jesus Christ."
5. First Peter 2:12: "Keep your behavior excellent among the Gentiles, so that in the thing in which they slander you as evildoers, they may on account of your good deeds, as they observe them, glorify God in the day of visitation."
6. See also Psalm 22:22-23; Isaiah 24:14-16; 25:3; 66:19; Daniel 5:22-23; Revelation 11:13; 14:6-7; 16:9.

Again, God's glory is the ultimate end or goal of particular virtues such as faith (Romans 4:20; Philippians 2:11), repentance (Joshua 7:19), generosity (2 Corinthians 8:19), thanksgiving (Luke 17:18), and praise (Psalm 50:23). Finally, 1 Corinthians 6:19-20 and 10:31 call upon us to seek God's glory in all that we are and all that we do.

Then, there are those doxological outbursts—that is, those declarations that "give vent to the virtuous and pious affections"[10] of the believer's heart:

1. Romans 16:27: "to the only wise God, through Jesus Christ, be the glory forever. Amen."

2. Galatians 1:5: "to whom be the glory forevermore. Amen."
3. Ephesians 3:21: "to Him be the glory in the church and in Christ Jesus to all generations forever and ever. Amen."
4. Philippians 4:20: "Now to our God and Father be the glory forever and ever. Amen."
5. Second Timothy 4:18: "to Him be the glory forever and ever. Amen."
6. Hebrews 13:21: "through Jesus Christ, to whom be the glory forever and ever. Amen."
7. Second Peter 3:18: "but grow in the grace and knowledge of our Lord and Savior Jesus Christ. To Him be the glory, both now and to the day of eternity. Amen."
8. Jude 25: "to the only God our Savior, through Jesus Christ our Lord, be glory, majesty, dominion and authority, before all time and now and forever. Amen."
9. Revelation 1:6: "to Him be the glory and the dominion forever and ever. Amen."
10. See also 1 Chronicles 16:28-29; Psalm 29:1-2; 89:17-18; 57:5; 72:18-19; 115:1; Isaiah 42:10-12.

We could also point to descriptions of the angelic host who always seem to be engaged in doxology: Isaiah 6:2-3; Luke 2:13-14; Revelation 4:9; 4:11; 5:11-14; 7:12.

In sum, says Edwards, "it is manifest that these holy persons in earth and heaven, in thus expressing their desires [for] the glory of God, have respect to it not merely as a subordinate end, or merely for the sake of something else; but as that which they look upon in itself valuable, and in the highest degree so."[11]

In particular, Edwards comments on the song of praise by the angels regarding the coming of Jesus. They declared to the shepherds, "Glory to God in the highest, and on earth peace among men with whom He is pleased" (Luke 2:14). "It must be supposed," says Edwards, "that they knew what was God's last end in sending Christ into the world: and that in their rejoicing on the occasion of His incarnation, their minds would be most taken up with, and would most rejoice in that which was most valuable and glorious in it."[12]

JESUS HIMSELF SEEKS GOD'S GLORY AS HIS HIGHEST END

1. John 7:18: "He who speaks from himself seeks his own glory; but He who is seeking the glory of the one who sent Him, He is true, and there is no unrighteousness in Him."
2. John 12:27-28: "'Now My soul has become troubled; and what shall I say, "Father, save Me from this hour"? But for this purpose I came to this hour. Father, glorify Thy name.' There came therefore, a voice out of heaven: 'I have both glorified it, and will glorify it again.'"
3. John 17:1: "These things Jesus spoke; and lifting up His eyes to heaven, He said, 'Father, the hour has come; glorify Thy Son, that the Son may glorify Thee.'"

"As this is His first request [in the great prayer of John 17]," notes Edwards, "we may suppose it to be His supreme request and desire, and what He ultimately aimed at in all. If we consider what follows to the end, all the rest that is said in the prayer seems to be but an amplification of this great request."[13]

4. John 17:4-5: "I glorified Thee on the earth, having accomplished the work which Thou hast given Me to do. And now, glorify Thou Me together with Thyself, Father, with the glory which I had with Thee before the world was."

5. John 13:31-32: "Now is the Son of Man glorified, and God is glorified in Him; if God is glorified in Him, God will also glorify Him in Himself, and will glorify Him immediately."

God's Glory Is the Purpose and End of His Redemptive Work in Christ

1. Psalm 79:9 (compare Isaiah 44:23): "Help us, O God of our salvation, for the glory of Thy name; and deliver us, and forgive our sins, for Thy name's sake."
2. Ephesians 1:6,12,14: "to the praise of the glory of His grace, . . . to the praise of His glory, . . . to the praise of His glory."
3. Philippians 2:11: "to the glory of God the Father."

The Ultimate End of God's Providential Government

The purpose for the establishment of public worship and the ordinances of the Mosaic Law was to glorify God: "'Go up to the mountains, bring wood and rebuild the temple, that I may be pleased with it and be glorified,' says the LORD" (Haggai 1:8).

The purpose for the fulfillment of all promises in Christ is the glory of God, as stated in 2 Corinthians 1:20: "For as many as may be the promises of God, in Him they are yes; wherefore also by Him is our Amen to the glory of God through us."

The purpose for the execution of divine judgments against the wicked and unbelieving is the glory of God: Exodus 14:17: "And as for Me, behold, I will harden the hearts of the Egyptians so that they will go in after them; and I will be honored through Pharaoh and all his army, through his chariots and his horsemen." So also Ezekiel 28:22: "and say, Thus says the Lord God, 'Behold, I am against you, O Sidon, and I shall be glorified in your midst. Then they will know that I am the LORD, when I execute judgments in her, and I shall manifest my holiness in her." And Ezekiel 39:13: "'Even all the people of the land will bury them; and it will be to their renown on the day that I glorify Myself,' declares the Lord God."

GOD'S GLORY IS THE END FOR WHICH THE REALM OF NATURE WAS CREATED

1. Psalm 8:1: "O LORD, our Lord, how majestic is Thy name in all the earth, who hast displayed Thy splendor above the heavens!"
2. Psalm 104:31: "Let the glory of the LORD endure forever; let the Lord be glad in His works."
3. Psalm 148:13: "Let them [that is, all aspects of creation] praise the name of the LORD, for His name alone is exalted; His glory is above earth and heaven."

THE PURPOSE OF ALL THAT GOD DOES IS EXALTATION AND PRAISE

1. First Samuel 12:22: "For the LORD will not abandon His people on account of His great name, because the LORD has been pleased to make you a people for Himself."

This declaration by Samuel comes on the heels of the wicked and faithless demand made by Israel that God give them a king. Samuel warns them of the disastrous consequences of not being satisfied with God as their king.

Nevertheless, despite their stubbornness, God declares, through Samuel, that He will not abandon them (1 Samuel 12:20-21). Israel is told not to fear. On what basis is this exhortation made? They are not to be afraid, says Samuel, · because God will not cast them away. But why will God not cast them away? The answer is: "for His great name's sake." The fundamental reason for God's commitment to His people is His prior commitment to His own name. But why is it that God's commitment to His own name results in His not casting away His people? Look again at verse 22. The point is that God's name is at stake in your destiny. What happens to you reflects on the glory of God's reputation. That is why He will not cast you away.

2. Psalm 23:3: "He restores my soul; He guides me in the paths of righteousness for His name's sake."
3. Psalm 31:3: "For Thou art my rock and my fortress; for Thy name's sake Thou wilt lead me and guide me."
4. Psalm 109:21: "But Thou, O GOD, the Lord, deal kindly with me for Thy name's sake."

There are several texts in which the purpose for God's having forgiven us is said to be the praise and glory of His name.

1. Psalm 25:7: "Do not remember the sins of my youth or my transgressions; according to Thy lovingkindness remember Thou me, for Thy goodness' sake, O LORD."
2. Psalm 25:11: "For Thy name's sake, O LORD, pardon my iniquity, for it is great."
3. Psalm 79:9: "Help us, O God of our salvation, for the glory of Thy name; and deliver us, and forgive our sins, for Thy name's sake."
4. Jeremiah 14:7: "Although our iniquities testify against us, O LORD, act for Thy name's sake!"
5. First John 2:12: "I am writing to you, little children, because your sins are forgiven you for His name's sake."

"These things seem to show," observes Edwards, "that the salvation of Christ is for God's name's sake. Leading and guiding in the way of safety and happiness, restoring the soul, the forgiveness of sin, and that help, deliverance and salvation that is consequent thereon, is for God's name."[14]

It is also likely that the redemption and deliverance of Israel from bondage in Egypt, and then again from Babylon, were types or figures of our redemption and deliverance from sin. If so, we should take note of numerous texts in which the former is said to have occurred for the sake of God's name or glory.

1. Second Samuel 7:23: "And what one nation on the earth is like Thy people Israel, who God went to redeem for Himself as a people and to make a name for Himself. . . ."

2. Psalm 106:8: "Nevertheless He saved them for the sake of His name, that He might make His power known."

3. Isaiah 63:12: "Who caused His glorious arm to go at the right hand of Moses, who divided the waters before them to make for Himself an everlasting name. . . ."

4. Ezekiel 20:9,14,22: "But I acted for the sake of My name, that it should not be profaned in the sight of the nations among whom they lived, in whose sight I made Myself known to them by bringing them out of the land of Egypt. . . . But I acted for the sake of My name, that it should not be profaned in the sight of the nations, . . . But I withdrew My hand and acted for the sake of My name."

5. Isaiah 48:9,11: "For the sake of My name I delay My wrath, and for My praise I restrain it for you, in order not to cut you off. . . . For my own sake, for My own sake, I will act; for how can My name be profaned? And My glory I will not give to another."

6. Ezekiel 36:21-23: "But I had concern for My holy name, which the house of Israel had profaned among the nations where they went. Therefore, say to the house of Israel, 'Thus says the Lord GOD, It is not for your sake, O house of Israel, that I am about to act, but for

My holy name, which you have profaned among the nations where you went. And I will vindicate the holiness of My great name. . . . Then the nations will know that I am the LORD, declares the Lord GOD, when I prove Myself holy among you in their sight.'"

7. Ezekiel 39:25: "Therefore thus says the Lord GOD, 'Now I shall restore the fortunes of Jacob, and have mercy on the whole house of Israel; and I shall be jealous for My holy name.'"

8. Daniel 9:19: "O Lord, hear! O Lord, forgive! O Lord, listen and take action! For Thine own sake, O my God, do not delay, because Thy city and Thy people are called by Thy name."

Several texts portray the purpose of human virtue and holiness as the glory and praise of God's name.

1. Matthew 19:29: "And everyone who has left houses or brothers or sisters or father or mother or children or farms for My name's sake, shall receive many times as much, and shall inherit eternal life."

2. Romans 1:5: "through whom we have received grace and apostleship to bring about the obedience of faith among all the Gentiles, for His name's sake."

3. Third John 7: "For they went out for the sake of the Name."

4. Revelation 2:3: "and you have perseverance and have endured for My name's sake, and have not grown weary."

JUDGMENTS AGAINST THE WICKED FOR THE SAKE OF GOD'S NAME

1. Exodus 9:16: "But, indeed, for this cause I have allowed you to remain, in order to show you My power, and in

order to proclaim My name through all the earth."

2. Nehemiah 9:10: "Then Thou didst perform signs and wonders against Pharaoh, against all his servants and all the people of his land; for Thou didst know that they acted arrogantly toward them, and didst make a name for Thyself as it is this day."

GOD PURSUES HIS OWN GLORY AND PRAISE IN ALL HE DOES

What we are now going to see is that God acts in a variety of ways to declare Himself as alone God, as alone the Lord, who does such mighty things. In other words, these passages that speak of God acting so that all would know He is God are simply another way of saying God acts for the glory and praise of who He is. There are more than sixty-five such verses just in the book of Ezekiel alone that make this point. Permit me to cite only a few.

1. Ezekiel 6:7: "And the slain will fall among you, and you will know that I am the LORD."

2. Ezekiel 7:4: "For My eye will have no pity on you, nor shall I spare *you*, but I shall bring your ways upon you, and your abominations will be among you; then you will know that I am the LORD!"

3. Ezekiel 11:10: "You will fall by the sword. I will judge you to the border of Israel; so you shall know that I am the LORD."

4. Ezekiel 12:15: "So they will know that I am the LORD when I scatter them among the nations, and spread them throughout the countries."

5. Ezekiel 13:9: "My hand will be against the prophets who see false visions and utter lying divinations. They will have no place in the council of My people, nor will they be written down in the register of the house of

Israel, nor will they enter the land of Israel, that you may know that I am the Lord GOD."

6. Ezekiel 14:8: "I shall set My face against that man and make him a sign and a proverb, and I shall cut him off from among My people. So you will know that I am the LORD."

7. Ezekiel 15:7: "and I set My face against them. *Though* they have come out of the fire, yet the fire will consume them. Then you will know that I am the LORD, when I set My face against them."

8. Ezekiel 16:62: "Thus I will establish My covenant with you, and you shall know that I am the LORD."

Are these texts in the book of Ezekiel sufficient to make this point? I certainly hope so. Clearly, God's principal motivation in all He does is to magnify and make known who He is in all His glory.

If you desire even greater confirmation of this truth, open your Bible to the book of Ezekiel and read 6:10,13-14; 7:9,27; 11:12; 12:16,20,25; 13:14,21,23; 20:5,7,12,19,20,26,38,42,44; 22:16; 23:49; 24:24,27; 25:5,7,11,17; 26:6; 28:22-24,26; 29:6,9,16,21; 30:8,19,25-26; 32:15; 33:29; 34:27; 35:4,9,15; 36:11,23,38; 37:6,13; 38:23; and 39:6-7,22,28. God is determined to make His point!

WHY GOD LOVES US[15]

The point I am laboring to make is that if God is going to lovingly seek our eternal happiness and welfare, He must first be committed above all else to the pursuit of His own glory and the esteem of His own name.

The extensive listing of biblical texts you have just read bears witness to this truth. My conclusion is that if God is going to love us passionately, He must first love Himself preeminently.

However, this latter statement is so bothersome to many people that I need to explain it in some detail.

Essential to true love is treating a person as valuable. To love someone you must esteem them highly and act sacrificially on their behalf and for their welfare. Although we should be cautious in saying that God *must* do this or that, of one thing I am certain: *God must love and thus value Himself supremely.*

Many find this offensive, and I can understand why. It strikes them as arrogant and egotistical of God to be so concerned with His own fame. We intuitively recoil from people who are always seeking their own glory and exploiting others to enhance their reputation or position. We value altruism and hold narrow self-seeking in contempt. And rightly so.

So, how does God escape our disdain? How can we be asked to admire God for seemingly doing what we condemn in others?

The answer is found in *the nature of moral excellence*, which demands that we value what is most valuable and honor what is most honorable. Both the Bible and common sense tell us it is morally incumbent that we cherish what is most worthy.

Everyone would agree that God is the supremely valuable being in the universe. His majesty exceeds that of all others, His holiness is incomparable and His beauty transcendently attractive. God is the preeminently worthy One and the most honorable Being in existence. That is why we worship only Him and ascribe all glory to His name (Exodus 20:3-4). Now follow carefully what Packer says:

> If it is right for man to have the glory of God as his goal, can it be wrong for God to have the same goal? If man can have no higher purpose than God's glory, how can God? If it is wrong for man to seek a lesser end than this, it would be wrong for God, too. The reason it cannot be right for man to live for himself, as if He were God, is because He is not God. However, it cannot be wrong for God to seek His own glory,

> simply because He is God. Those who insist that God
> should not seek His glory in all things are really
> asking that He cease to be God. And there is no
> greater blasphemy than to will God out of existence.[16]

How could we describe God as righteous and good if He ever failed to pursue and preserve what is supremely valuable and of greatest worth? That is why God must take ultimate delight in His own glory or He would be unrighteous. It is incumbent on everyone to take delight in a person in proportion to the excellence of that person's glory. Whose glory can compare with that of God's? If God were not to delight supremely in God He would not be God, or at least He would be an unrighteous one and thus unworthy of our delight.

For God to fail or refuse to value Himself preeminently would implicate Him in the sin of idolatry. Idolatry is honoring anyone or anything as god, instead of God. If God were ever to act in such a way that He did not seek His own glory, He would be saying that something more valuable than Himself exists, and that is a lie. Worse still, it is idolatrous.

The reason it is sinful for us to seek our own glory is because there is something more valuable and important than ourselves. God. We are but creatures. For the same reason it is righteous for God to seek His own glory because nothing is more important or more worthy than God. He is the Creator.

It follows from this that everything God does is designed to win praise for that glory from His people. Says Piper,

> All the different ways God has chosen to display his
> glory in creation and redemption seem to reach their
> culmination in the praises of his redeemed people. God
> governs the world with glory precisely that he might be
> admired, marveled at, exalted and praised. The climax
> of his happiness is the delight he takes in the echoes of
> his excellence in the praises of the saints.[17]

How, then, can He be a God of love? If God loves Himself above all others, how can He love others at all? If He is passionately committed to doing everything for His own sake, how can He be passionately committed to ours? So again, if God is for Himself, how can He be for us?

Here is my answer. If God were to cease loving Himself supremely He would cease being God, for He will have committed an unrighteous and idolatrous act. If this were to occur, we are the ones who stand to lose most. Whom, then, should we adore? On whom, then, should we rely? Where, then, would we turn for strength and sustenance and joy and life?

Now answer two questions. First, what is the most loving thing that God could do for us? Piper puts it like this: "What could God give us to enjoy that would prove him most loving? There is only one possible answer: himself! If he withholds himself from our contemplation and companionship, no matter what else he gives us, he is not loving."[18]

Now for the second question. What do we all do when we are given or shown something beautiful or excellent? We praise it! In fact, our joy in the gift is incomplete until we praise it. Our praise is the consummation of our enjoyment.

What this means is that if God loves us, and He does, He will do two things. First, He will give Himself to us. He is Himself the greatest gift. Second, He will work to secure from our hearts the praise of His glory. As Piper explains, this isn't "because he needs to shore up some weakness in himself or compensate for some deficiency, but because he loves us and seeks the fullness of our joy that can be found only in knowing and praising him, the most magnificent of all Beings."[19] That is why if God is going to be for us He must be for Himself. In other words,

> God is the one Being in all the universe for whom
> seeking his own praise is the ultimately loving act.
> For him, self-exaltation is the highest virtue. When

he does all things 'for the praise of his glory,' he preserves for us and offers to us the only thing in all the world which can satisfy our longings. God is for us! And the foundation of this love is that God has been, is now, and always will be, for himself.[20]

Now, how would a God like this go about loving us? Would it not be by providing us with the highest good possible? And is not God Himself the highest good? Therefore, if God really loves us, He must work to bring us into the enjoyment of who He is (there's our happiness) and thereby win from our hearts praise for Himself (there's His glory). He must do everything in His infinite power to lead us into praise and honor of His name. By winning for Himself our worship as the God of all glory, we experience the greatest possible satisfaction, namely, enjoying God. There's our happiness again. And God is most glorified by our enjoyment of Him. Or, to put it in words we already heard, God is most glorified in us when we are most satisfied in Him.

Thus, for God to seek His own glory and for God to seek our happiness are not separate or antithetical endeavors. For us to seek our own happiness is thus perfectly consistent with our pursuit of God's glory. That is because God is most glorified in us (there's His glory) when we are most satisfied in Him (there's our happiness). Therefore, if God were not committed first to His own glory, He would not be at all committed to our good.

Our highest good (that is, our happiness) is in the enjoyment of God. God's highest good is in being enjoyed. Thus, for God to work for your enjoyment of Him (that's His love for you) and for His glory in being enjoyed (that's His love for Himself) are not properly distinct. Whereas I used to think that these concepts were on two different tracks moving at the speed of light in opposite directions, I now recognize that they are gloriously inseparable. That is the gospel of Christian hedonism. And it is our only hope for holiness. So I'll say it again. The aim of God in all He does is His delight in our delight in Him.

CONCLUSION

So what conclusion may we draw from this as it pertains to the pursuit of holiness? Simply that:

> It is impossible that anyone can pursue happiness with too much passion and zeal and intensity. This pursuit is not sin. Sin is pursuing happiness where it cannot be lastingly found (Jeremiah 2:12 and following), or pursuing it in the right direction, but with lukewarm, halfhearted affections (Revelation 3:16). Virtue, on the other hand, is to do what we do with all our might in pursuit of the enjoyment of all that God is for us in Jesus.[21]

> That, my friend, breaks the power of cancelled sin.

So there it is: do what you do with all your might in pursuit of the enjoyment of all that God is for you in Jesus. In this way, and only in this way, will sin lose its grip on our hearts.

CHAPTER FIVE

OH!

WHAT HAVE WE LEARNED SO FAR? FIRST OF ALL, THE AIM OF GOD in all He does is His delight in our delight in Him. Thus we are by God's creative design delighters. We are hedonists. We yearn for pleasure. We were built for excitement. We find within our hearts an irrepressible impulse to be fascinated. Our passion for joy and satisfaction is relentless and inescapable. And that's okay.

Second, although this passion for pleasure is not in itself sinful, it is the reason why we sin. We say Yes to temptation because it feels good. The sin to which it invites us injects into our spiritual veins an immediate rush that we stupidly believe is more satisfying than anything God might provide.

Third, finding the strength to say No comes from believing in, banking on, drawing and drinking from God's promise of a superior pleasure found only in the arms of Jesus. Neither threats nor fear can break the cycle of sin in which so many of us daily live. Neither shame nor the prospects of painful retribution are adequate to stifle the inward surge of sinful desire.

Volitional restraint and abstinence are only effective against sin when the soul embraces a pleasure superior to the one denied. There is little sanctifying value in depriving our souls of fleshly entertainment if steps are not taken to feast on all that God is for us in Jesus. Suppressed desire will always resurface, desperate for satisfaction. Finding fullness of joy and everlasting pleasure in God's presence alone will serve to woo our wayward hearts from the power of the world, the flesh, and the Devil. Therefore, falling in love with the Son of God is the key to holiness.

SAYING NO TO THE SOUNDS OF SIRENS

Most of you will remember the story from Greek mythology of Odysseus, also known as Ulysses. Having kissed his tearful wife, Penelope, good-bye, he set sail from his much-beloved home of Ithaca, destined for the city of Troy. The reason for his journey was that Paris, the prince of Troy, had seduced (or stolen) Helen, the wife of Menelaus, king of Greece. Menelaus, together with his brother Agamemnon, Ulysses, and a mighty Greek army, undertook the daunting task of recapturing Helen and restoring dignity to their beloved Greece. Hiding in the belly of a Trojan horse, Ulysses and his men gained access to the city, slaughtered its inhabitants, and rescued the captive Helen (she whose "face launched a thousand ships"). The return voyage to Ithaca, however, would prove far more daunting.

Much could be said of Ulysses' encounter with the witch Circe and his careful navigation between the treacherous Scylla and Charybdis. Hollywood has done an admirable job of portraying for us the adventures of our Greek hero. My fascination, however, has always been with the infamous Sirens. Countless were the unwitting sailors who, on passing by their island, succumbed to the outward beauty of the Sirens and their seductively irresistible songs. Once lured close to shore, their boats crashed on the hidden rocks lurking beneath the surface of the sea. The demonic cannibals whose alluring disguise and mesmerizing melodies had drawn them close wasted little time in savagely consuming their flesh.

Ulysses had been duly warned about the Sirens and their lethal hypocrisy. Upon reaching their island, he ordered his crew to put wax in their ears lest they be lured to their ultimate demise. "Look neither to the left nor right," he commanded them. "And row for your lives." Ulysses had other plans for himself. He instructed his men to strap him to the mast of the ship, leaving his ears unplugged. "I want to hear their song," said the curious, but foolish, leader. "No matter what I say or do, don't untie me until we are safely at a distance from the island."

Ulysses was utterly seduced by the songs of the Sirens. Were it not for the ropes that held him fast to the mast, Ulysses would have succumbed to their invitation. Although his hands were restrained, his heart was captivated by their beauty. Inwardly he said Yes, though outwardly the ropes prevented such indulgence. His "No" was not the fruit of a spontaneous revulsion but the product of an external shackle.

Such is the way many live as Christian men and women. Their hearts pant for the passing pleasures of sin. They struggle through life saying No to sin, not because their hearts are so inclined but because their hands have been shackled by the laws, rules, taboos, and prohibitions of their religious environment. *Their obedience is not the glad product of a transformed nature but a reluctant conformity born of fear and shame.* Is that the way you want to live? How do you account for your "obedience"? Are you bound tightly to the mast of religious expectations, all the while wanting to do the opposite of what is done? Is there not a better way to say No to the sinful sounds of Sirens?

Jason, like Ulysses, was himself a character of ancient mythology. Again, like Ulysses, he faced the temptation posed by the sonorous tones of the Sirens. But his solution was of a different order. Jason brought with him a certain Orpheus, the son of Oeager. Orpheus was a musician of incomparable talent, especially on the lyre and flute. When it came time, Jason declined to plug the ears of his crew. Neither did he strap himself to the mast to restrain his otherwise lustful yearning for whatever pleasures the Sirens might sing. Instead, he ordered Orpheus to play his most beautiful, most alluring songs. The Sirens didn't stand a chance! Notwithstanding their collective allure, Jason and his men paid no heed to the Sirens. They were not in the least inclined to succumb. Why? Because they were captivated by a transcendent sound. The music of Orpheus was of a different order. Jason and his men rebuffed the sounds of the Sirens because they had heard something far sweeter, far more noble, far more soothing.

It is only for you to answer. No one can choose on your behalf. The options are clear. Will you continue to fight against the restrictive influence of legal ropes and the binding power of fear, reprisal, and guilt, while your heart persists in yearning for what your hand is denied? Or do you long to shout a spontaneous and heartfelt "No!" at the Sirens because you've heard a sweeter sound? Personally, I want my No to sin to arise from a prior Yes to the Son of God. I want to love the things that God loves and hate what He hates, not simply because that is what I'm supposed to do but because that is what I long to do. I want to look upon the things that offend God and feel that same offense in my heart. I want to experience the same revulsion that God experiences. My most intense spiritual pain is when I find myself drawn to those things that repel God and repelled by those things that draw Him. My most satisfying spiritual pleasure is when I find myself drawn to those things that draw God and repelled by those things that repel Him. I want to be attuned to God's heart, to be of one mind, one spirit, one disposition with Him.

If this occurs, it will only occur as the fruit of fascination with all that God is in Himself and all that He is for me in Jesus. That sinful habit you struggle with daily, that low-grade addiction that keeps you in the throes of guilt and shame, that inability to walk with consistency in the things you know please God, ultimately will only be overcome when your heart, soul, mind, spirit, and will are captivated by the majesty, mercy, splendor, beauty, and magnificence of who God is and what He has and will do for you in Jesus. I must confess that I have ransacked the dictionary for words to describe what

I have in mind. Here is what I mean by falling in love with Jesus. Here is what God had in mind when He created and fashioned your heart and stamped His indelible image upon it. I, you, we were made to be *enchanted, enamored,* and *engrossed* with God; *enthralled, enraptured,* and *entranced* with God; *enravished, excited,* and *enticed* by God; *astonished, amazed,* and *awed* by God; *astounded, absorbed,* and *agog* with God; *beguiled* and *bedazzled; startled* and *staggered; smitten* and *stunned; stupefied* and *spellbound; charmed* and *consumed; thrilled* and *thunderstruck; obsessed* and *preoccupied; intrigued* and *impassioned; overwhelmed* and *overwrought; gripped* and *rapt; enthused* and *electrified; tantalized, mesmerized,* and *monopolized; fascinated, captivated,* and *exhilarated* by God; *intoxicated* and *infatuated* with God!

Does that sound like your life? Do you want it to? Or is your greatest struggle in the Christian life resisting the urge to yawn from boredom and lifelessness? Do you realize how difficult it would be to sin if this were true of you? This is what God made you for. There is an ineradicable, inescapable impulse in your spirit to experience the fullness of God in precisely this way—and God put it there! Don't feel guilty for it. Glut yourself in it!

I believe with all my heart that if the public face of Christianity is going to change, God's people (you and I) must change, and if God's people are going to change, God Himself must take steps to kindle afresh in our hearts the flame of fascination with who He is, the marvel and the wonder at what He has done and will do. God must restore in His people the mystery and excitement of the knowledge of all that He is for us in Jesus. That and that alone will enable us to win the war against sin.

AN APOSTOLIC OH!

Romans is the deepest and most profound book of the New Testament. In terms of historical impact, it is second to none. The grand sweep of its vision of God's eternal purpose and the remarkable depths of its portrayal of divine grace render it first among equals in the New Testament canon.

It is little wonder that, at the close of his theological musings, the apostle Paul should break forth into doxology:

> Oh, the depth of the riches both of the wisdom and knowledge of God! How unsearchable are His judgments and unfathomable His ways! For who has known the mind of the Lord, or who became His counselor? Or who has first given to Him that it might be paid back to Him again? For from Him and through Him and to Him are all things. To Him be the glory forever. Amen. (Romans 11:33-36)

We would do well to drink deeply at this fountain of revelation. But my purpose here is well-served by directing you to one word. It is, perhaps, the least likely word to attract your attention. Yet, it is rich and powerful and life-changing. "Oh!" That's right, "Oh!" This is no insignificant particle. It is no mere transitional exclamation. This is the apostle's passionate proclamation of the impact on his own soul of all that has preceded in his theological narrative.

I ask myself, I ask you: where is the "Oh!" in our response to God. Where is the intensity of awe and amazement that a true knowledge of the Holy One of Israel ought to evoke? Much of the church has lost the "Oh!" in her relationship with and response to God. Do you want to know why so many believers are muddling through the Christian life, just trying to stay out of hell and to get by with as little discomfort and risk as possible? It is because when they think of God, instead of "Oh!" their response is a "Who?" of ignorance, or a "Huh?" of disinterest, or a "So what?" of indifference. It isn't exclamatory excitement but a religious snore that emanates from the soul of so many in the church today when the character of God is at issue.

It grieves me to say this, but *the primary reason people are in bondage to sin is because people are bored with God.* One of Satan's most effective tactics is to convince us that God is a drag. And the church has contributed in its own way to this dismal image that God has among His people. For example, some have humanized God by denying His foreknowledge of future events. Others have drained Him of His power or ignored His holiness or presumed upon His grace. The way many have recast God in the image of man, it's little wonder that we're bored with the prospect of investigating His character. We have trivialized God, having reduced Him to moral irrelevancy. It's not just that God seems unfathomable. For many, God is quite unnecessary.

How different this is from the cry of the psalmist who, when he ran out of adjectives, resorted to interjections: "*How great is Thy goodness* which Thou hast stored up for those who fear Thee, which Thou hast wrought for those who take refuge in Thee" (Psalm 31:19, emphasis added). David would tell us how great God is, if he could. But he can't. "There are no measures," said C. H. Spurgeon, "which can set forth the immeasurable greatness of Jehovah, who is goodness itself. . . . Notes of exclamation suit us when words of explanation are of no avail. If we cannot measure we can marvel; and though we may not calculate with accuracy, we can adore with fervency."[1]

rOHmans

So where did this apostolic "Oh!" come from and why is it so important that you and I feel it deep down in our spiritual bones? It assuredly must have come from Paul's reflections and meditations on the truths of Romans 1–11. It had been building up in Paul for eleven chapters and finally burst forth in this hymn of adoration. As he ruminated on the magnificence of divine grace, the very fountain from which all blessings flow, he could contain himself no longer. As he pondered the joy of forgiveness and justification and adoption and the gift of the Spirit and the mysteries of election and the purposes of God for Israel, Paul lost himself in wondrous praise.

This "Oh!" that burst forth from the depths of his soul may well have been ignited by any number of passions. It may have been the "Oh!" of enchantment, borne of his knowledge that he, like us, is the bride of Christ. It may have been the "Oh!" of sheer excitement, or perhaps stunned disbelief ("Can all I've written really be true?"). For us, it may be the "Oh!" of bewilderment. How does one get a grip on God's providence and His sovereign purposes for broken, sinful people? Do we really understand Romans 9? For us, it may be the "Oh!" of surprise ("Wow! I had no idea!"). It may be the "Oh!" of amazement, wonder, and fascination. It may be the "Oh!" of yearning for yet more of God's presence and peace and joy. It may be the "Oh!" of hunger and thirst. It may be the "Oh!" of urgency ("Oh, God! I've got to see You more clearly. Where can I find You? What must I do?").

Perhaps it is the "Oh!" of awe and adoration, or the "Oh!" of reverential fear ("How dare I sin against such a God as this!"). It may be the "Oh!" of submission ("I'll happily do whatever He asks of me"). It may be the "Oh!" of joy and satisfaction ("How could I ever look to anyone or anything else when I have this God for my God?"). It may be the "Oh!" of comparison and contrast ("He is truly incomparable. None can compare. Nothing can compete."). Perhaps it is the "Oh!" of Paul's painful realization of how utterly opposite he is from God when it comes to holiness ("Yet He loves me anyway!"). On any account, it is the "Oh!" that drives us to our knees in humility. It is the "Oh!" that energizes us to dance with happiness.

This is what Edwards had in mind when he said that "happiness and delight of soul arise always from the sight or apprehension of something that appears excellent."[2] If that is true, then even God Himself takes greatest delight in "looking in the mirror"! Nothing pleases God more than the delight of enjoying His own beauty. God looks at God and cries "Oh!" But let's stay with our "Oh!" in God and leave God's "Oh!" in God for another time. Says Edwards:

There is very great delight the Christian enjoys in the sight he has of the glory and excellency of God. How many arts and contrivances have men to delight the eye of the body. Men take delight in the beholding of great cities, splendid buildings and stately palaces. And what delight is often taken in the beholding of a beautiful face. May we not well conclude that great delights may also be taken in pleasing the eye of the mind in seeing the most beautiful, the most glorious, the most wonderful Being in the world?[3]

All well and good, you say. But what does this have to do with holiness? What does this have to do with my struggle with sin? How does "pleasing the eye of the mind in seeing the most beautiful, the most glorious, the most wonderful Being in the world" affect my battle with temptation? Why spend time and energy on the character and beauty of God and Jesus? The answer is easy. It is so that you will walk around spiritually dazed, with your mouth wide open and your eyes bulging from your head. Why? Because spiritually stunned people are not easily seduced by sin. People in awe of God find sin less appealing. When you are dazzled by God it is hard to be duped by sin. When you are enthralled by His beauty it is hard to become enslaved by unrighteousness. People whose attention has been captured by the beauty of Christ find little appeal in the glamour of this world. People whose hearts are enthralled with the revelation of God's greatness turn a deaf ear to the sounds of Sirens. They've heard a sweeter song.

"Oh!" in Action

During the First Great Awakening in New England (1740-1742), countless people were powerfully affected by what they claimed was a fresh outpouring of the Holy Spirit. Many lives were gloriously transformed. But others were skeptical. One life that was never to be the same was that of Sarah Edwards, wife of Jonathan, and mother of eleven children. Jonathan was only twenty when he met Sarah, she herself only thirteen. Years later, during the revival known to history as The First Great Awakening, God visited Sarah with great power and passion. Jonathan was so impressed and awed by what God had done in his wife that he prevailed upon her to write it down. I don't think it's going too far to say that if Sarah had been asked to sum up her experience in one word, that word would be: "Oh!" Consider these few short excerpts from her testimony.[4]

> Under a delightful sense of the immediate presence and love of God, these words seemed to come over and over in my mind, "My God, my all; my God, my all." *The presence of God was so near and so real that I seemed scarcely conscious of anything else* [emphasis added]. God the Father, and the Lord Jesus Christ, seemed as distinct persons, both manifesting Their inconceivable loveliness and mildness and gentleness and Their great and immutable love to me. I seemed to be taken under the care and charge of my God and Saviour, in an inexpressibly endearing manner; and Christ appeared to me as a mighty Saviour, under the character of the Lion of the tribe of Judah, taking my heart, with all its corruptions, under His care and putting it at His feet.

≈ ≈ ≈

> The peace and happiness which I hereupon felt was altogether inexpressible. It seemed to be that which came from heaven; to be eternal and unchangeable. I seemed to be lifted above earth and hell, out of the reach of everything here below, so that I could look on all the rage and enmity of men or devils with a kind of holy indifference and an undisturbed tranquillity. At the same time I felt compassion and love for all mankind, and a deep abasement of soul, under a sense of my own unworthiness. . . . I also felt myself more perfectly weaned from all things here below

than ever before. The whole world, with all its enjoyments and all its troubles seemed to be nothing: — My God was my all, my only portion.

≈ ≈ ≈

I was entirely swallowed up in God, as my only portion, and His honor and glory was the object of my supreme desire and delight.

Sarah particularly recalls one night in which she continued:

in a constant, clear, and lively sense of the heavenly sweetness of Christ's excellent and transcendent love, of His nearness to me, and of my dearness to Him; with an inexpressibly sweet calmness of soul in an entire rest in Him. I seemed to myself to perceive a glow of divine love come down from the heart of Christ in heaven, into my heart, in a constant stream, like a stream or pencil of sweet light. At the same time, my heart and soul all flowed out in love to Christ; so that there seemed to be a constant flowing and re-flowing of heavenly and divine love, from Christ's heart to mine; and I appeared to myself to float or swim in these bright, sweet beams of the love of Christ, like the motes swimming in the beams of the sun or the streams of His light which come in at the window. My soul remained in a kind of heavenly Elysium. So far as I am capable of making a comparison, I think that what I felt each minute, during the continuance of the whole time, was worth more than all the outward comfort and pleasure which I had enjoyed in my whole life put together. It was a pure delight which fed and satisfied the soul. It was pleasure, without the least sting or any interruption. It was a sweetness which my soul was lost in. It seemed to be all that my feeble

frame could sustain, of that fullness of joy which is felt by
those who behold the face of Christ and share His love in
the heavenly world. There was but little difference whether
I was asleep or awake, so deep was the impression made on
my soul; but if there was any difference, the sweetness was
greatest and most uninterrupted while I was asleep.

What was it that proved more powerful and winsome than all
the pleasures and outward comforts this present world could
afford? It was the glorious knowledge of the beauty of Christ's love
and His nearness to her soul. Read between the lines. You might
hear a barely muffled "Oh!"

The spiritual beauty of the Father and the Savior seemed
to engross my whole mind; and it was the instinctive feeling of my heart, "Thou art; and there is none beside Thee."
I never felt such an entire emptiness of self-love or any
regard to any private, selfish interest of my own. It seemed
to me that I had entirely done with myself. I felt that the
opinions of the world concerning me were nothing, and
that I had no more to do with any outward interest of my
own than with that of a person whom I never saw. The
glory of God seemed to be all, and in all, and to swallow
up every wish and desire of my heart.

Again we see that the temptation of self-love and the alluring
pleasures of this world and the fear of man are no match for the excellencies of what Sarah calls "the spiritual beauty" of God in Christ!
"Oh!"

A PRACTICAL QUESTION

Does it really work? Can fascination with God and delight in Jesus
really help me overcome my failures? Can my life be changed? Can

this truth really make a difference down in the gutter of lust and greed and pride and envy and shame where I live? Yes! Let's look for a moment at how this "Oh!" in the heart of Paul revolutionized his life. He describes it for us in Philippians:

> But whatever things were gain to me, those things I have counted as loss for the sake of Christ. More than that, I count all things to be loss in view of the surpassing value of knowing Christ Jesus my Lord, for whom I have suffered the loss of all things, and count them but rubbish in order that I may gain Christ, and may be found in Him, not having a righteousness of my own derived from the Law, but that which is through faith in Christ, the righteousness which comes from God on the basis of faith, that I may know Him, and the power of His resurrection and the fellowship of His sufferings, being conformed to His death; in order that I may attain to the resurrection of the dead. (Philippians 3:7-11)

This passage is all about a transformation, a personal revolution, a moral and mental 180 degree turn in one man's life and how it can happen in our life as well. It is as if Paul envisions himself walking down a certain path in life, heading in a specific direction, believing certain things, honoring and valuing what he was convinced would bring him life, cherishing and nourishing his earthly achievements, only to find himself suddenly walking in the opposite direction. It is as if he is saying, "Those things of which I once boasted and loved and pursued, those things that energized me and gave me joy and got my juices flowing, I now look upon and say, YUK!"

How did he do it? Why did he do it? How do you explain this phenomenal experience that all of us yearn for so deeply?

First, we must look at what Paul used to prize. There are seven things in which he had once placed his confidence. The first four relate to birth and upbringing, the last three to personal choice:

1. He was circumcised the eighth day.
2. He was of the nation of Israel.
3. He was of the tribe of Benjamin.
4. He was a Hebrew of Hebrews.
5. He was, as to the Law, a Pharisee.
6. He was, as to zeal, a persecutor of the church.
7. He was, as to righteousness, blameless.

One can almost hear Paul's prideful reminder: "No one did it better than I. I was the best. I was number one. If it is possible to have good reason and warrant for boasting in human achievement and religious excellence and ethnic purity, I did it!"

Perhaps it would be wise for each of us to pause at this point and draw up our own list. They will undoubtedly be different from Paul's, but that's OKAY. So let me ask you: What are the seven things in this world, in your life, that compete with the most intensity to win your heart away from Jesus? If you were of a mind to boast in earthly achievements and accolades, what would they be?

The second thing of importance is for us to recognize we are not going to simply wake up one morning and discover that we suddenly hate what we used to love. The things of this world will never appear as "dung" when viewed in and of themselves. They will smell good and taste good and feel good and bring satisfaction and we will treasure and value them and fight for them and work for them and find every excuse imaginable to get them at any and all cost; they will retain their magnetic appeal and allure and power until they are set against the surpassing value and beauty of Christ Jesus.

MOSES' MOTIVE

We see this in the life of Moses, no less than with Paul. It was by faith that Moses made a critical decision: he refused to be called the son of Pharaoh's daughter (Hebrews 11:24). He looked at "the passing pleasures of sin" and chose instead "to endure ill-treatment with the people of God" (11:25). This didn't occur in a vacuum. Something happened that recast Moses' vision and altered his evaluation of worldly pleasures and treasures. The key is stated in Hebrews 11:26 where we read that he considered "the reproach of Christ [in other words, the abuse and stigma incurred as a result of identifying with God's people] greater riches than the treasures of Egypt, for he was looking to the reward."

What exactly happened to Moses? It would appear that Moses took a long, hard, honest look at all that life in Egypt offered him as the son of Pharaoh's daughter. He was neither naïve nor ignorant. He knew exactly what lay ahead for him, were he to want it. We can only guess at what this involved. Surely it entailed wealth beyond our wildest dreams, unlimited and unimaginable sexual opportunities, power, influence, comfort, authority, fame, and respect. Collectively, cumulatively, it is called, in verse 26, the "treasures" of Egypt. Yet Moses said no. Wow! He chose the path of pain and sacrifice and endurance and reproach instead. How did he do it? How can we do it?

The answer is also found in verse 26. Quite simply, Moses didn't simply look at the "treasures" of Egypt and suddenly find them repelling and repulsive. There was no magical alteration in their appeal. Indeed, according to verse 25 there was great "pleasure" to be found in all they offered. So how did the pleasures and treasures of Egypt lose their grip on Moses' heart? It's really simpler than you might think. He looked at the reproach, that is, the suffering and stigma, that comes with following Christ and considered it "greater riches" than anything Egypt could produce. He looked at the glitter, the grandeur, the thrill of all that Egypt had to offer (and it was a lot!) and in view of what he saw in Christ (and that's the key), he said: "Are you kidding me? Is that the best you can do? You're going to have to make a better offer than that. What do you think I am, stupid or something?" *It was from his desire for a greater pleasure that he said No to a lesser pleasure.* He didn't disregard his desires or repent of them or deny they existed. He made a careful, spiritually informed evaluation of what Egypt offered versus what God offered and came to the conclusion that the latter would prove eminently and eternally more satisfying to his soul. "Why would I want pleasures that are fleeting," he must have said, "when I can have pleasures that are evermore!"

This is precisely what Paul is describing in Philippians 3. The things of the world (what we value, do, purchase, think about, possess, want, and so on) will not, in and of themselves, cease to be appealing. There is no magical transformation. In fact, their power to draw you into their trap will actually increase. Transformation will never happen until your heart is captivated by a rival attraction that is comparatively superior. Merely praying for sin to lose its grip on your heart won't work. Merely fighting against sin won't work.

In other words, to give up something simply for the sake of giving it up may work for a time, but in the long run you'll return to it. Saying No to sin simply because you recognize it as evil may have momentary impact, but in the long run you will find a way to rationalize and excuse and justify your return to it. Saying No for no other reason than "my parents told me it was the right thing to do," or "my teachers taught me . . . ," or "my pastor preached that . . . ," or even "the Bible says so . . ." has limited value in loosening the vice-grip of sin on our souls.

One might also have expected Paul to say that his previous personal advantages, although still good, are being left behind because he has found something better. But this was not a decision to go from good to better. Once he saw the "surpassing value" of knowing Jesus, he reevaluated what he formerly regarded as gain, was struck with revulsion at it, realizing that it was actually working against him, that it blinded him to his need for Christ as well as to the beauty of Christ. Now he views it all as loss, as dung.

The key is found in what Paul identifies as the ground or motive for his decision: it was because of Christ. It was the prospect of gaining Christ, the promise of all that God is for him in Jesus that provoked and stirred and stimulated him and accounts for his re-evaluation of everything in his life. Paul actually makes this point in Philippians 3 no fewer than eight times!

First, it was "for the sake of Christ" (verse 7), with a view to a personal relationship of love and prayer and praise and guidance with the Son of God, that he now counted all things as loss.

Second, Paul made this momentous decision "in view of the surpassing value of knowing Christ" (verse 8). Or, to put it in other words, Paul wanted to experience "the overwhelming gain" and "the unparalleled worth" of Jesus. He yearned for "the supreme advantage" and "the ultimate value" of walking and talking with the second person of the Trinity. His vision was fixed on "the surpassing greatness" and "the incomparable excellence" of knowing Jesus! Paul said No to earthly achievements and fleshly pleasures because his heart and will were energized and empowered by the prospect of a superior delight—knowing Jesus.

Third, he refers to Jesus as the one "for whom I have suffered the loss of all things" (verse 8). Again we see that he didn't suffer loss in a vacuum. He willingly suffered loss *for a living, loving person,* to gain intimacy and peace *with a person,* to embrace and be embraced *by a person:* Jesus. Lest you think that Paul's decision carries no relevance for you, observe that he refers to "whatever things" in verse 7 and "all things" in verse 8. It doesn't matter who is confronted with this decision, when it occurs, or what it is that one forsakes for the sake of knowing Jesus. The reward is the same.

Fourth, his decision was made "in order that I may gain Christ" (verse 8). To lose or to give up or to forfeit or to turn away from something without a reason, namely, to get something infinitely better, is crazy. Paul makes it clear that it is Christ Himself, not His blessings or favor or gifts but the person of the Son of God Himself that accounts for this transformation in the allegiance of his soul. His decision was not grounded in fear, shame, boredom, or any other negative incentive. It was "because of Christ"—that is, on the hope of getting more and better and greater and more beautiful and more satisfying experience of the knowledge and fellowship found only in Christ—that explains his revolutionary decision.

Fifth, it was "in order that I may be found in Him" (verse 9) that he regarded the formerly fragrant achievements of life to be a repugnant stench of refuse. Whether in Rome or Philippi or Colorado Springs or Kansas City; whether healthy or sick or worried or carefree or wealthy or poor; it only matters that he (we) be "in Him." If I may be allowed to paraphrase Paul, "Not only do I want to get Christ; I want to get in Christ! I want to find Him and then be found in Him."

Sixth, echoing his earlier statement in verse 8, it was "in order that I may know Him" (verse 10). When I hear words such as this I am reminded of Paul's reference in 2 Corinthians 2:14 to "the sweet aroma of the knowledge of Him." Knowing Jesus stimulates olfactory delights! There is a spiritual and emotional pleasure in knowing Jesus that can best be compared to the physical delight we experience when our nostrils are filled with the fragrance of the choicest of perfumes or the soothing aroma of our favorite food. Simply put, knowing Jesus smells good!

The seventh and eighth of his assertions pertain to his desire to "know the power of His resurrection" and "the fellowship of His death" (verse 10).

Is the "Oh!" of adoration, awe, longing, and love a practical exclamation? Or is it a mere waste of emotional energy? You be the judge.

"OH!" AND ONE MAN'S WAR WITH LUST

One man who knows the power of "Oh!" in the human heart is the anonymous author of the highly praised article entitled "The War Within." First published in *Leadership* magazine in 1982, this testimonial is the stirring, first-person account of one man's battle with the destructive impact of lust.[5]

The author, a pastor, husband, and father, describes in vivid and disturbing detail his ten-year war with pornography, peep-shows, and strip bars. His story is a seemingly endless cycle of sin, tears of conviction, repentance, restoration, more sin, more tears, repentance yet again, restoration, sin—well, you get the picture. Countless hours of counseling, deliverance ministry, self-imposed discipline, agonizing prayer, Bible reading, and virtually every known remedy available in both the Christian and secular community proved fruitless to set him free from the shackles of lust and its paralyzing shame.

Not long ago I read in a denominational newspaper a similar story of another man's battle with pornography. At the conclusion of the article this man recommended a four-step approach to breaking free from the cycle of addiction. He suggested that a person begin with counseling, preferably with someone who is experienced in dealing with sexual addiction. The second step he recommends is to get in a relationship of accountability with someone who is not afraid of asking the tough questions. The third step, advises the author, is maintenance, a process by which the addict takes steps to avoid putting himself in a position or place of vulnerability where he is likely to fall back into old habits. Finally, the writer says that one must rely on the power of God.

I don't want to sound critical or unappreciative of this author's advice. It's not as if his counsel is wrong. It's simply inadequate. Perhaps it has proven effective in his own case. But I'm not convinced it will prove fruitful in the long term. Six months or a year down the road, when the watchful eye of concerned friends and family is turned in the other direction, when loneliness and boredom and frustration with God set in, four steps to freedom or seven principles to deliverance or whatever program one has embraced will prove no match for the deceitful lies of the Enemy and the powerful throb in the human heart for satisfaction. One's craving for pleasure will not magically disappear or even dissipate. Odds are it will only increase. Every loss must be for the sake of or with a view to a superior gain. Not giving in to the pleasure pornography brings will last only if one finds pleasure in fascination and fellowship with the person and presence and splendor of Jesus.

The courageous author of "The War Within" didn't discover this until he read a simple book of memoirs entitled *What I Believe,* by the Roman Catholic Francois Mauriac. Mauriac, he explains, "concludes that there is only one reason to seek purity. It is the reason Christ proposed in the Beatitudes: 'Blessed are the pure in heart, for they shall see God.' Purity, says Mauriac, is the condition [of] a higher love—for a possession superior to all possessions: God himself."[6] Hear now the impact of this discovery on one tormented pastor's soul:

> The thought hit me like a bell rung in a dark, silent hall. So far, none of the scary, negative arguments against lust had succeeded in keeping me from it. Fear and guilt simply did not give me resolve; they added self-hatred to my problems. But here was a description of what I was missing by continuing to harbor lust: I was limiting my own intimacy with God. The love he offers is so transcendent and possessing that it requires our faculties to be purified and cleansed before we can possibly contain it. Could he, in fact, substitute another thirst and another hunger for the one I had never filled? Would Living Water somehow quench lust? That was the gamble of faith.[7]

Moses took that "gamble." So did Paul. Likewise, this pastor. So I ask you, as I ask myself: How have the scary, negative arguments against sin fared in your war with the world, the flesh, and the Devil? If there is a negative incentive to saying No to sin, it is the prospect of missing out on the "surpassing excellencies of knowing Christ Jesus" in all His tenderness and compassion and power and peace. Sounds to me like it is worth the gamble.

CHAPTER SIX

LOOKING UNTO JESUS

IN THE SPRING OF 1958 I WAS SEVEN YEARS OLD — AND FAST. I'm a lot slower now, needless to say, but when I was in the first grade at Woodrow Wilson Elementary School in Shawnee, Oklahoma, no one in my class was faster. Each year the Kiwanis Club of Shawnee hosted a track meet for all those in grades 2-6. It was the highlight of the year for the kids and it seemed that half the town showed up to watch.

Those in the first grade were not allowed to participate, except for one. Each school selected one young boy to be its mascot. A special fifty-yard dash was held to determine the fastest first-grader in the city. Yours truly proudly represented Woodrow Wilson.

As I said (humbly?), I was fast. I did have a problem, however. I had a hard time running in a straight line! For some unknown reason, I tended to veer off course when I ran. One of the first things we all learn growing up is that the shortest distance between two points is a straight line. You would think I'd know enough to apply this to the fifty-yard dash, but to no avail. My father worked with me every day. He tried everything. Speed wasn't the problem. Direction was.

On the day before the race, my dad asked a special favor of the officials in charge. They agreed to let him stand in my lane just beyond the finish line. His instructions to me were simple: "Sambo (yeah, I know; but that's what he called me). All you have to do is keep your eye on me. When the starter fires his gun, you run like the dickens and look at me. No matter what happens, no matter whether you are in first place or dead last, you look at me. Don't worry about the other boys in the race. Look at me. Don't listen to the crowd. Just look at me, and run!" My dad was convinced that if I only obeyed him, my tendency to veer off line would be remedied.

It's been over forty years since that day, but I can still remember everything that happened. When the gun sounded, I burst out of the starting blocks and looked down the lane. There was Dad shouting and clapping his hands and stomping his foot, and no doubt praying that I would not take my eyes off him as I ran. As he told the story in the years since, I supposedly took my eyes off him momentarily and began to veer into the lane next to me. Hearing his voice, as Dad put it, I fixed my gaze back on him just in time, regained my sense of direction, and raced toward the finish line. I have a home movie of the event and, yes, a first-place blue ribbon in my scrapbook, just in case you were wondering!

Aside from it being a sweet, nostalgic story, what's the point? Simply this. Holiness, like winning the race, will come only to the degree that we keep our eyes fixed on the Son of God. To our left and to our right the world clamors for our attention. It shouts at us with claims of something better. It hurls its seductive alternatives to following Christ. It tempts us with lavish pleasures, hoping to divert our attention, distract our focus, and lead us into another lane. In track, that's grounds for immediate disqualification.

My aim in this book is to persuade you that the battle with sin can only be won if we rivet our spiritual eyes on Jesus. Good advice from a track coach alone won't do it. It doesn't matter how skilled or educated you might be. Warnings about disqualification are soon forgotten once the gun sounds. The only thing that will keep us running in the right direction is having our hearts fixed on Jesus.

There are numerous biblical texts that say this very thing, but in this chapter I want to direct our attention to five. After all, it doesn't matter how intriguing or effective my arguments may be. If they're not biblical, they aren't worthy of consideration.

FIXING OUR EYES ON JESUS

Many Christians memorize Hebrews 12:1-3 early after their conversion. Listen to what the author of that book says about running the Christian race:

> Therefore, since we have so great a cloud of witnesses surrounding us, let us also lay aside every encumbrance, and the sin which so easily entangles us, and *let us run with endurance the race that is set before us, fixing our eyes on Jesus,* the author and perfecter of faith, who for the joy set before Him endured the cross, despising the shame, and has sat down at the right hand of the throne of God. *For consider Him* who has endured such hostility by sinners against Himself, so that you may not grow weary and lose heart. (Emphasis added)

I'd like to pose two questions whose answers are so patently obvious that I'm a little embarrassed to ask them. But here goes. First, would you like to find the strength to say No to sin? And second, would you like to find the strength to say Yes to endurance? I ask these questions because my experience has been that Christians everywhere, if they complain, complain of two things: their inability to break free of the entangling web of sin and their strong temptation to quit. So look with me at four things that stand out in this passage.

1. *Victory over sin* is achieved by "looking to Jesus," by "considering Jesus." The strength to "lay aside every encumbrance"

and "entangling sin" comes from having our souls captivated and entranced by the Son of God. Sin turns ugly and is subject to defeat only when seen in the light of Christ's beauty.

The author of Hebrews is not opposed to mentioning the inevitable consequences of sin. There are severe warnings in this book that are designed to deter disobedience. But our author is no less pointed about how one should exercise such restraint and abstinence. It is by looking unto Jesus. It is by pursuing the blessings in Him that everywhere in this epistle are portrayed as "better" than any alternative option.

2. Encouragement to persevere is also achieved by "looking to Jesus," by "considering Jesus." Are you "weary" from fighting a losing battle with your flesh? Are you "weary" from worldly opposition and ostracism? Are you about to "lose heart" (verse 3)? Tempted to quit? To throw in the towel? Then "consider" Jesus. Once again, the strength to endure, to hang on when everyone else is letting go, comes from having our souls captivated and entranced by the Son of God. Look to Jesus. Consider Jesus. Think of Jesus. Meditate on Jesus. Ponder Jesus. Drink from the One who gives water that truly quenches spiritual thirst. Eat at the table of Him who serves up the most exquisite of culinary feasts.

3. But what in particular about Jesus are we to "look at" and "consider" that is supposed to help us in the fight against sin and despondency? Amazing! It isn't what you might think at first. It isn't Jesus on His throne or Jesus performing miracles. It isn't Jesus denouncing the Pharisees or Jesus cursing a fig tree or casting out a demon. It is His willingness to embrace suffering and shame heaped on Him

by sinners! It is Jesus "enduring the cross" (verse 2) and
"despising the shame" (verse 2). It is Jesus "enduring hos-
tility" (verse 3) to whom we should look.

There is something powerfully transforming and uplift-
ing to the spirit that comes from meditating on the
sufferings of Jesus. There is nothing morbid in doing so. We
find strength and encouragement in His sufferings because
they are precisely what secured for us the "fullness of joy"
and "pleasures evermore" that keep our hearts from wandering from His presence.

Knowing that Jesus suffered as we do (Hebrews 2:16-18;
4:14-16), yet without sin, is a constant reminder that there is
no struggle or pain or hassle in our lives with which He can't
identify and sympathize. He knows the seductive power of
temptation. Furthermore, when we look to Jesus in His sufferings we see a model of how a man is to live in utter
dependence on the Holy Spirit. In His sufferings we see with
the greatest clarity His trust in the Father. It is in His sufferings
that we are given hope that sin will not ultimately win. And in
His sufferings we see and feel the depths of His affection for
us. How can we go on sinning or even consider giving up when
One so pure and kind and gentle and merciful endured so
much for us?

4. Lastly, what motivated Jesus to willingly endure suffering
   and shame? Joy! The joy that Jesus contemplated, the joy
   that He held and nurtured in His heart, the joy that was ever
   before Him and to which He relentlessly pressed forward,
   the joy that, like a magnet, drew His heart and soul, was *the
   joy of being exalted to God's right hand* in the assembly of a
   redeemed people who will glorify God forever and ever. His
   joy was our redemption which overflows to God's glory.
   This is not to suggest that Jesus was a masochist. He didn't

enjoy the cross. He endured it. He didn't delight in shame. He despised it. What He did was indescribably hard and painful and distressing. But what energized His soul not to give up was the prospect of the joy that awaited Him on the other side of Calvary, and that joy was the joy that He would experience in bringing many sons and daughters to glory.

When Jesus thought about spending eternity with you in unbroken intimacy and fellowship, He said: "Yes! I can face anything. I can endure anything. I can and I will embrace shame and suffering because it means a bride with whom I can spend an eternity in glad fellowship and indescribable intimacy, all to the glory of My Father."

Here, then, is how we can run to win: look unto Jesus.

SEEKING THINGS ABOVE

There are two enemies, theological twins, if you will, that stand staunchly opposed to what I've been saying. They are legalism and asceticism. They are like a life-threatening virus that repeatedly infects the body of Christ, draining it of vitality and making it miserable. The church at Colossae in the first century was especially vulnerable to this dual assault. And you'll never guess Paul's remedy.

Legalism itself comes in two forms. On the one hand are those legalists who insist on obedience to the law, especially their law, as a condition for acceptance with God. To be saved one must submit to rules and regulations, sometimes biblical ones, sometimes not. But at the heart of this variety of legalism is the idea that works are a condition for justification. Paul encountered such people in his epistle to the Galatians and spared no words in denouncing them as heretics. The other kind of legalist may well affirm salvation by grace through faith, but demands that others submit to his image of what constitutes true spirituality. Invariably he or she sets extra-biblical guidelines, identifies morally proscribed activities, and then severely judges those who fail to measure up. *unduly strict*

The twin brother to legalism is asceticism. Not all asceticism is bad. Many in the church could do with a little self-discipline and self-restraint. We live in an overly indulgent society in which at times the only sin seems to be abstinence. Paul referred to godly asceticism when he spoke of buffeting his body and making it his slave, preparatory to running a race so that he might win (1 Corinthians 9:24-27).

Sinful asceticism, on the other hand, is the sort that he describes in Colossians 2:20-23. Note especially verses 20-21:

> If you have died with Christ to the elementary principles
> of the world, why, as if you were living in the world, do
> you submit yourself to decrees, such as "Do not handle, do
> not taste, do not touch!"

Here he has in mind those who impose man-made rules concerning the body and one's behavior as a means for enhancing one's relationship with God. For the ascetic, the body is a thing to be punished, denied, even abused. The body is regarded as evil and the only way to defeat it is to starve it of anything that might spark desire. Steps are taken to diminish the intake of food and drink to an irreducible minimum. In brief, asceticism is the belief that if you add up enough physical negatives you will get a spiritual positive. Mere avoidance becomes the pathway to holiness.

Paul's assessment of this approach to the Christian life is unmerciful. He faults it on four grounds. First, he tells the church at Colossae that all such things are "destined to perish with the using" (2:22). The things included in their list of taboos are perishable objects of the material world, destined to dissipate even as they are being used.

Second, such rules are man-made, not divinely given. They are, Paul says, "in accordance with the commandments and teachings of men" (2:22). As noted above, this is the essence of legalism: the demand that others conform to your conscience when God has remained silent. Such rules come not by divine revelation but by human ingenuity.

Third, this approach to spiritual living only seems to be wise. "These are matters," writes Paul, "which have, to be sure, the appearance of wisdom in self-made religion and self-abasement and severe treatment of the body" (2:23). When you look at someone so dedicated and disciplined denying themselves the ordinary amenities of life, it is easy to be deceived by the appearance of spirituality. Such people look committed and pious and holy. But appearances can indeed be deceiving.

Finally, Paul makes perhaps his most important statement. Notwithstanding the surface spirituality that such religious activities produce, they "are of no value against fleshly indulgence" (2:23). Rules and prohibitions and self-denial that spring from man's own religious creativity are utterly ineffective in curbing the desires of the flesh. The flesh mocks any such attempt to inhibit its expression. Asceticism, in and of itself, won't help you keep sinful urgings in check or energize you in the war with temptation.

What will? Surely Paul will do more than merely denounce what is ineffective. Surely he will offer a more biblical alternative. Well, of course he will. Unfortunately, the division made between chapters 2 and 3 in his epistle to the Colossians tends to obscure his point. Paul was not responsible for this division. Like all chapter and verse divisions in the New Testament, it was the work of religious scribes and biblical scholars of subsequent generations.

Paul does indeed have a remedy for fleshly indulgence. A remarkably simple one. It is found in the immediately following verses of chapter 3:

If then you have been raised up with Christ, *keep seeking the things above,* where Christ is, seated at the right hand of God. *Set your mind on the things above,* not on the things that are on earth. (Verses 1-2, emphasis added)

The italicized phrases in these two verses are simply another way of saying what we've already seen: Holiness, in this case the ability to say No to "fleshly indulgence" (2:23), comes not from rigorous asceticism or self-restraint but from a mind captivated and controlled by the beauty and majesty of the risen Christ and all that we are in Him in the heavenlies!

Yielding to fleshly urges is overcome by "seeking" the things above. Fixing our minds on "things above" leaves little time or mental energy for earthly fantasies. The heart that is entranced by the risen Christ is not easily seduced by "the things that are on earth" (verse 2b). Paul uses language that requires both the energetic orientation of our will ("keep seeking") as well as the singular devotion of our mind ("set your mind"). This is a conscious and volitionally deliberate movement of the soul to fix and ground itself on, indeed to glut itself in, if you will, the beauty of spiritual realities as opposed to the trivial and tawdry things of this world.

The reason we must seek the things above is because that is "where Christ is" (verse 1). The appeal of heavenly things is the presence of Jesus. It is the glory and beauty and multifaceted personality and power and splendor of the risen Christ to which Paul directs our attention. The apostle is not averse to calling us away from the earthly and transient temptations of the flesh. In fact, in verses 5-6 he grounds his appeal to abstain from immorality, impurity, and idolatry in the impending reality of divine wrath. But only after, and I believe because he has something incomparably more grand and glorious to which he has already called us, namely, Jesus and the grandeur of heaven. This, I believe Paul would have us know, is of great value against fleshly indulgence!

BEHOLDING HIS GLORY

Earlier I said that *beholding is a way of becoming*. Becoming like Jesus is the fruit of beholding Jesus. We will take on the characteristics, values, and qualities of whatever we most cherish and to which we devote our hearts and minds. To put it in more contemporary terms, what you see is what you be! This is Paul's point in 2 Corinthians 3:18 where he says that "we all, with unveiled face beholding as in a mirror the glory of the Lord, are being transformed into the same image from glory to glory, just as from the Lord, the Spirit."

Paul's mirror analogy suggests that we see the "glory of the Lord" indirectly, "mirrored," as it were, in "the face of Jesus" who is "the image of God." But where exactly do we "see" or "behold" that glory? After all, Peter tells us that we "do not see Him now" (1 Peter 1:8). How, then, can we "behold" Him?

Paul saw the glory of Christ on the road to Damascus (compare Acts 22:11 ["the brightness of that light"]; 26:13). In 2 Corinthians 4:3-6 he suggests that God shines the glory of that light "in our hearts" through "the gospel." Thus as commentator Paul Barnett explains, "paradoxically, therefore, Paul's readers see the glory of Christ as they hear the gospel, which in turn gives the knowledge of God."[1] In other words, the transforming vision of the glory of Jesus is found in the anointed portrayal of Him in Holy Scripture. When we humbly kneel before the inspired authority of the written Word and diligently seek out the rich treasures buried within it, the Spirit of God shines a light in our hearts awakening us to the person of Jesus. He quickens our minds and illumines our thoughts, enabling us to do more than merely recite words on a page. When we eat and drink from the fountain of Scripture, Jesus comes alive in our souls and His beauty and kindness and loving presence are indelibly stamped on our hearts.

It is important to point out that Paul's mirror analogy is not meant to suggest that we see the glory of Christ indistinctly or in a distorted way, but simply indirectly as compared with seeing Him "face to face" when He returns to the earth. It's a genuine "seeing." It's a very real and powerful personal encounter, yet it falls short of the beatific vision that will come only at the end of the age.

Of what practical benefit is our encounter with Jesus in the

Word? Does it really help in our struggle with sin? Can it actually make a difference when we feel the overwhelming temptation to give up? Yes, and again, yes!

Paul speaks of an experience wherein we are transformed from one likeness into another, namely, from our fallen and rebellious image into that of Jesus Himself. The verb rendered "transformed" is the Greek *metamorphoumetha* (compare English "metamorphosis") which is used of the "transfigured" Christ in Mark 9:2 and Matthew 17:2. The apostle thus envisions a transformation that consists of more than merely the doing of deeds. Looking unto Jesus effects an inward change in the core of our souls. He envisions an alteration in how we think and feel and choose. "Seeing" Jesus in the Word reconfigures our emotional chemistry and transforms the disposition of our hearts in terms of what we love, desire, cherish, and hate.

Would that this change might happen once and for all, forever putting to rest the daily struggle! But that isn't God's way of doing things. This experience of sanctification is progressive. It unfolds incrementally, taking us from one stage of glory (first "seen" in the gospel when we turn to Christ) to another (that final glory of the glorified Jesus, whose glory we will see on the final day).

HOPING IN HIM

No matter how great the change, there is a continuing frustration that it doesn't happen faster and more fully. The good news, however, is that we have greatly misjudged God's intentions if we think that what is visible now is the consummation of His blessings for us. What we now see and feel and do is only temporary, for we shall be made wholly holy (Philippians 3:20-21; Colossians 3:3-4). God has not yet made a public display of the glory that He has reserved for His children, of the inheritance incorruptible, unstained, unfading, reserved for us in heaven (1 Peter 1:4).

Whereas the indirect vision of Christ in the present (in

Scripture) sanctifies us progressively, seeing Him face to face in the future will sanctify us wholly. In either case, it is our apprehension of Christ that sanctifies. If progressive assimilation to the likeness of Christ results from our present beholding of Him through a glass darkly, to behold Him face to face—that is, "to see Him as He is"—will result in instantaneous perfection or glorification. This is John's point in his first epistle:

> Beloved, now we are children of God, and it has not appeared as yet what we shall be. We know that, when He appears, we shall be like Him, because we shall see Him just as He is. And every one who has this hope fixed on Him purifies himself, just as He is pure. (1 John 3:2-3)

There is some dispute as to the precise causal relationship between the vision of Christ and our final glorification. Some argue that we shall see Christ because we are like Him. That is to say, likeness is the condition of seeing Him (see Matthew 5:8; Hebrews 12:14). This view says that holiness is a prerequisite to the vision of Christ and thus must precede it. Those who advocate this position, however, are quick to point out that this holiness "without which no one shall see the Lord" (Hebrews 12:14) is a divine and gracious gift, not a meritorious reward for personal diligence.

More likely, though, is the view that when Christ appears we will see Him and, *as a result of seeing Him, we shall be made like Him.* That is to say, in His presence sin will be eradicated from us and we will reflect His glory, and through the majesty of that moment we will be made like Him. How could it be otherwise? Sin doesn't stand a chance in the presence of the risen and glorified Jesus. When Jesus appears the Father will unleash a power in His people that will forever expel every sinful impulse from their souls and replace them with the mind, will, disposition, and character of Christ Himself. What a day that will be!

But here's the really important and immediately practical point of it all. The possession now of such hope is *the strongest imaginable incentive to purity of life*. It is no passing fancy; it is a hope securely fixed *upon Him*. Simply stated, the Christian hope is incompatible with moral indifference. The mind that is singularly fixed on meeting Jesus at His return will discover a renewed power to pursue righteousness.

The words John uses here, both purify and pure, stress the personal, internal dimensions of moral change. This transformation will not merely touch our external appearance or physical constitution. It will go far beyond a mere alteration in how we act and talk and look. The emphasis is no less on our sensitivity to sin. We will not merely decline to sin, we will despise sin itself. It takes my breath away to think of a day when my mind will be utterly free and void of greedy, lustful, envious, bitter thoughts. It's not that in heaven I'll have the strength I now lack to say No to sin. I won't need the strength because I'll be forever delivered of a nature that could even want to sin.

Oh, for the day when our hearts will instinctively recoil from the slightest contact with sin. Oh, for the day when, upon seeing Jesus, we will forever disdain contamination by the world and the flesh and the Devil. John's vision is thus of an intense, inner purification from sin because of a deep sensibility to it. And those who now long for that moment, who have fixed their hope on that day, whose souls now pant for the presence of Jesus, purify themselves now even as Jesus Himself is pure.

His Holiness and Ours

Have you ever noticed how frequently and flippantly we use the word *holy*? We say *holy Moses, holy cow, holy mackerel, holy Toledo, holy smoke,* and *holy roller,* just to mention a few. It should come as no surprise to us that people are singularly unimpressed when the Bible talks about God as being holy.

What does it mean to say that God is holy? Most people think of moral rectitude or righteousness or goodness, and that is certainly true. To be holy is to be characterized by purity and blamelessness and integrity, both in terms of one's essence and one's activity. In this sense, God's holiness and His righteousness are somewhat synonymous. He is described in the Old Testament as "too pure to behold evil" and intolerant of evil (Habbakuk 1:12-13). But this is only a secondary way in which God is said to be holy. We need to understand the primary thrust of the word.

The Biblical Meaning of Holiness

God is regularly identified in Scripture as "the Holy One" (see Job 6:10; Isaiah 40:25; 43:15; Ezekiel 39:7; Hosea 11:9; Habbakuk 1:12; 3:3). He is also called "the Holy One of Israel" in 2 Kings 19:22; Isaiah 1:4; 43:3 (a total of twenty-five times in Isaiah alone); Jeremiah 50:29; 51:5; and elsewhere. In Isaiah 57:15 God is described as "the high and lofty one who inhabits eternity, whose name is Holy." God's holiness is often associated with His majesty, sovereignty, and awesome power (Exodus 15:11-12; 19:10-25; Isaiah 6:1-4).

Holiness is so much the essence of who God is that Amos speaks of Him as swearing "by His holiness" (4:2). This is simply another way of saying that "the Lord God has sworn by Himself" (6:8). In fact, God's name is qualified by the adjective "holy" in the Old Testament more often than all other qualities or attributes combined!

The root meaning of the Hebrew noun "holiness" *(qodes)* and the adjective "holy" *(qados)* comes from a word that means "to cut" or "to separate." The Greek equivalent is *hagios* and its derivatives. The point is that God is separate from everyone and everything else. He alone is Creator. He is altogether and wholly other, both in His character and His deeds. He is transcendently different from and greater than all His creatures in every conceivable respect. To put it in common terms, "God is in a class all by Himself."

We often speak of something that is outstanding or has superior excellence as being "a cut above" the rest. That is what God is, to an infinite degree. Holiness, then, is not primarily a reference to moral or ethical purity. It is a reference to transcendence. So where does the concept of purity come from? R. C. Sproul explains:

> We are so accustomed to equating holiness with purity or ethical perfection that we look for the idea when the word holy appears. When things are made holy, when they are consecrated, they are set apart unto purity. They are to be used in a pure way. They are to reflect purity as well as simply apartness. Purity is not excluded from the idea of the holy; it is contained within it. But the point we must remember is that the idea of the holy is never exhausted by the idea of purity. It includes purity but is much more than that. It is purity and transcendence. It is a transcendent purity.[2]

Holiness, then, is that in virtue of which God alone is God alone. Holiness is moral majesty.

There is an interesting paradox in the title for God, "Holy One of Israel." The words "Holy One" point to God's otherness, His "set-apartness," so to speak. As we shall see, to be holy is to be transcendently above the creation. Yet, He is the Holy One "of Israel"! He has given Himself to an unholy people. They are His people and He is their God. Although transcendent and lofty, He is also immanent and loving. His eternal distinctiveness as God does not prohibit or inhibit Him from drawing near in grace and mercy to those with whom He is in covenant relationship:

> For thus says the high and exalted One who lives forever, whose name is Holy, "I dwell on a high and holy place, and also with the contrite and lowly of spirit in order to revive the spirit of the lowly and to revive the heart of the contrite." (Isaiah 57:15)

And again,

> Thus says the LORD, "Heaven is My throne, and the earth
> is My footstool. Where then is a house you could build for
> Me? . . . But to this one I will look, to him who is humble
> and contrite of spirit, and who trembles at My word."
> (Isaiah 66:1-2)

An Encounter with the Holiness of God

The encounter that Isaiah the prophet had with the majestic holiness of God (6:1-8) is more instructive than any in Scripture. A careful reading of this passage will show that Isaiah saw three things: the Lord, the angels, and himself.

We are told in verse 1 that he saw "the Lord sitting on a throne, lofty and exalted, with the train of His robe filling the temple."

King Uzziah, one of the more godly kings who ruled Judah, died in roughly 740 B.C. (see 2 Kings 15:1-7; 2 Chronicles 26). He ascended the throne at the age of sixteen and ruled for fifty-two years. One king was dead, but Isaiah was about to make contact with the King who never dies. One king had lost his power. The Other never will. One king has seen his authority pass to the next generation. The Other will rule from generation to generation. An earthly nation mourns the passing of its monarch. A heavenly nation praises the perpetuity of its Monarch's reign. Uzziah's power was limited and fleeting. God's power is limitless and forever. The contrasts are striking.

Second, Isaiah sees the angels (6:2-4). This is the only place in Scripture where the seraphim are mentioned. The word literally means "burning ones." Observe what is said about their posture and their praise. As for their posture (verse 2), they covered their faces and eyes, for even among the angels it is forbidden to gaze directly at the glory of God. As Alec Motyer put it, "They covered their eyes, not their ears, for their task was to receive what the Lord would say, not to pry into what he is like."[3] They cover their feet, perhaps an allusion to Moses' experience of being on "holy ground." Others have suggested it points to their humility. Or perhaps because it is our feet that connect us to the earth, they are symbolic of our creatureliness. Although angels are not earthbound or human, they acknowledge their status as mere creatures in the presence of the Creator. Thus, Motyer points out, "in covering their feet they disavowed any intention to choose their own path; their intent was to go only as the Lord commanded."[4]

As for their praise (verses 3-4), they ascribe holiness unto the Lord. Holiness is the only "attribute" of God raised to the third power! Some have argued that it implies triunity, one "holy" for each person of the Godhead. Most likely the Trisagion, as it has come to be known, is simply an example of a Hebrew literary device in which repetition is used for the sake of great emphasis. Note several things.

First, He is the Lord of "hosts," a reference to His military role. God is the warrior who engages the enemies of His people. He stands at the head of a mighty heavenly host, an army of angelic powers against whom no one can stand. That certainly ought to inspire our confidence in His ability to fight our battles.

Second, although God is holy and therefore transcendent, He is not remote. The infinite loftiness of God, implied by the reference to His holiness, does not entail His aloofness. God is great but He is not geographically distant. Observe the threefold emphasis on "fullness" or God's "filling" the temple and the earth (verses 1,3,4). This thrice-holy God is intimately near those who love Him.

Third, the impact is shattering! There is trembling (compare Exodus 19:18; Acts 4:31) and the presence of smoke (Isaiah 4:5). "A recent survey of ex-church members," notes R. C. Sproul, "revealed that the main reason they stopped going to church was that they found it boring. It is difficult for many people to find worship a thrilling and moving experience. We note here, when God appeared in the temple, the doors and the thresholds were moved. The inert matter of doorposts, the inanimate thresholds, the wood and metal that could neither hear nor speak had the good sense to be moved by the presence of God."[5]

What is important to remember is that *we are now the Temple of God!* If the inanimate structure of the old covenant trembled and shook at God's presence, what is *our* response, we *in whom* this same glorious and holy God now lives? How can there be the slightest indifference or coldness or routine or mere ritual or mindless habit in our worship when this same God lives and abides in us?

Lastly, Isaiah sees himself (verses 5-8). Seeing God does not produce rapture or giddiness or religious flippancy. It produces terror and self-loathing. Isaiah does not respond with pride or elitism, boasting that he alone has experienced this wonderful privilege. He is undone! He sees himself as insufferably unrighteous compared to the resplendent purity and transcendence of the King. We arrogantly measure sin solely in terms of its effects both within the created order and upon us. Isaiah, on the other hand, measures it by the majesty and purity of the One against whom it is perpetrated.

Isaiah's experience is instructive in another respect. This man was already aware of his sinfulness and had made great strides in his growth in spiritual things. But now, in the unmediated presence of the Holy God, he sees himself as filthier than ever before. So intensely aware is he of his sin that he, in effect, calls down the curse of God on his own head. "Woe is me" is a cry of judgment. It is a cry of anathema. Sproul explains, "It is one thing for a prophet to curse another person in the name of God; it was quite another for a prophet to put that curse upon himself."[6]

This is no small twinge of a sensitive conscience. Isaiah cries out: "I am ruined"—that is, "I am coming apart at the seams! I am unraveling! I am experiencing personal disintegration!" Contrast this with the modern obsession with "personal wholeness," "having it all together," and being "integrated." Says Sproul:

> If ever there was a man of integrity, it was Isaiah Ben Amoz. He was a whole man, a together type of a fellow. He was considered by his contemporaries as the most righteous man in the nation. He was respected as a paragon of virtue.

Then he caught one sudden glimpse of a Holy God. In that single moment all of his self-esteem was shattered. In a brief second he was exposed, made naked beneath the gaze of the absolute standard of holiness. As long as Isaiah could compare himself to other mortals, he was able to sustain a lofty opinion of his own character. The instant he measured himself by the ultimate standard, he was destroyed— morally and spiritual annihilated. He was undone. He came apart. His sense of integrity collapsed.[7]

Surprisingly, his sudden sense of sinfulness and personal ruin were linked to his lips. He cried out, in essence, "Woe is me, for I am ruined! *Because I've got a dirty mouth!"* Why the focus on his mouth? I don't think there is any reason to conclude that Isaiah was guilty of profanity or telling dirty jokes! Instead, there are two reasons for this conviction on his part. First, mention is made of his mouth because what we say betrays what we are. The mouth is like a phonograph speaker, it simply manifests what is impressed on the record of the heart (see Matthew 15:11,18; James 3:2,6-12).

But more important still is the fact that the one area in his life which Isaiah thought he had under control, in which he no doubt prided himself, because of which the people honored and respected him, because of which he was highly esteemed, because of which he had position and prestige, was the power of his mouth. He was a prophet! If there was one arena in his life of which he had no fear or concern, related to which he felt God's most overt approval, which he regarded as his greatest strength, and which was above reproach and beyond falling or failure *was his tongue!* His speech! His mouth! His verbal ministry! He was God's mouthpiece! He was God's voice, His spokesman on the earth! Yet the first thing he felt was the sinfulness of his speech!

I am reminded of a statement by Oswald Chambers to the effect that an "unguarded strength is double weakness."[8] Beware of that in your life which you regard as invulnerable to attack, failure, or demonic assault.

At this point Isaiah must have felt hopeless. Sproul says:

[Isaiah] was groveling on the floor. Every nerve fiber in his body was trembling. He was looking for a place to hide, praying that somehow the earth would cover him or the roof of the temple would fall upon him, anything to get him out from under the holy gaze of God. But there was nowhere to hide. He was naked and alone before God. He had no Eve to comfort him, no fig leaves to conceal him. His was pure moral anguish, the kind that rips out the heart of a man and tears his soul to pieces. Guilt, guilt, guilt. Relentless guilt screamed from his every pore.[9]

But here is the good news of the gospel: The infinitely holy God is also a gracious and merciful God! This God of mercy immediately provides cleansing and forgiveness. Isaiah's wound was being cauterized. The dirt in his mouth was washed away as the corruption of his heart was forgiven. He was refined by holy fire. As Motyer says, the fact that the coal was placed on his lips points to the principle that "God ministers to the sinner at the point of confessed need."[10]

So What?

The practical implications of this vision of divine holiness are immense. Remember what we've seen thus far. Personal transformation is the product, not so much of seeing the ugliness of sin as of seeing the beauty of the Savior. Isaiah was awakened to the horror of his sin only because he saw the holiness of his God. Nothing on earth in the course of what must have been a full and fascinating life had ever awakened Isaiah to the presence and depth of his sin the way this experience did. No teaching he had received, no exhortation from parent or friend or colleague, no warning about verbal sins, . . . nothing had brought him the quality of conviction that truly transforms. It was only when he saw the indescribably surpassing and incomparable character of

God that his heart was stung with the anguish of conviction. Personal holiness thus begins with an awareness of who God is. Perhaps that's why so few people are or care to be holy; they've never "seen" God; they know little if anything of the magnitude of His holy majesty, His infinite, uncreated righteousness.

Awareness of who God is leads inevitably to an awareness of who we are. Self-image, the concept we have of ourselves, must begin not by looking in the mirror but by looking into the face of God. Few have expressed this more cogently than John Calvin (1509-1564), who insisted that no one ever achieves

> a clear knowledge of himself unless he has first looked upon God's face, and then descends from contemplating Him to scrutinize himself. For we always seem to ourselves righteous and upright and wise and holy—this pride is innate in all of us [even in Isaiah, I might add]— unless by clear proofs we stand convinced of our own unrighteousness, foulness, folly, and impurity. Moreover, we are not thus convinced if we look merely to ourselves and not also to the Lord, who is the sole standard by which this judgment must be measured.[11]

Calvin concludes that man is never sufficiently "touched and affected by the awareness of His lowly state, until he has compared himself with God's majesty."[12]

This self-awareness in turn inevitably leads to brokenness and pain, followed by confession and repentance. One need only reflect on the emotional and spiritual anguish of Isaiah. His physical agony was but a portrait of his spiritual discomfiture. True knowledge of God always leads to repentance. This in turn leads to cleansing and forgiveness. The holiness of God that first hurts, then heals. Finally, cleansing leads to commissioning. Mercy leads to ministry. Having seen God, what else is there to say but: "Here am I [Lord]. Send me" (Isaiah 6:8).

CHAPTER SEVEN

Transformed by Beauty

Nepal is a Hindu state of some sixteen million people that lies nestled in the Himalayas between northern India and southwestern China. Until recently, it has been overtly antiChristian. The missionaries there are courageous and few.

One such person lived and ministered in Katmandu. An encounter she had one day with a Hindu woman is indelibly planted in my memory. It was a religious holy day. Schools, businesses, and other establishments were closed. It was a day of worship for those whose Hindu faith gave them the option of bowing before any one of several million deities (literally!).

This missionary thought she had seen it all. Until that day. There in the middle of a busy street was a Hindu woman bowing low, chanting and prostrating herself before a pile of yak dung! In case you didn't know, a yak is a domesticated ox. I realize that doesn't diminish the ugliness of the image, but at least you know now what she was dealing with. Scattered amidst the dung were flowers, worshipfully placed there by this devotee of an obviously unusual "god." There in public, for everyone to see, was a lady who was quite serious about her religion, about her "god." She suffered no embarrassment. She showed no signs of hesitation. She had no fear of disrupting traffic or provoking opposition or incurring the ridicule of those who

145

might find her act of devotion a bit out of the ordinary.

Think about it for a moment. Let it sink in. Better still, let it stink in! Try to grasp the quality of zeal, misguided though it be, that would prompt someone to worship yak dung. Try to get a mental handle on the depth and intensity of such religious commitment. I'm sorry to put it this way, but in all seriousness, this woman would have died for that pile of dung.

So what's the point of this distasteful story? I can't know what it is for you, but for me it's quite simply this: Just how serious am I about the kingdom of God? I worship the One, True, Living God and yet probably do so with less zeal than this woman worships a pile of dung. It forces me to ask: How devoted am I to the King of kings and the Lord of lords? Am I as unashamedly dedicated to the God of heaven and earth as that Hindu woman is to the droppings of a yak? How passionate is my pursuit of the living God and His will? That's the point of the story for me. Resist the urge to laugh at her. She shames us.

If the key to holiness is falling in love with Jesus, there must be reasons why He, rather than someone or something else, should be the object of our affection. Why have passion for Jesus? What is it about the carpenter from Nazareth that makes intimacy with Him a pleasure superior to all competing pleasures? What is it about Jesus that leads us to believe setting our hearts and minds on Him will empower us to say No to sinful indulgence? There was something about yak dung (don't ask me what) that attracted this Hindu woman and so captivated her heart that she was willing to pay any price to praise it. Why, then, Jesus? It may seem like a silly question, especially when one thinks of yak dung as a potential rival! But why should we believe that Jesus is sufficiently worthy of our passion and focus that for Him we willingly forsake the "passing pleasures of sin"?

DEFINING BEAUTY

Beauty is _____. Can you fill in the blank? Can beauty even be defined or does it exist outside the lines? When we think of beauty we typically imagine visual properties such as color ("That's a beautiful shade of blue!") or brilliance to which we respond with an intuitive affirmation. Or perhaps audible properties such as melody, pitch, rhythm, harmony, and resolution come to mind. Others might say that the concept of beauty evokes thoughts of a sweet, pleasing aroma. It's not uncommon to overhear a comment at the cosmetic counter, "Oh, my, that's beautiful," as a customer samples the latest fragrance from *L'air Du Temps*. Some predicate beauty as whatever soothes the soul or challenges the imagination or stretches our powers of perception or stirs the depths of our senses.

Beauty is whatever stuns and surprises and takes our breath away, whether the golden glow of a lingering sunset, the cavernous depths of the Grand Canyon, or the inaugural steps of a first-born child. Beauty is whatever causes our hearts to beat with increasing rapidity and sends chills down our spines or causes goose bumps to rise on our arms. Beauty is whatever stirs up worth in the human spirit and enables us to feel the dignity of self and the hope of tomorrow.

But beauty can also be moral in nature. I believe it also has spiritual dimensions. For example, tenderness and humility and gladness of heart and compassion and faithfulness and graciousness and joy and patience and understanding and loyalty and mercy and perseverance and forgiveness and power and love and kindness are qualities of beauty, especially when they are all found in the same person! When I speak of the beauty of Jesus, it has nothing to do with His physical frame. I don't know what Jesus looked like. Probably like His mom. For all we know, He couldn't carry a tune in a bucket. We have no way of knowing how competent a carpenter He was. Perhaps He often hit His thumb with a hammer or split a board with an errant nail.

The beauty of Jesus has nothing to do with how He smelled or looked or the sound of His voice or the strength of His arms or the color of His hair or the way He dressed. Jesus is beautiful

because He perfectly embodied everything we need in a friend. His
beauty emanates from His having expressed all one might hope for
in a savior. What do you need most in a man, in a God? You will
find it only in Jesus—so perfectly in Him that everything else can't
help but be seen as disfigured and distorted and shameful and repulsive and unworthy of our devotion or love.

Wherein is the beauty of Jesus? Jonathan Edwards has made
an effort to answer this question with a series of questions. As you
read, ask them of yourself:

> What are you afraid of, that you dare not venture your
> soul upon Christ? Are you afraid that He cannot save
> you; that He is not strong enough to conquer the enemies
> of your soul? But how can you desire one stronger than
> the "mighty God" as Christ is called in Isaiah 9:6? Is
> there need of greater than infinite strength? Are you
> afraid that He will not be willing to stoop so low as to
> take any gracious notice of you? But then, look on Him,
> as He stood in the ring of soldiers, exposing His blessed
> face to be buffeted and spit upon by them! Behold Him
> bound with His back uncovered to those that smote Him!
> And behold Him hanging on the cross! Do you think that
> He that had condescension enough to stoop to these
> things, and that for His crucifiers, will be unwilling to
> accept of you if you come to Him? Or, are you afraid that
> if He does accept of you, that God the Father will not
> accept of Him for you? But consider, will God reject His
> own Son, in whom His infinite delight is, and has been,
> from all eternity, and who is so united to Him, that if he
> should reject Him he would reject Himself?
>
> What is there that you can desire should be in a
> Savior that is not in Christ? Or, in what way would you
> desire a Savior to be otherwise than Christ is? What
> excellency is there lacking? What is there that is great or

good; what is there that is venerable or winning; what is there that is adorable or endearing; or what can you think of that would be encouraging, which is not to be found in the person of Christ?

Would you have your Savior to be great and honorable, because you are not willing to be beholden to a mean person? And, is not Christ a person honorable enough to be worthy that you should be dependent on Him; is He not a person high enough to be appointed to so honorable a work as your salvation? Would you not only have a Savior of high degree, but would you have Him, notwithstanding His exaltation and dignity, to be made also of low degree, that He might have experience of afflictions and trials, that He might learn by the things that He has suffered, to pity them that suffer and are tempted? And has not Christ been made low enough for you and has He not suffered enough?

Would you not only have Him possess experience of the afflictions you now suffer, but also of that amazing wrath that you fear hereafter, that He may know how to pity those that are in danger, and are afraid of it? This Christ has had . . . a greater sense of it, a thousand times, than you have, or any man living has.

Would you have your Savior to be one who is near to God, so that His mediation might be prevalent with Him? And can you desire Him to be nearer to God than Christ is, who is His only-begotten Son, of the same essence with the Father? And would you not only have Him near to God, but also near to you, that you may have free access to Him? And would you have Him nearer to you than to be in the same nature, united to you by a spiritual union, so close as to be fitly represented by the union of the wife to the husband, of the branch to the vine, of the member to the head; yea, so as to be one spirit? For so He will be united to you, if you accept of Him. Would you have a Savior that has given some great and extraordinary testimony of mercy and love to sinners, by something that He has done, as well as by what He says? And can you think or conceive of greater things than Christ has done? Was it not a great thing for Him, who was God, to take upon Him human nature; to be not only God, but man thenceforward to all eternity? But would you look upon suffering for sinners to be a yet greater testimony of love to sinners, than merely doing, though it be ever so extraordinary a thing that He has done? And would you desire that a Savior should suffer more than Christ has suffered for sinners? What is there lacking, or what would you add if you could, to make Him more fit to be your Savior?[1]

On several occasions I've insisted that holiness is the fruit of savoring all that God is for us in Jesus. What is God for us in Jesus? Edwards just gave us one answer. But the beauty of Jesus that enthralls and excites and satisfies and soothes is yet so much more. I can only begin to unpack it. But before I do so, let's be sure we know why we should. As I said in chapter five, to the degree that your mind is in a perpetual state of Oh!, that is to say, captivated and enthralled with the transcendent splendor of who God is in Christ, sin will diminish in its capacity to keep you in its grip. Houses and microwaves and mistresses and money carry little appeal to those whose thoughts and dreams are filled with the mystery of the uncreated God in human flesh!

THE WORD BECAME FLESH

Let's think for a moment of the beauty of Jesus as revealed in the act of incarnation. For some of you that's a new and unfamiliar word. It may sound esoteric, but without it we are a hopeless people. Without it, Jesus is nothing to us and we are nothing to Him.

So what exactly do I mean by the word "Incarnation"? The idea is found in several texts which speak of Jesus as "coming in the flesh" (1 John 4:2; 2 John 7), being "sent in the flesh" (Romans 8:3), "revealed in the flesh" (1 Timothy 3:16); He also "suffered in the flesh" (1 Peter 4:1), "died in the flesh" (1 Peter 3:18), made peace by abolishing "in the flesh the enmity" (Ephesians 2:15), and "made reconciliation in the body of his flesh" (Colossians 1:21-22). In sum, "the Word became flesh" (John 1:14).

Thus, by the Incarnation we mean that the eternal Word or second Person of the Trinity became a man or assumed human flesh at a point in time, yet without ceasing to be God. Think of it: "The Word became flesh" (John 1:14). The contrasts posed by this equation are stunning:

John 1:1	**John 1:14**
The Word *was*	The Word *became*
The Word *was with God*	The Word *dwelt among us*
The Word *was God*	The Word *became flesh*

John does not say simply that the Word became a *man* (although that's true). Nor does he say He became a *human*, or even that He took to Himself a body (although both are again true). Rather, the Word became *flesh,* a strong, almost crude way of referring to human nature in its totality: true body, soul, spirit, will, and emotions.

We also note that the Word did not pretend to be a man or play at being human. The Word became flesh. The Word did not "beam down" in full bodily form. The Word did not enter into flesh, as if to suggest that there was a man, a human being, into which the Word made entrance. He doesn't say the Word "dwelled" or "abided in" human flesh. What John means is that the eternal Word, God the Son, entered into this world by being born as a human being. Therefore, it isn't correct to say that *Jesus* has always existed or that *Jesus* was in the beginning with God (John 1:1). The *Son of God* has always existed. The second Person of the Trinity, the Word, was in the beginning with God. But Jesus is the human name given to the second Person of the Trinity *when* He took to Himself flesh. The Word was never called *Jesus* until Joseph did so in obedience to the command of the angel in Matthew 1.

The doctrine of the Incarnation means that two distinct natures (divine and human) are united in one Person: Jesus. Jesus is not two people (God and man). He is one Person: the God-man. Jesus is not schizophrenic. When the Word became flesh He did not cease to be the Word. The Word veiled, hid, and voluntarily restricted the use of certain divine powers and prerogatives. But God cannot cease to be God. In other words, when the Word became flesh He did not commit divine suicide.

When the Word once became flesh He became flesh forever. After His earthly life, death, and resurrection, Jesus did not divest Himself of the flesh or cease to be a man. He is a man even now at the right hand of God the Father. He is also God. He will always be the God-man. Thus, we might envision Jesus saying: "I am now what I always was: God (or Word). I am now what I once was not: man (or flesh). I am now and forever will be both: the God-man."

A REAL HUMAN, REALLY!

If there is a downside to the confession of Christ's deity (and I hesitate even using such language), it is that many are led to minimize the reality of His humanity. But the New Testament simply will not allow this. Indeed, the confession that Jesus was Christ come "in the flesh" became the touchstone of orthodoxy (see 1 John 1:1; 1 Timothy 3:16; Luke 24:39,43; John 20:17,20,27). Jesus hungered (Matthew 4:2), thirsted (John 19:28), grew weary (John 4:6), wept and cried aloud (John 11:35; Luke 19:41), sighed (Mark 7:34), groaned (Mark 8:12), glared angrily (Mark 3:5), and felt annoyance (Mark 10:14).

It makes me wonder: Did Jesus ever get sick? When He hit His thumb with a hammer while working in His father's carpenter shop, would He have been susceptible to getting an infection? Did Jesus ever get headaches from prolonged exposure to the hot Palestinian sun? Could Jesus have caught the flu from one of His family members? Could Jesus have suffered from a twenty-four hour stomach virus (nausea, vomiting, diarrhea) caused by drinking dirty water from the Jordan river?

How human was He? We read that His soul was "overwhelmed with sorrow to the point of death" (Matthew 26:38). It was to the divine purpose that He subjected His will (Luke 22:42). It was into the Father's hands that He committed His spirit (Luke 23:46). He felt compassion (Matthew 9:36; 20:34; Mark 1:41; 6:34; 8:2; Luke 7:13), love (John 11:3; 15:8-12; Mark 10:21), anger (Mark 3:5; John 2:13-17), and joy (Luke 7:34; 10:21; John 15:11; 17:13).

GLORIOUS PARADOXES

Take a deep breath and ponder what this means. Don't dismiss it as theological speculation. This is a truth on which your eternal destiny hangs suspended. This is a truth that will evoke an "Oh!" in your spirit the likes of which you may never before have known. This is a truth the beauty and majesty of which will captivate your attention and cause sin to sink in your estimation. Wherein lies the power to turn from iniquity and say No to sin? It lies in the power and irresistible appeal of an uncreated God who would dare to become a man!

The Word became flesh! God became human! The invisible became visible! The untouchable became touchable! Eternal life experienced temporal death! The transcendent one descended and drew near! The unlimited became limited! The infinite became finite! The immutable became mutable! The unbreakable became fragile! Spirit became matter! Eternity entered time! The independent became

dependent! The almighty became weak! The loved became
the hated! The exalted was humbled! Glory was subjected
to shame! Fame turned into obscurity! From inexpressible
joy to tears of unimaginable grief! From a throne to a
cross! From ruler to being ruled! From power to weakness!

Max Lucado put it this way:

The omnipotent, in one instant, made himself breakable.
He who had been spirit became piercable. He who was
larger than the universe became an embryo. And he who
sustains the world with a word chose to be dependent upon
the nourishment of a young girl. God as a fetus. Holiness
sleeping in a womb. The creator of life being created. God
was given eyebrows, elbows, two kidneys, and a spleen.
He stretched against the walls and floated in the amniotic
fluids of his mother.[2]

As Paul said in 1 Timothy 3:16, "great is the mystery of godliness: He who was revealed in the flesh!"
Stay with me for just a moment more. If it hasn't hit home yet,
perhaps the following will do the trick:

- **Conception:** God became a fertilized egg! An embryo.
  A fetus. God kicked Mary from within her womb!
- **Birth:** God entered the world as a baby, amid the stench
  of manure and cobwebs and prickly hay in a stable. Mary
  cradled the Creator in her arms. "I never imagined God
  would look like that," she says to herself. Envision the
  newborn Jesus with a misshaped head, wrinkled skin,
  and a red face. Just think: angels watched as Mary
  changed God's diapers! Tiny hands that would touch and
  heal the sick and yet be ripped by nails. Eyes (what color
  were they?). Tiny feet (where would they take Him?) that

likewise would be pierced by nails. She tickled His side (which would one day be lanced with a spear).

- **Infancy:** God learned to crawl, stand, and walk. He spilt His milk and fell and hit His head.
- **Youth:** Was He uncoordinated? How well did He perform at sports? Perhaps Jesus knew the pain of always being picked last when the kids chose up sides for a ballgame. God learned His ABCs!
- **Teenager:** Jesus probably had pimples and body odor and bad breath. God went through puberty! His voice changed. He had to shave. Girls probably had a crush on Him and boys probably teased Him. There were probably some foods He didn't like (no doubt squash among them).
- **Adulthood** (as a carpenter)**:** Calloused hands. Dealings with customers who tried to cheat Him or complained about His work. How did He react when they short-changed Him?

Some are bothered when I speak of Jesus like this. They think it is irreverent and shocking! As Max Lucado has said,

It's not something we like to do; it's uncomfortable. It is much easier to keep the humanity out of the incarnation. Clean the manure from around the manger. Wipe the sweat out of his eyes. Pretend he never snored or blew his nose or hit his thumb with a hammer. He's easier to stomach that way. There is something about keeping him divine that keeps him distant, packaged, predictable. But don't do it. For heaven's sake, don't. Let him be as human as he intended to be. Let him into the mire and muck of our world. For only if we let him in can he pull us out.[3]

The marvel of it all is that He did it for you and me! It was an expression of the depths of His love for you that the Word entered the depths of human ugliness, human weakness, human humiliation.

MORE OF THE MYSTERY

- He was conceived by the union of divine grace and human disgrace.
- He who breathed the breath of life into the first man is now Himself a man breathing His first breath.
- The King of kings sleeping in a cow-pen.
- The Creator of oceans and seas and rivers afloat in the womb of His mother.
- God sucking His thumb.
- The Alpha and Omega learning His multiplication tables.
- He who was once surrounded by the glorious stereophonic praise of adoring angels now hears the lowing of cattle, the bleating of sheep, the stammering of bewildered shepherds.
- He who spoke the universe into being now coos and cries.
- Omniscient Deity counting His toes.
- Mary playing "this little piggy went to market" on the toes of God (well, being Jewish, maybe it was "this little pony").
- From the robes of eternal glory to the rags of swaddling clothes.
- The omnipresent Spirit, whose being fills the galaxies, confined to the womb of a peasant girl.
- Infinite power learning to crawl.
- Mary playing "patty-cake" with the Lord of lords!

HE WAS GOD TOO

There is no better place than the book of Revelation to learn about and meditate upon the excellencies of Christ's deity. In particular, chapter 1, verses 12-18, presents us with an unparalleled portrait of the glory and power of the risen Christ. There then follows in chapters 2-3 an interesting application of these verses. Each of the seven letters to the seven churches, with one exception, is prefaced with a description of Jesus taken from 1:12-18. Furthermore, in most cases the description is especially relevant to the circumstances of the church being addressed.

Many are surprised by the perspective taken toward the person of Christ in the book of Revelation. It is almost exclusively concerned with Him as exalted and glorified, not humbled and oppressed. What little is said of His life pertains almost exclusively to His death on the cross. But we must remember that the book of Revelation is largely concerned with encouraging believers who are persecuted and oppressed. Whereas it would certainly be appropriate to speak of Jesus' humiliation and suffering as a man in order to comfort those who themselves are suffering, we have instead a vivid description of His deity, His triumph, and the glories of His exalted status at the right hand of the Father. The point is this: *We should be encouraged and strengthened in our struggle with persecution and pain by reflecting on the triumphant exaltation of the God-man, Jesus.* His resurrection and exaltation remind us that no matter how intense the battle may be, in the end we win because He won.

We must also be careful not to become overly obsessed with the particulars of this portrait of Jesus. Whereas each element in this portrait has theological significance, G. B. Caird warns us not "to unweave the rainbow."[4] In other words,

John uses his allusions not as a code in which each symbol requires separate and exact translation, but rather for their evocative and emotive power. This is not photographic art. His aim is to set the echoes of memory and association ringing. The humbling sense of the sublime and the majestic which men experience at the sight of a roaring cataract [waterfall] or the midday sun is the nearest equivalent to the awe evoked by a vision of the divine. John has seen the risen Christ, clothed in all the attributes of deity, and he wishes to call forth from his readers the same response of overwhelming and annihilating wonder which he experienced in his prophetic trance.[5]

Let's look briefly at the portrait of Jesus in all His glorified beauty as John described it in Revelation 1:12-18.

John calls Jesus the *Son of Man* (compare Daniel 7:13-14), a descriptive phrase that not only points to our Lord's humanity, but even more to His role as *Messianic King* through whom God's dominion and power are exercised over all creation.

The robe and girdle that adorn Him evoke images of the high priest under the Mosaic Covenant (Exodus 28:4; 39:29) and thus point to Christ's function as He who has obtained for us immediate access into God's presence. The white hair reminds us of the Ancient of Days in Daniel 7:9 and thus points again to His deity, His essential oneness with the Father in the eternal Godhead. His eyes *were like a flame of fire.* J. A. Seiss explains:

Here is intelligence; burning, all-penetrating intelligence. Here is power to read secrets, to bring hidden things to light, to warm and search all hearts at a single glance. . . . But his sharp look is one of inspiring warmth to the good, as well as discomfiting and consuming terror to the hypocritical and the godless. Will you believe it, my friends, that this is the look which is upon you, and which is to try you in the great day! Well may we pray the prayer of David: "Search me, O God, and know my heart; try me, and know my thought; and see if there be any evil way in me, and lead me in the way everlasting"[6]

His feet *were like burnished bronze* and His voice *was like the sound of many waters.* The sword is not in His hand, but proceeds *from His mouth,* indicating that *His spoken word is in view.* A sword that cuts two ways points to the gospel as that which both brings either life or judgment. *His face was like the sun shining in its strength.* Again Seiss paints the scene in words that evoke wonder:

> Something of this was seen in the mount of transfiguration, when "his face did shine as the sun, and his raiment was white as the light." Something of the same was manifest when he appeared to Saul of Tarsus in "a light above the brightness of the sun." And so glorious and pervading is this light which issues from his face, that in the New Jerusalem there will be neither sun, nor moon, nor lamp, nor any other light, and yet rendered so luminous by his presence, that even the nations on the earth walk in the light of it: And so the lightning brilliancy, which is to flash from one end of heaven to the other at the time of his coming, and the glory which is then to invest him and the whole firmament, is simply the uncovering or revelation of that blessed light which streams from his sublime person.[7]

A PURITAN'S VISION OF THE BEAUTY OF JESUS

I've already referred to Jonathan Edwards and his wife, Sarah. From what little I've said I suspect you are beginning to see that he had an unrelenting passion for the Son of God. In his personal diary, Edwards spoke often of what he called "vehement longings of soul"[8] for Jesus. He described feeling "a burning desire to be in every thing a complete Christian; and conformed to the blessed image of Christ, and that I might live in all things, according to the pure, sweet and blessed rules of the gospel."[9] He had "an eager thirsting"[10] after holiness. He engaged daily, through God's enabling grace, in "pursuing and pressing"[11] after them.

Edwards was keenly aware, as we all are I hope, of his "extreme feebleness and impotence"[12] when it came to doing what pleases God. He spoke honestly of "the innumerable and bottomless depths of secret corruption and deceit"[13] in his heart. Yet he pressed forward in the strength that God supplies, desperate for a deeper experience of Christlike holiness. Edwards' love for holiness is captured in the following words. Would that we all might view it in this light:

> Holiness . . . appeared to me to be of a sweet, pleasant, charming, serene, calm nature. It seemed to me it brought an inexpressible purity, brightness, peacefulness and ravishment to the soul and that it made the soul like a field or garden of God, with all manner of pleasant flowers; that is all pleasant, delightful and undisturbed; enjoying a sweet calm, and the gently vivifying beams of the sun. The soul of a true Christian . . . appeared like such a little white flower as we see in the spring of the year; low and humble on the ground, opening its bosom, to receive the pleasant beams of the sun's glory; rejoicing as it were, in a calm rapture; diffusing around a sweet fragrance; standing peacefully and lovingly in the midst of other flowers round about; all in like manner opening their bosoms to drink in the light of the sun.[14]

How many Christians do you know who describe obedience and holiness in those terms?

One might well ask: How did Edwards come to have such a view of obedience? Why did he find such delight in what he calls "gospel rules"? The answer comes in his own words. Edwards was so much in love with Jesus, so utterly enthralled with the transcendent beauties of his Savior, so swallowed up in the adequacy of the Son of God in all things that nothing appeared so sweet to him as obedience to His commands. In one place Edwards describes his experience of

> the excellent fullness of Christ, and His meetness and suitableness as a Savior; whereby He has appeared to me,

far above all, the chief of ten thousands. And His blood
and atonement has appeared sweet, and His righteousness
sweet; which is always accompanied with an ardency of
spirit, and inward strugglings and breathings and groan-
ings, that cannot be uttered, to be emptied of myself, and
swallowed up in Christ.[15]

He goes on to speak of

the glory of the Son of God as mediator between God
and man, and His wonderful, great, full, pure and sweet
grace and love, and meek and gentle condescension. This
grace that appeared to me so calm and sweet appeared
great above the heavens. The person of Christ appeared
ineffably excellent, with an excellency great enough to
swallow up all thought and conception, . . . which kept
me, the bigger part of the time, in a flood of tears and
weeping aloud. I felt an ardency of soul to be . . . emptied and annihilated, to lie in the dust and to be full of
Christ alone; to love Him with a holy and pure love; to
trust in Him; to live upon Him; to serve and follow Him,
and to be totally wrapped up in the fullness of Christ,
and to be perfectly sanctified and made pure, with a
divine and heavenly purity.[16]

Edwards was so completely consumed by the beauty of Jesus that
he could scarcely look upon anything in natural creation and not see
a reflection of the splendor of his Savior. Here is but one example:

When we are delighted with flowery meadows and gentle
breezes of wind, we may consider that we see only the
emanations of the sweet benevolence of Jesus Christ.
When we behold the fragrant rose and lily, we see His love
and purity. So the green trees and fields and singing of

birds are the emanations of His infinite joy and benignity
[that is, kindness]. The easiness and naturalness of trees
and vines are shadows of His beauty and loveliness. The
crystal rivers and murmuring streams are the footsteps of
His favor, grace, and beauty. When we behold the light
and brightness of the sun, the golden edges of an evening
cloud, or the beauteous rainbow, we behold the adum-
brations of His glory and goodness; and in the blue sky of
His mildness and gentleness. There are also many things
wherein we may behold His awful majesty, in the sun in
His strength, in comets, in thunder, in the hovering thun-
der-clouds, in ragged rocks, and the brows of mountains.
That beauteous light with which the world is filled in a
clear day, is a lively shadow of His spotless holiness, and
happiness and delight in communicating Himself.[17]

But will Jesus be enough? The world seems to offer so much more,
so much easier, so much faster. Is there in the beauty of all that Jesus
is and offers sufficient joy to keep my soul satisfied and to stem its
search for other delights? Jesus, and only Jesus, says Edwards,

has true excellency, and so great excellency, that when
[weary souls] come to see it they look no further, but the
mind rests there. It sees a transcendent glory and an inef-
fable sweetness in Him; it sees that till now it has been
pursuing shadows, but that now it has found the substance;
that before it had been seeking happiness in the stream,
but that now it has found the ocean. The excellency of
Christ is an object adequate to the natural cravings of the
soul, and is sufficient to fill the capacity. It is an infinite
excellency, such a one as the mind desires, in which it can
find no bounds. . . . Every new discovery makes this
beauty appear more ravishing, and the mind sees no end;
here is room enough for the mind to go deeper and deeper,

and never come to the bottom. The soul is exceedingly ravished when it first looks on this beauty, and it is never weary of it. The mind never has any satiety, but Christ's excellency is always fresh and new, and tends as much to delight, after it has seen a thousand or ten thousand years, as when it was seen the first moment.[18]

What will turn our hearts from the passing pleasures of sin? What can strengthen our wills to reject the temptations of the flesh? What will energize our souls to turn from worldly delusions? What has the power to transform our desires and reconfigure our longings and stir our emotional chemistry that we might love what God loves and hate what He hates? Only one thing. Not rules and threats and fear and punishment. Only one thing. Jesus, in all His beauty. Jesus, in all that He is for us now and will be tomorrow. Edwards is certain that only Jesus can satisfy our soul's desire. He says:

[In Jesus] the longing soul may be satisfied and the hungry soul may be filled with goodness. The delight and contentment that is to be found here, passeth understanding, and is unspeakable and full of glory. It is impossible for those who ever tasted of this fountain, and know the sweetness of it, ever to forsake it. The soul has found the river of water of life, and it desires no other drink; it has found the tree of life, and it desires no other fruit.[19]

This is God's mission in my life: to maximize my "delight and contentment" in His Son. This is my mission in ministry: to portray Jesus in such a light that, turning to Him, others will find complete satisfaction and lose their taste for sin. Edwards says:

There is every kind of thing dispensed in Christ that tends to make us excellent and amiable, and every kind of thing that tends to make us happy. There is that which shall fill every faculty of the soul and in a great variety. What a glorious variety is there for the entertainment of the understanding! How many glorious objects set forth, most worthy to be meditated upon and understood! There are all the glorious attributes of God and the beauties of Jesus Christ, and manifold wonders to be seen in the way of salvation, the glories of heaven and the excellency of Christian graces. . . . The blessings are innumerable.[20]

Do you fear that it might one day run dry, that the capacity of God to "entertain" and "thrill" your soul with Christ will soon dissipate as eventually do all earthly pleasures? Then you have not yet considered the inexhaustible resources for joy in the inexhaustible heart of God:

There is [in God] an inexhaustible fountain of blessings. Every kind of dainty is in inexhaustible plenty. Therefore 'tis called a river of life, rivers of pleasure forevermore (Revelation 22:1). Here the soul [your soul] manifests itself abundantly without danger of spending the provision. Therefore Christ says to His people, "Eat, O friends; drink, yea, drink abundantly, O beloved" (Song of Songs 5:1). There is no such thing as excess in our taking of this spiritual food. There is no such virtue as temperance in spiritual feasting. . . . At God's right hand there are pleasures forevermore. There you may always eat and drink, and always be satisfied and yet never be glutted. You may eat and drink abundantly and never be in danger of excess.[21]

The key to holiness? Eating and drinking and enjoying and delighting in all that God is for you in His Son. The key to holiness is *falling in love with Jesus.*

CHAPTER EIGHT

What to Eat When You're Fasting

IF IT IS IN GOD'S PRESENCE THAT FULLNESS OF JOY IS TO BE found and at God's right hand that pleasures evermore are to be experienced, how do we get there? It's all well and good to talk about fascination with God and being entranced by His beauty, but how do I posture my soul to see that beauty and to encounter this God at whose "river of delights" I've been invited to drink?

The answer to that question could come in any number of shapes and sizes, but I want us to consider three possibilities. When I think of the most effective way to tenderize my spirit and enlarge my heart to receive the fullness of God, my mind (not my stomach) turns to fasting. Sometimes my stomach just plain turns! Meditation also comes immediately to mind, as does worship. These pursuits are simply three (but by no means all) of God's prescribed means for posturing our thirsty souls beneath the spout of His ever-flowing blessings. They are conduits of His mercy and channels for the free-flow of His presence into our experience. We neglect them to our peril.

FASTING IS FEASTING

"Are you nuts? Or have you joined one of those bizarre cults that believes there's a space ship in the tail of a comet?" Don't be surprised

165

if you hear a question like that should you choose to let your friends in on the fact that you voluntarily fast every so often. Nothing seems as silly to the natural mind or as repulsive to the body as fasting. It's not hard to figure out why. As Kevin Springer has noted, "we live in a consumer oriented society that bombards us with messages of instant gratification. 'You can have it all!' 'Go for the gusto!' 'Have it your way!' (And have it now). To this mindset, fasting does not make any sense at all."[1]

Even from a Christian point of view, it seems a little odd. If God has generously created food "to be gratefully shared in by those who believe and know the truth" (1 Timothy. 4:3), what possible reason could there be for abstinence? It seems like something reserved for the weird, the odd, or at worst, the masochist.

The reputation of fasting has also suffered because of its association in the minds of many with the ascetic abuses of medieval monks and hermits. In centuries past, fasting often was subjected to rigid regulations and was combined with extreme forms of self-mortification and self-denial. Little wonder, then, that fasting seems so often to contribute to that "holier-than-thou" mentality we all want to avoid. There is no getting around the fact that fasting is inseparable, in the minds of many, from showy and ostentatious self-righteousness.

Richard Foster points out that "the constant propaganda fed us today convinces us that if we do not have three large meals each day with several snacks in between, we are on the verge of starvation. This, coupled with the popular belief that it is a positive virtue to satisfy every human appetite, has made fasting seem obsolete."[2]

FASTING IS NOT PRIMARILY ABOUT NOT EATING

One thing that will help us in our attitude toward fasting is to distinguish it from other reasons why people don't eat. For example, fasting must be distinguished from a hunger strike, the purpose of which is to gain political power or to draw attention to some social cause. Some of us are old enough to remember the protest fasting of jailed Irish militants as well as the highly visible fast of black comedian and social critic Dick Gregory.

We must also distinguish fasting from health dieting, which insists on abstaining from certain foods for physical reasons. Saying No to burgers and shakes so you can look better in this summer's swimsuit is not what this chapter is about. Biblical fasting has nothing to do with anorexia nervosa, an emotional disorder in which a person starves herself to lose weight, either out of self-contempt or in hope of becoming fashionably and loveably thin. Finally, fasting must be distinguished from how it is practiced in numerous pagan religions: to control or appease the gods, or perhaps to make contact with spirits in order to manipulate their power.

Are We Commanded to Fast?

No. But according to Matthew 6:16-18, Jesus simply assumes that we will. Twice Jesus says, "when you fast" (verses 16,17). As Foster notes, "It is as if there is an almost unconscious assumption that giving, praying, and fasting are all part of Christian devotion. We have no more reason to exclude fasting from the teaching than we do giving or praying."[3] Therefore, although Jesus does not say, "If you fast," neither does He say, "You must fast." He says, simply: "When you fast . . ." Matthew 9:14-17 is especially instructive on this point. When the Pharisees queried why Jesus' disciples didn't fast, He explained it in terms of His own physical presence on earth. "But the days will come," He said, "when the bridegroom is taken away from them, and then they will fast" (Matthew 9:15).

The point here is that the Messiah has come like a bridegroom to a wedding feast. Such a moment is too joyful and stunning and exciting to mingle with fasting. This indicates, by the way, that in those days fasting was by and large associated with mourning. People fasted as an expression of deep personal longing for something more precious than mere food. Their self-denial was symptomatic of a heart-sickness borne of desperation. Fasting is for times of yearning and longing. When the bridegroom is no longer physically with us on earth, then it is appropriate to fast. In this age there is an ache, a homesickness of sorts, inside every Christian because Jesus is not as intimately and powerfully and visibly and personally present as we want Him to be and as we know one day He will be (see 1 Peter 1:8). And that is why we are to fast.

There is in this regard a fascinating parallel between fasting and the Lord's Supper. The latter is a feasting that looks backward in time, whereas fasting is a feasting that looks forward in time. The breaking of bread and drinking the cup is done "in remembrance" of our Lord's historic, and therefore past, act of sacrifice. Thus by eating and drinking we celebrate the finality and sufficiency of that atoning death and that glorious resurrection. We should never fast from the supper of the Lord, even when we are fasting from other ordinary "suppers." On the other hand, as Piper explains,

> by not eating—by fasting—we look to the future with an aching in our hearts saying: "Yes, he came. And yes, what he did for us is glorious. But precisely because of what we have seen and what we have tasted, we feel keenly his absence as well as his presence. . . . we can eat and even celebrate with feasting because he has come. But this we also know: he is not here the way he once was. . . . And his [physical] absence is painful. The sin and misery of the world is painful. . . . We long for him to come again and take up his throne and reign in our midst and vindicate his people and his truth and his glory."[4]

When we sit at Christ's table with other believers, we gratefully, fearfully, joyfully feast upon that food and drink that remind us of what has happened. And when we turn away from the table where otherwise daily meals are served we declare our deep yearning for what has not yet happened.

How may we sum up these thoughts concerning our obligation

to fast? Richard Foster comes right to the point: "There simply are no biblical laws that command regular fasting. Our freedom in the gospel, however, does not mean license; it means opportunity. Since there are no laws to bind us, we are free to fast on any day."[5]

WHY SHOULD WE FAST?

I have identified fifteen reasons in the Bible for fasting. There may be more, but these will give us a good start.

The key is to remember that fasting is always motivated by deep desire. I realize that it may have come as something of a jolt to you when I turned from a discussion of the centrality of pleasure to a practice that most people associate with deprivation and discomfort. Whereas there is certainly a measure of physical pain that comes with fasting, I want to insist that, contrary to popular opinion, fasting is not the suppression of desire but the intense pursuit of it. We fast because we want something more than food. We say No to food for a season only to fill ourselves with something far more tasty, far more filling, far more satisfying. That is to say, if one suppresses the desire for food it is only because he or she has a greater and more intense desire for something more precious — something of eternal value.

We don't fast because we hate our bodies and look to punish them. Whatever immediate discomfort we may experience, it is a sacrifice that pays immeasurable long-term benefits. We do not fast for pain, but for the pleasure of experiencing still more of Christ Jesus and the revelation of His powerful presence. In other words, fasting is perfectly consistent with Christian Hedonism! More on this later.

1. *Fasting was practiced to avert God's judgment and displeasure against His people.* Fasting per se could not turn away God's wrath, but only insofar as it was an expression of conviction for sin. See 1 Samuel 7:6; Joel 2:12; Jonah 3:5-8; Judges 20:26 (compare Esther 4; 1 Kings 21:9; Jeremiah 36:6,9).

2. *The people of God often fasted in preparation for war, with a view to seeking God's protection and blessing.* Thus, fasting is especially appropriate in times of national emergency. See 2 Chronicles 20:1-4; Joel 2:15.

3. *Fasting was one way of seeking God's help for deliverance from personal troubles and oppression.* It was a sign of utter reliance on God alone to help and save. See 1 Kings 21:27-29.

4. *Fasting was often an expression of sincere and heartfelt repentance from sin and humility before God.* Indeed, the only fast day for Israel was the Day of Atonement (Leviticus 16:29-31). See also Nehemiah 9:1-2; Psalm 35:13 ("I humbled my soul with fasting"); Daniel 9:3; Joel 2:12-13; Jonah 3:5-8.

5. *Fasting also signified or expressed mourning, sorrow, deep grief, and sadness.* See especially 1 Samuel 31:13 (fasting following the death of Saul and his sons); 2 Samuel 1:12 (David fasted on hearing of Saul's and Jonathan's death); 2 Samuel 12:15-23 (David fasted while grieving over the fatal illness of his son); 1 Samuel 20:34 (Jonathan fasted out of grief over his father's treachery against David). It is as if one says: "It would not be proper to enjoy the pleasures of food at a time of such tragedy and sadness and loss."

6. *Ezra fasted as part of his request that God provide him with a safe journey* (Ezra 8:21-23). Here we see that Ezra refused an army escort so that he could testify to king Artaxerxes about the power and faithfulness and sufficiency of God in protecting His people. Instead of the king's help he sought God's help and he sought it through fasting. Notice also that here again fasting is an expression of humility (verse 21). Fasting is a humbling of ourselves because in it we feel and express our absolute dependence

on God and our refusal to trust ultimately in any human resource or power. Fasting is also portrayed here as an expression of seeking God with life-and-death seriousness: "so we fasted and sought our God" (verse 23).

7. *Fasting is a way of expressing one's concern for the success of God's work* (Nehemiah 1:3-4). Daniel was well into his seventies when he sought the Lord by "prayer and supplications, with fasting, sackcloth, and ashes," all of which was the fruit of his desire to see Israel set free from her captivity in Babylon (Daniel 9:3).

8. *Fasting serves to humble and rebuke us as it reveals how much of our happiness depends on the external pleasures of eating.* See Psalm 69:10.

9. *Fasting teaches us self-control and self-discipline.* Our belly must not be our god, as it is with some (Philippians 3:19; Romans 16:18). See especially 1 Corinthians 9:25-27.

Richard Foster put it this way:

More than any other single Discipline, fasting reveals the things that control us. This is a wonderful benefit to the true disciple who longs to be transformed into the image of Jesus Christ. We cover up what is inside us with food and other good things, but in fasting these things surface. If pride controls us, it will be revealed almost immediately. David said, "I humbled my soul with fasting" (Psalm 69:10). Anger, bitterness, jealousy, strife, fear—if they are within us, they will surface during fasting. At first we will rationalize that our anger is due to our hunger, then we know that we are angry because the spirit of anger is within us. We can rejoice in this knowledge because we know that healing is available through the power of Christ.[6]

John Piper agrees:

What are we slaves to? What are our bottom-line passions? Fasting is God's testing ground—and healing ground. Will we murmur as the Israelites murmured when they had no bread? Will we leave the path of obedience and turn stones into bread? Or will we "live by every word that proceeds out the mouth of God?" Fasting is a way of revealing to ourselves and confessing to God what is in our hearts.[7]

10. *Fasting is a powerful weapon in spiritual warfare.*
    Fasting heightens our complete dependence upon God and forces us to draw on Him and His power, and to believe fully in His strength. This explains why Jesus fasted in preparation for facing the temptations of Satan in the wilderness (Matthew 4:1-11; Mark 9:29; Matthew 17:14-21).

It is important to note that as Jesus was standing on the brink of the most important public ministry the world had ever seen, He chose to fast! Have you ever paused to reflect on the eternal consequences of what transpired in the wilderness of Judea those forty days? Heaven and hell hung in the balance. Had Jesus wavered, had He faltered, had He balked, all hope of heaven would have been dashed on the very rocks with which the Enemy tempted Him. Of the dozens of things Jesus might have done to withstand this temptation, He is led by the Spirit to fast. Piper reminds us that "we owe our salvation, in some measure (not to overstate it), to the fasting of Jesus, [which] is a remarkable tribute to fasting."[8]

11. *Fasting opens our spiritual ears to discern God's voice.*
    The gentle words of the Spirit are more readily heard during times of fasting. During times of fasting God

often grants insights and understanding into His will and purpose, or perhaps new applications of His Word to our lives. The following incident is recorded in Acts 13:1-3:

> Now there were at Antioch, in the church that was there, prophets and teachers . . . . And while they were ministering to the Lord and fasting, the Holy Spirit said, "Set apart for Me Barnabas and Saul for the work to which I have called them." Then, when they had fasted and prayed and laid their hands on them, they sent them away.

Here we see Saul (Paul) and Barnabas, together with leaders of the church in Antioch, seeking direction from the Lord as to where they should go as a church, in terms of ministry. Their desperation to hear God's voice and follow God's will could find no more appropriate expression than through bodily denial. As they turned away from physical dependence on food they cast themselves in spiritual dependence on God. "Yes, Lord, we love food. We thank You for it. We enjoy it as You want us to. But now, O Lord, there is something before us more important than filling our mouths and quenching our thirst. Where would You have us go? Whom shall we send? How shall it be financed? Lord, we hunger to know Your will. Lord, we thirst for Your direction. Feed us, O God!"

There is much to learn here about the importance of fasting. Note four things in particular.[9]

1. They were fasting after the death and resurrection of Jesus. This is important for the simple reason that some argue that fasting was an Old Testament practice no longer relevant for people in the church age.
2. They fasted together as a group. Clearly they did not believe that Jesus' warning about fasting to be seen by men (Matthew 6:17-18) precluded corporate fasting. When you fast as a group others obviously know, but

this is evidently not a violation of Christ's instruction. Evidently the church leaders at Antioch take Jesus to mean not that we sin if someone knows that we are fasting, but that we sin if our motive is to be known for our fasting so that men applaud us. Group fasting has marked God's people all through biblical and post-biblical history.

3. Their fasting became the occasion for the Spirit's guidance to be communicated to them. Don't miss the obvious causal link that Luke draws. It was while or when they were ministering to the Lord and fasting that the Holy Spirit spoke. Indeed, it would not be too much to say it was because they ministered to the Lord and fasted that He spoke. I'm not suggesting that fasting puts God in our debt, as if it compels Him to respond to us. But God does promise to be found by those who diligently seek Him with their whole heart (Jeremiah 29:12-13). People who are merely "open" to God rarely find Him. God postures Himself to be found by those who wholeheartedly seek Him, and fasting is a single-minded pursuit to know, hear, and experience God.

4. What God said to them in the course of their fasting changed history. This revelatory word was spoken in a moment of spiritual hunger for God's voice to fill the void left by mere human wisdom. The results, both immediate and long-term, are stunning, for prior to this incident the church had progressed little, if at all, beyond the eastern seacoast of the Mediterranean. Paul had as yet taken no missionary journeys westward to Asia Minor, Greece, Rome, or Spain. Neither had he written any of his epistles. All his letters were the result of the missionary journeys he was to take and the churches he was to plant. This occasion of prayer and fasting, notes Piper, "resulted in a missions movement that would catapult Christianity from

obscurity into being the dominant religion of the Roman Empire within two and a half centuries, and would yield 1.3 billion adherents of the Christian religion today, with a Christian witness in virtually every country of the world. And thirteen out of the twenty-seven books of the New Testament (Paul's letters) were a result of the ministry that was launched in this historic moment of prayer and fasting.[10]

John Wesley recorded in his journal a time of fasting that seemed to have altered the course of history. The king of England called for a solemn day of prayer and fasting because of a threatened invasion of the French (1756). Wesley wrote: "The fast day was a glorious day, such as London has scarce seen since the Restoration. Every church in the city was more than full, and a solemn seriousness sat on every face. Surely God heareth prayer, and there will yet be a lengthening of our tranquility." In a footnote he later added, "Humility was turned into national rejoicing for the threatened invasion by the French was averted."[11]

12. *Fasting sharpens and intensifies our intercessory prayers.* On Monday, April 19, 1742, David Brainerd recorded in his journal that he set apart this day for fasting and prayer. He said of his experience that day:

I felt the power of intercession for precious, immortal souls; for the advancement of the kingdom of my dear Lord and Savior in the world; and withal, a most sweet resignation and even consolation and joy in the thoughts of suffering hardships, distresses, and even death itself, in the promotion of it. . . . My soul was drawn out very much for the world, for multitudes of souls. I think I had more enlargement for sinners than for the children of God, though I felt as if I could spend my life in cries for both. I enjoyed great sweetness in communion with my dear Savior. I think I never in my life felt such an entire weanedness from this world and so much resigned to God in everything.[12]

13. *To fast is to worship.* Anna (Luke 2:36-37) worshiped "by fastings and prayers" (verse 37; compare Acts 13:1-3). The example of Anna, in a certain sense, stands as a rebuke to us. She fasted for years in anticipation of the coming of Messiah. But He has now come. We now have the blessings He came to provide. Piper applies this to us in pointed fashion:

Shall we long for him less than Anna longed for him? Does the fact that we have had him with us for 30 years and have his Spirit now make you long less or more? O what an indictment of our blindness if the answer is less. I say, let us long for him and yearn for him and look for him with more intensity than Anna and Simeon. Shall we have less devotion than these pre-Christian saints? We have beheld his glory, glory as of the only begotten of the Father. And shall we hunger less for his appearing?[13]

14. *Fasting can be an expression of our generosity and compassion toward those in need.* In Isaiah 58:1-3, God issues an indictment against His people. But what Isaiah calls sin looks amazingly like godly religious fervor! Five things are noted:

1. They are "seeking God" (verse 2).
2. They "delight to know God's ways" (verse 2).

3. They ask God for "just decisions" (verse 2).
4. They "delight in the nearness of God" (verse 2).
5. They fast and humble themselves (verse 3).

Yet their fasting does not please the Lord! Why? The reason is made clear in verses 3-5. The ethical accompaniments of their fasting are abominable: they are motivated by selfish desire (verse 3), they are unfair and harsh to those who work for them (verse 3), they are irritable and contentious and stir up strife and get into fights (verse 4)! This is not the kind of fast that God chooses or desires. If your fasting leaves you selfish, grumpy, abrasive, angry, and insensitive to the needs of those around you, please, for heaven's sake (and for the sake of everyone else), eat something!

The fast that God chooses or desires results in several activities. There are thirteen of them but Piper has helpfully reduced them to seven general categories:[14]

1. In this fasting, we are called to lift the burden of bondage. (verses 6, 9)
2. In this fasting, we are called to feed the hungry. (verse 7)
3. In this fasting, we are called to house the homeless. (verse 7)
4. In this fasting, we are called to clothe the naked. (verse 7)
5. In this fasting, we are called to be sympathetic; to feel what others feel because we have the same flesh as they do. (verse 7; compare Hebrews 13:3. The point of this latter text is, you have the same flesh they do. So put yourself in their place and feel what they feel.)
6. In this fasting, we are called to put away gestures and words that show contempt for other people. (verse 9)
7. In this fasting, we are called not just to give food, but to give ourselves, our souls, and not just to satisfy the stomach of the poor, but the soul of the afflicted. (verse 10)

The results are equally explicit:

1. If we fast like this, the darkness in our lives will become light. (verses 8a,10)
2. This sort of fasting results in physical strengthening. (verses 8,11)
3. God will be in front of us and behind us and in the midst of us with righteousness and glory when we fast His way. (verses 8,9)
4. If we fast like this, God promises to guide us continually. (verse 11)
5. If we fast like this, God will satisfy our souls. (verse 11)
6. If we fast like this, God will make us like a well-watered garden with springs that do not fail. (verse 11)
7. If we fast like this, God will restore the ruins of His city—and His people. (verse 12)

15. *Fasting is feasting!* Or, what to eat when you're on a fast! The ironic thing about fasting is that it really isn't about not eating food. It's about feeding on the fullness of every divine blessing secured for us in Christ. Fasting tenderizes our hearts to experience the presence of God. It expands the capacity of our souls to hear His voice and be assured of His love and be filled with the fullness of His joy. Dallas Willard explains:

Fasting confirms our utter dependence upon God by finding in him a source of sustenance beyond food. Through it, we learn by experience that God's word to us is a life substance, that it is not food ("bread") alone that gives life, but also the words that proceed from the mouth of God (Matthew 4:4). We learn that we too have meat to eat that the world does not know about (John 4:32,34). Fasting unto our Lord is therefore feasting—feasting on him and on doing his will.[15]

Look again at Jesus' words to His disciples in John 4. I'm sure Jesus appreciated their concern for His welfare, but He wanted to make a point. So when they insisted that He eat something, His response was startling: "I have food to eat that you do not know about" (4:32). No, Jesus didn't have a double-meat Big Mac hidden inside His robe. Nor were His words, as Foster explains, "a clever metaphor, but a genuine reality. Jesus was, in fact, being nourished and sustained by the power of God."[16] Wesley Duewel put it this way:

> Fasting in the biblical sense is choosing not to partake of food because your spiritual hunger is so deep, your determination in intercession so intense, or your spiritual warfare so demanding that you have temporarily set aside even fleshly needs to give yourself to prayer and meditation.[17]

The point is that fasting is a feast. Fasting is all about eating! It is about ingesting the Word of God, the beauty of God, the presence of God, the blessings of God. Fasting is all about spiritual gluttony! It is not a giving up of food for its own sake. It is about a giving up of food for Christ's sake. As Jesus Himself made clear in Matthew 6:16-18, either we abstain from food for the praise of men or for the reward of our heavenly Father. The point is: we are always driven to fast because we hunger for something more than food. As strange as it may sound, fasting is motivated by the prospect of pleasure. The heart that fasts cries out, "This I want more than the pleasure of food!" And "this" can be the admiration that men give to people with will power, or it can be the reward we seek from God alone without regard to the praise of men.[18]

THE DANGERS OF FASTING

The real danger of fasting is more than the potential physical side effects. Jesus warns us in Matthew 6:16 not to be like the hypocrites.

Hypocrites are those who undertake spiritual disciplines, such as fasting, to be seen by men. This is the reward they are after. All of us at some time have felt the satisfaction of this kind of reward: the ego boost that comes from being admired for our "spirituality" and acknowledged publicly for our "zeal." It truly gratifies the flesh when people make much of our accomplishments, especially our religious accomplishments. Jesus says that if this is the reward that motivates our fasting, we shall surely receive it. But that's all we will receive! If the praise of men is what we desire, we shall have it, but none from God.

Jesus calls this sort of fasting "hypocrisy." Why? Because true, godly fasting is motivated by a heart for God, not human admiration. If these Pharisees wanted to be totally open about their reason for fasting, they should have distributed an explanatory tract that read: "The ultimate reason why we're fasting is to solicit the praise and admiration of men and women." Then they would no longer be hypocrites. It wouldn't make their fasting godly, but it would at least eliminate hypocrisy from their list of sins! Their hypocrisy consists of putting a public face on their fasting, which purports to be their way of seeking God's approval when in fact it is their way of seeking man's approval. As Piper explains,

> there are two dangers that these fasting folks have fallen into. One is that they are seeking the wrong reward in fasting, namely, the esteem of other people. They love the praise of men. And the other is that they hide this with a pretense of love for God. Fasting means love for God— hunger for God. So with their actions they are saying that they have a hunger for God. But on the inside they are hungry to be admired and approved by other people. That's the god that satisfies them.[19]

Someone might understandably ask at this point, "Does this mean that if someone discovers I've been fasting, I've sinned or

I'm a hypocrite?" No, not necessarily. The value of your fasting is not undermined if someone notices that you skipped dinner. This statement by Jesus does not rule out group fasting either. It is possible to fast with others or that it be known that you are fasting and it not be sin or hypocrisy. The deciding factor is your motive for fasting. Simply put, "being seen fasting and fasting to be seen are not the same."[20] Being seen fasting is merely an external, and often unavoidable, event. But fasting to be seen is a self-exalting motive of the heart.

> What, then, is the "reward" that God promises to give if our motive is only to be seen by him in secret (Matthew 6:18)? God sees us fasting and knows that we are motivated by a deep longing in our hearts for him and for his purposes to be fulfilled in the earth. He knows that we are not fasting to obtain the applause of people. He sees that we are acting not out of strength to impress others with our discipline, or even out of a desire to influence others to imitate our devotion. But we have come to God out of weakness to express to him our need and our great longing that he would manifest himself more fully in our lives for the joy of our soul and the glory of his name.[21]

And when He sees this, He responds. He responds by giving to us more of Himself and the blessings secured for us in Christ. He "rewards" us by answering the prayers we pray in accordance with His instruction in Matthew 6:9-13 (that His name be hallowed, that His kingdom come, that His will be done on earth). Surely God can and does give us other things that we seek through fasting (physical healing, guidance, and so on). But chief among the results of fasting is the exaltation of God's name and the expansion of God's kingdom.

So here's how to avoid hypocrisy in fasting. If at any point, while fasting, you find yourself thinking, "God will love me more . . . God will surely be impressed with me now!" get in your car and go eat a McDonalds' Quarterpounder! If you are in the least way tempted to believe, "God will bless me more . . . He will have no choice but to reward my righteousness!" go eat the biggest, greasiest pizza you can find! If it crosses your mind, "I'm better than others who don't fast, and I sure hope they recognize it as clearly as I do!" go to an all-you-can-eat smorgasbord!

HOW SHOULD WE FAST?

Now for a few practical guidelines. First of all, a progression should be observed in your fasting, especially if this discipline is new to you and you are unfamiliar with its physical effects. Don't start out with a two-week water fast! Begin by skipping one meal each day for three to five days and setting aside the money it would have cost to give to the poor. Spend the time praying that you would have used for eating.

Remember also that there are degrees of fasting. There is a regular fast, which consists of abstaining from all food and drink except water (Matthew 4:2-3; Luke 4:2). Apart from supernatural enablement, the body can function only three days without water. A partial fast is when one abstains from some particular kind of food, as in the case of Daniel while in Babylon (Daniel 10:3; compare 1:8,12). A liquid fast means that you abstain only from solid foods. Most who choose this path are sustained by fruit juices and the like. A complete or absolute fast that entails no food or liquid of any kind (Ezra 10:6; Esther 4:16; Acts 9:9) should only be for a very short period of time. For anything longer, seek medical advice. There is also what can only be called a supernatural fast, as in the case of Moses (Deuteronomy 9:9), who abstained from both food and water for forty days (enabled to do so only by a miraculous enabling from God).

In the early stages you may get dizzy and have headaches. This is part of the body's cleansing process and will pass with time. Be sure that you break the fast gradually with fresh fruit and vegetables. Do not overeat after the fast. Chili and pizza may sound good after several days of not eating, but please, exercise a little restraint and say No!

How long you fast is entirely up to you and the leadership of the Holy Spirit. In the Bible are examples of fasts that lasted one day or part of a day (Judges 20:26; 1 Samuel 7:6; 2 Samuel 1:12; 3:35; Nehemiah 9:1; Jeremiah 36:6), a one-night fast (Daniel 6:18-24); three-day fasts (Esther 4:16; Acts 9:9), seven-day fasts (1 Samuel 31:13; 2 Samuel 12:16-23), a fourteen-day fast (Acts 27:33-34), a twenty-one day fast (Daniel 10:3-13), forty-day fasts (Deuteronomy 9:9; 1 Kings 19:8; Matthew 4:2), and fasts of unspecified lengths (Matthew 9:14; Luke 2:37; Acts 13:2).

Finally, never lose sight of the fact that what you don't eat or how long you don't eat isn't paramount. What you do eat, spiritually speaking, is critical. Feed on God. Don't simply taste, don't nibble, don't snack. Feast on Him! Seek Him. Cry out to Him. Focus on Him. Invite Him to fill you up "to all the fulness of God" (Ephesians 3:19). Entreat Him to sustain you and supply you and succor you. Then, when your fast is finished, rejoice in the food He has provided and give Him thanks for all good things.

CHAPTER NINE

Pleasures of the Mind

WHAT DOES MEDITATION HAVE TO DO WITH HOLINESS? MORE
to the point, what does it have to do with maximizing our pleasure in God and minimizing our enjoyment of sin?

Scripture has many functions but none more vital than fuel-
ing and feeding our appetite for God. Sin tells me that pursuing
purity will preclude experiencing life's greatest adventures and most
satisfying pleasures. But the Word of God reinforces my decision
to obey by reminding me that in obedience is the fullness of joy,
and in honor there is the blessing of God, and in righteousness there
is a thrill that not even on its best day could the sweetest of sins
begin to touch. "And as I pray for my faith to be satisfied with God's
life and peace," notes Piper, "the sword of the Spirit carves the sugar-
coating off the poison of lust. I see it for what it is. And by the grace
of God, its alluring power is broken."[1]

All of us want to not sin. That's why I wrote this book and that's
why you're reading it. The apostle Paul said in Romans 3:23 that
"all have sinned and fall short of the glory of God," by which I take
him to mean that sin is failing to glorify God because of having
cherished other things as more valuable and enjoyable than He. The
key to not sinning is therefore to enjoy God above all else, for in
our enjoyment of Him is His glory in us. The psalmist declares that

185

the way not to sin, that is, the way to enjoy God above all else, is by treasuring His Word in our hearts (Psalm 119:11). Making God's Word our heart's treasure is another way of describing one aspect of meditation. More than merely "confessing" His Word, "treasuring" it "in our hearts" means placing ultimate value on its truth, prizing it as something precious and dear and of supreme excellence, and then ingesting it through memorization and meditation so that it flows freely through our spiritual veins. When this happens, the Holy Spirit energizes our hearts to believe and behave in conformity with its dictates. In other words, we sin less.

The problem we face is that meditation has become a dirty word in many Christian circles, almost as dirty as fasting(!), due primarily to its association with Eastern religions and New Age philosophy. But meditation is a thoroughly biblical concept, apart from which the believer will never fully embrace and experience the depths of communion with God that He has made available to His children. We simply must not permit the abuse and distortion of this biblical practice to rob us of the delights God intends for it to impart.

WHAT IS MEDITATION?

Meditation begins, but by no means ends, with thinking on Scripture. To meditate properly our souls must reflect upon what our minds have ingested and our hearts must rejoice in what our souls have grasped. We have truly meditated when we slowly read, prayerfully imbibe, and humbly rely upon what God has revealed to us in His Word—all of this, of course, in conscious dependence on the internal, energizing work of the Spirit.

Meditation, then, is being attentive to God. It is one way we "keep seeking the things above where Christ is" (Colossians 3:1). It is a conscious, continuous engagement of the mind with God. This renewing of the mind (Romans 12:1-2) is part of the process by which the Word of God penetrates the soul and spirit with the light of illumination and the power of transformation. Don

Whitney uses the analogy of a cup of tea:

> You are the cup of hot water and the intake of Scripture is
> represented by the tea bag. Hearing God's Word is like one
> dip of the tea bag into the cup. Some of the tea's flavor is
> absorbed by the water, but not as much as would occur
> with a more thorough soaking of the bag. In this analogy,
> reading, studying, and memorizing God's Word are repre-
> sented by additional plunges of the tea bag into the cup.
> The more frequently the tea enters the water, the more
> effect it has. Meditation, however, is like immersing the
> bag completely and letting it steep until all the rich tea
> flavor has been extracted and the hot water is thoroughly
> tinctured reddish brown.[2]

VARIETIES OF MEDITATION

Meditation may take one of several forms, depending on the object
upon which we focus our mental and spiritual energy.

Meditation on Scripture

If I have a hobby, it would be books, or better still, reading them
(I hope). I have many books. Novels, nonfiction, treatises on
theology, encyclopedias and dictionaries and commentaries and who
knows what else, all line the shelves of my office. But for all their
worth and depth and literary excellence, they are merely books. They
are but ink on paper encased by two covers. None of them is infal-
lible and their advice is occasionally pathetic. The power of such
books to change my life is minimal. They can expand my vocabulary, inform me of facts hitherto unknown, even add spice to my
romantic fantasies (were I to read a certain sort, which, thank God,
I don't!). But when my heart faints from despair, such books cannot
supply hope. When doubts rise up like flood waters, threatening to
drown out reasons to believe, such books fail to bring faith. When

I struggle to break free of sinful habits, such books are powerless to help me. When I wake up wondering if anyone really cares for my soul, such books cannot impart the joy of knowing I'm loved by God. When I'm sad and sullen and fed up with life, I need a book whose words are anointed with the power of the Holy Spirit, a book empowered by God to bring about the changes it calls for. And the only book that can do what I need done is the Word of God.

The power of the written Word of God to transform how we think, feel, and behave must be embraced before the value of meditation will be acknowledged. Consider for a moment the ways in which Scripture—and Scripture alone—can influence our lives.

In the first place, the Word of God is the means or instrument by which the Holy Spirit regenerates the human heart. The proclamation or communication of the Word is the catalyst for the inception of spiritual life. Peter declares that we "have been born again not of seed which is perishable but imperishable, that is, through the living and abiding word of God. . . . And this is the word which was preached to you" (1 Peter 1:23,25). Paul said much the same thing when he spoke of the Word of God in the gospel as the power by which we are saved (see especially Romans 1:16-17; 10:14-15; and 1 Corinthians 1:18-25).

The Word of God is also the spring from which the waters of faith arise. Paul says in Romans 10:17 that "faith comes from hearing" and that hearing comes "by the word of Christ." It is from or through the Scriptures that the Spirit imparts perseverance and encouragement: "For whatever was written in earlier times was written for our instruction, that through perseverance and the encouragement of the Scriptures we might have hope" (Romans 15:4).

I have a pastor friend who once told me that on virtually every Monday morning he struggles to suppress the cry: "I quit!" When I laughed, he assured me that it was no idle threat. The disillusionment that being in ministry can produce is often overwhelming. So why didn't he quit? Because he stems the rising tide of frustration by immersing himself in Scripture, bathing his mind and soaking his soul in the promises of God. Sure enough, it does what it says. His heart is infused with new hope and reasons to endure and the power to press on. He still gets discouraged, almost like clockwork. But he knows where to look for help.

It is from or through the Scriptures that joy, peace, and hope arise. Paul prays in Romans 15:13 that God would "fill you with all joy and peace in believing, that you may abound in hope by the power of the Holy Spirit." Both joy and peace are the fruit of believing, which in turn yields hope. But believe "what"? Belief is confidence placed in the truth of what God has revealed to us in Scripture about who He is and our relationship to Him through Jesus. Belief does not hover aimlessly in mid-air, but plants itself in the firm foundation of inspired, revelatory words inscripturated for us in the Bible.

It is the Word of God that accounts for the ongoing operation of the miraculous in the body of Christ. We read in Galatians 3:5, "Does He then, who provides you with the Spirit and works miracles among you, do it by the works of the Law, or by hearing with faith?" Paul's question is this: "Why does God supply you with power for miracles? Does He do it because of all the rules you keep, as if somehow religious diligence might put Him in your debt? Or is it a gracious response to your faith?" Let me make three observations about Paul's answer, each of which builds on the other.

First, it is God who continually and generously supplies you with the Spirit. Although you have already received the Spirit, there is yet more in terms of an experiential encounter with His power! Second, this fresh supply of the Spirit finds expression in miracles, a phenomenon that Paul obviously finds neither unusual nor controversial. Third, and most important of all, the instrument God uses is the faith that we experience upon hearing the Word of God! When we hear the Word of God (in preaching and teaching and in times of meditation), our thoughts and hearts become God-centered. Our focus is on His glory and thus our faith in His greatness expands and deepens, all of which is the soil in which the seeds of the supernatural are sown. Apart from the truths of biblical texts, there can be no genuine, long-lasting, Christ-exalting faith; and apart from such faith there can be no (or at best, few) miracles.

It is the Word of God, expounded and explained and applied, that yields the fruit of sanctification and holiness in daily life. Consider the following:

> And for this reason we also constantly thank God that when you received from us the word of God's message, you accepted it not as the word of men, but for what it really is, the word of God, which also performs its work in you who believe. (1 Thessalonians 2:13)

> In pointing out these things to the brethren, you will be a good servant of Christ Jesus, constantly nourished on the words of the faith and of the sound doctrine which you have been following. (1 Timothy 4:6)

> Like newborn babes, long for the pure milk of the word, that by it you may grow in respect to salvation. (1 Peter 2:2)

> For the word of God is living and active and sharper than any two-edged sword, and piercing as far as the division of soul and spirit, of both joints and marrow, and able to judge the thoughts and intentions of the heart. (Hebrews 4:12)

Transformation does not descend upon us like dew from heaven. Each of these passages resonates with a common theme: change is the fruit of fascination with the glory of God as revealed in Scripture. "We change," notes Piper, "because we have seen a superior beauty and worth and excellence. If you look into the face of Christ and then look into *Sports Illustrated* or *Glamour* and are not moved by the superior beauty and worth and excellence and desirability of Christ, then you are still hard and blind and futile in your thinking. You need to cry out, 'Open my eyes to see wonderful things out of your Word!' And your life will show it. Where your treasure is—your desire, your delight, your beauty—there will your heart be also—and your evenings and your Saturdays and your money. We are changed by seeing the glory of God in the Word of God."[3]

The power of the Word of God is perhaps nowhere better seen than in Psalm 19. There we find six declarations that tell us what the Bible is and does: six nouns, six adjectives, six verbs. The focus is on the identity (the nouns), the quality (the adjectives), and the function (the verbs) of Scripture.

First, "the law of the LORD is perfect, restoring the soul" (Psalm 19:7). As for its identity, it is a "law," or instruction, pointing us in the direction of what is right and away from what is wrong. It does this "perfectly," without the slightest defect, never lacking what is needed to address our circumstances. Its function is to "restore" our souls, to refresh and renew and to remind us that the pleasures of obedience to God's "law" are delightfully superior to all rival claims that would lead us in another direction.

Second, "the testimony of the LORD is sure, making wise the simple" (verse 7). Scripture is the record of God's own witness to who He is and what He will provide for us in Jesus. This testimony is "sure," it is true in principle and verifiable in life's situations. The Bible takes the undiscerning and naïve and gullible person and makes him wise. After all, "every fork in the road does not have a biblical arrow."[4] We need wisdom for decision making. It comes from Scripture. She who is immersed in the Word is equipped to choose wisely where no explicit direction is found.

Third, "the precepts of the LORD are right, rejoicing the heart" (Psalm 19:8a). God's rules are never wrong. We can always rely on them to provide truth and accuracy. She whose heart is fixed on the precepts of the Lord is never at the whim of public opinion polls or the fickle fluctuations of human advice. In God's precepts one finds cause for joy and reason for rejoicing. This is God's remedy for a sinking, sad, broken heart. If your heart is sour and embittered and could use an injection of joy, memorize and meditate and mull over God's precepts.

Fourth, "the commandment of the LORD is pure, enlightening the eyes" (verse 8). That word "pure" may also be rendered "radiant" (NIV). God's commandments shine and shimmer and glow and glimmer. They are brilliant and bright and dispel the darkness of human ignorance and senseless advice. Here we see again the inseparable link God has forged between Word and Spirit. Piper expresses the matter thus:

> God has ordained that the eye-opening work of his Spirit always be combined with the mind-informing work of his Word. His aim is that we see the glory of his Son (and be changed). So he opens our eyes when we are looking at the Son—not at soaps or sales. The work of the Spirit and the work of the Word always go together in God's way of true spiritual self-revelation. The Spirit's work is to show the glory and beauty and value of what the mind sees in the Word.[5]

Fifth, "the fear of the Lord is clean, enduring forever" (Psalm 19:9). David has in mind the fear of God that the Bible produces in us. It is "clean" both in terms of its essence and its impact on our hearts. Its power and purpose never end; we can always count on God's Word to do its work; God's Word does not change with the seasons or with fashions; it is always "in"!

Finally, "the judgments of the LORD are true, they are righteous altogether" (verse 9). What God says in His Word is never false or off the mark. His Word is the only barometer for reality. One need never again live in doubt and hesitation concerning what is righteous. Guesswork is gone. The certainty of God's Word is our foundation.

And the best part of all? The Word of God brings us satisfaction and joy and delight so that we will not be enticed and tempted by the passing pleasures of sin:

They [that is, the laws, precepts, commandments of God's Word] are more desirable than gold, yes, than much fine gold; sweeter also than honey and the drippings of the honeycomb. Moreover, by them Thy servant is warned; in keeping them there is great reward. (Psalm 19:10-11)

Yes, there is "great reward" in the treasuring of God's Word in our hearts. For starters, there are the six things just noted: God's Word rewards you with restoration of your soul, wisdom for your walk, joy for your heart, enlightenment for your eyes, truth you can count on, and the provision of righteousness. Wow!

Psalm 19 isn't the only place we find this truth. Consider these texts:

This book of the law shall not depart from your mouth, but you shall meditate on it day and night, so that you may be careful to do according to all that is written in it; for then you will make your way prosperous, and then you will have success. (Joshua 1:8)

How blessed is the man who does not walk in the counsel of the wicked, nor stand in the path of sinners, nor sit in the seat of scoffers! But his delight is in the law of the LORD, and in His law he meditates day and night. (Psalm 1:1-2)

Thy word I have treasured in my heart, that I may not sin against Thee. (Psalm 119:11)

O how I love Thy law! It is my meditation all the day. (Psalm 119:97)

How sweet are Thy words to my taste! Yes, sweeter than honey to my mouth! (Psalm 119:103)

See also: Psalm 119:15,23,48,78,99, and 148.

Boring? Tedious? Hardly! When the seed of the Word sprouts and sinks its roots deeply into our souls, the fruit it yields is sheer gladness. The psalmist declares him "blessed" who "greatly delights" in God's commandments (Psalm 112:1). In the hymnic celebration of God's Word, Psalm 119, we read of him finding more joy in God's testimonies than in all riches and what they might buy (Psalm 119:14). He committed himself to "delight" in God's statutes (Psalm 119:16,24,35,47,70,77) and to relish the joy they bring even in the midst of affliction (Psalm 119:92,143).

Jonathan Edwards' journey into an all-absorbing love affair with the sweetness of God's presence began with his meditation on but one verse of Scripture.

> The first that I remember that ever I found any thing of that sort of inward, sweet delight in God and divine things, that I have lived much in since, was on reading those words, 1 Tim. 1:17, "Now unto the king eternal, immortal, invisible, the only wise God, be honor and glory for ever and ever, Amen." As I read the words, there came into my soul, and was as it were diffused thro' it, a sense of the glory of the Divine Being; a new sense, quite different from any thing I ever experienced before. Never any words of scripture seemed to me as these words did. I thought with myself, how excellent a being that was; and how happy I should be, if I might enjoy that God, and be wrapped up to God in Heaven, and be as it were swallowed up in Him. I kept saying, and as it were singing over these words of scripture to myself; and went to prayer, to pray to God that I might enjoy Him; and prayed in a manner quite different from what I used to do; with a new sort of affection.[6]

In summary, says Piper,

> the challenge before us . . . is not merely to do what God says because He is God, but to desire what God says

because He is good. The challenge is not merely to pursue righteousness, but to prefer righteousness. The challenge is to get up in the morning and prayerfully meditate on the Scriptures until we experience joy and peace in believing "the precious and very great promises of God" (Romans 15:13; 2 Peter 1:4). With this joy set before us the commandments of God will not be burdensome (1 John 5:3) and the compensation of sin will appear too brief and too shallow to lure us.[7]

Meditation on Creation

I'm still growing, often imperceptibly, in my appreciation for the splendor of natural creation. I have to be honest, though, and admit that I'd rather be sitting at my desk with book in hand, under the refreshing breeze of a well-oiled air conditioner, than on the beach or in the woods or walking in a grassy meadow. I have much to learn from the Scriptures in this regard. Jonathan Edwards has helped me, as he describes the impact of one particular encounter with the power and wonder of creation:

And as I was walking there [in his father's pasture], and looked up on the sky and clouds; there came into my mind, a sweet sense of the glorious majesty and grace of God, that I know not how to express. . . . The appearance of everything was altered: there seemed to be, as it were, a calm, sweet cast, or appearance of divine glory, in almost everything. God's excellency, His wisdom, His purity and love, seemed to appear in everything; in the sun, moon and stars; in the clouds, and blue sky; in the grass, flowers, trees; in the water, and all nature; which used greatly to fix my mind. I often used to sit and view the moon, for a long time; and so in the day time, spent much time in viewing the clouds and sky, to behold the sweet glory of God in these things: in the mean time, singing forth with a low

voice, my contemplations of the Creator and Redeemer.
And scarce any thing, among all the works of nature, was
so sweet to me as thunder and lightning. Formerly, nothing
had been so terrible to me. I used to be a person uncom-
monly terrified with thunder: and it used to strike me with
terror, when I saw a thunder-storm rising. But now, on the
contrary, it rejoiced me. I felt God at the first appearance
of a thunder-storm. And used to take the opportunity at
such times to fix myself to view the clouds, and see the
lightning's play, and hear the majestic and awful voice of
God's thunder: which often times was exceeding entertain-
ing, leading me to sweet contemplations of my great and
glorious God. And while I viewed, used to spend my time,
as it always seemed natural to me, to sing or chant forth
my meditations; to speak my thoughts in soliloquies, and
speak with a singing voice.[8]

Meditation on God and His Works
Just thinking about thinking about God can be a mind-altering experience. Actually thinking about Him is even better.

One thing I have asked from the LORD, that I shall seek:
that I may dwell in the house of the LORD all the days of
my life, to behold the beauty of the LORD, and to meditate
in His temple. (Psalm 27:4)

When I remember Thee on my bed, I meditate on Thee in
the night watches. (Psalm 63:6)

I have considered the days of old, the years of long ago. I
will remember my song in the night; I will meditate with
my heart; and my spirit ponders. . . . I shall remember the
deeds of the LORD; surely I will remember Thy wonders of

old. I will meditate on all Thy work, and muse on Thy deeds. (Psalm 77:5-6, 11-12)

Great are the works of the LORD; they are studied by all who delight in them. (Psalm 111:2)

Make me understand the way of Thy precepts, so I will meditate on Thy wonders. (Psalm 119:27)

I remember the days of old; I meditate on all Thy doings; I muse on the work of Thy hands. (Psalm 143:5)

On the glorious splendor of Thy majesty, and on Thy wonderful works, I will meditate. (Psalm 145:5)

If then you have been raised up with Christ, keep seeking the things above, where Christ is, seated at the right hand of God. Set your mind on the things above, not on the things that are on earth. (Colossians 3:1-2)

Fixing our eyes on Jesus, the author and perfecter of faith . . . for consider Him. (Hebrews 12:2-3)

Once more, Edwards writes:

I began to have a new kind of apprehensions and ideas of Christ, and the work of redemption, and the glorious ways of salvation by Him. I had an inward, sweet sense of these things, that at times came into my heart; and my soul was led away in pleasant views and contemplations of them. And my mind was greatly engaged, to spend my time in reading and meditating on Christ; and the beauty and excellency of His person, and the lovely way of salvation, by free grace in Him. . . . [And I] found, from time to time, an inward sweetness, that used, as it were, to carry me away in my contemplations; in what I know not how to express otherwise, than by a calm, sweet abstraction of soul from all the concerns of this world; and a kind of vision, or fixed ideas and imaginations, of being alone in the mountains, or some solitary wilderness, far from all mankind, sweetly conversing with Christ, and wrapped and swallowed up in God. The sense I had of divine things, would often of a sudden as it were, kindle up a sweet burning in my heart; an ardor of my soul, that I know not how to express.[9]

When my spirit needs a boost like that and my heart lacks the energy to say No to sin, I often turn to Psalm 145. This psalm was apparently used in the ancient church as a prayer to be recited over the midday meal (largely because of verses 15-16): "The eyes of all look to you, and you give them their food at the proper time. You open your hand and satisfy the desires of every living thing" (Psalm 145:15-16, NIV). Its title has but one word: "Praise" (found only here in the Psalter). What is most important about it is the way it portrays the majesty of God and His works on which we are to meditate.

David extols God's " greatness" in verses 3 ("Great is the LORD, and most worthy of praise") and 6 ("They will tell of the power of your awesome works . . ."). Unfortunately, the word "great" has become commonplace in our society and means very little. We use "great" to describe everything from deodorants to athletes. Historically, many have taken the adjective great and made it part of their name: Alexander the Great, Peter the Great, and in our own day the comedian Jackie Gleason simply went by the title, The Great One. NO! God is alone and infinitely The Great One! Furthermore, "his greatness no one can fathom," it is unsearchable (verse 3). No one ever has or ever shall fully comprehend the depths of His greatness. Not all the minds of all the ages using all the best scientific equipment can capture all that God is. He is beyond and past finding out.

He is not only majestic ("They will speak of the glorious splendor of your majesty," verse 5), His majesty is characterized by a glorious splendor! There is a great light or luster or spiritual brilliance that emits from the magnificence of His majesty. No less marvelous is His goodness ("They will celebrate your abundant goodness and joyfully sing of your righteousness," verses 7,9). Try to envision living in a universe in which the one true God were bad rather than good! Thank Him for His goodness.

Our God on whom we muse is a righteous God (verse 7). To say that God is righteous is not to say He conforms to human standards of right and wrong. It is to say He conforms perfectly to the standards of His own perfections. But if He is wholly and holy righteous, how can unholy and unrighteous people like you and me enter His presence? It is only because He is also "gracious" (verse 8) and "merciful" (verses 8,9). Oh! What a wondrous God He is!

This God of grace and mercy is also long-suffering ("slow to anger and rich in love," verse 8). God has a holy temper, but He has a very long fuse! Even those who deny and blaspheme His name are recipients of His patience and long-suffering. He permits His enemies to live, to spew forth their horrid blasphemies, all the while blessing them with food and air and earthly pleasures (see Romans 2:4-5).

He is a God of immeasurable lovingkindness (verse 8). This is the translation of the Hebrew word *hesed,* elsewhere rendered by such terms as *mercy, merciful, goodness, merciful kindness, loyal love,* and occasionally by the word *grace.* Its primary emphasis is on God's covenant love, His steadfast commitment to His people.

That is but a glimpse of who He is. These attributes are, as Job said, the mere "fringes of His ways" (Job 26:14). This God, our God, on whom our minds are to meditate, does great and mighty things.

He works! Here in Psalm 145:4-6,9,12 we read of God's works, His mighty works, His wonderful works, His awesome acts, and His merciful works "so that all men may know of your mighty acts and the glorious splendor of your kingdom."

And He rules (verses 11-13). God is in office for life (see Daniel 4:3,34)! There is no transition team to move from one heavenly administration to another. There are no inaugural ceremonies. God has always been on the throne. There is no concern over the qualifications of a vice-God should the Almighty be unable to serve out the full extent of His term. There are no tearful good-byes to the staff, no waving "so-long" from the steps of a helicopter, no cleaning out of the desk in the heavenly oval office to make way for His successor. In English history especially, we see kings — James I and James II and Charles I and Charles II and Charles III, and so on. Not in the heavenly kingdom! God is first and last! And "there will be no end to the increase of His government" (Isaiah 9:7).

The God who rules also sustains ("The Lord upholds all those who fall and lifts up all who are bowed down," verse 14). It is important to read this verse in connection with verse 13 and "admire the unexpected contrast: he reigns in glorious majesty, yet condescends to lift up and hold up those who are apt to fall" (also see Isaiah 66:1-2).[10]

He bountifully supplies (verses 15-16) those who are in need (see Psalm 147:9; Luke 12:24; Hebrews 4:16), satisfying "the desire of every living thing" (verse 16).

His ways are righteous (verse 17). That is easy for us to believe when things are going well. But God is righteous in all His ways, not just in the ways that favor us. Nothing is more difficult to acknowledge when we are in trouble, or when He afflicts us, or when we feel He has been unfair. Yet, no matter how incoherent life may become, He is kind in all His deeds ("The LORD is righteous in all his ways and loving toward all he has made," verse 17, NIV). God is both righteous and kind ("loving") in what He does. It may be difficult for us to balance the two, but not with God. We swing to one or the other extreme and find it difficult to be both righteous and kind in any particular situation. But God is perfectly both. This was revealed most perfectly in the person of Jesus, as we saw in chapter seven. Whom else do you know that is

> high, yet humble . . . strong, yet sensitive . . . righteous,
> yet gracious . . . powerful, yet merciful . . . authoritative,
> yet tender . . . holy, yet forgiving . . . just, yet com-
> passionate . . . angry, yet gentle . . . firm, yet friendly?

He is a prayer-answering God ("The LORD is near to all who call on him, to all who call on him in truth," verses 18-19). He is nearby, not simply by virtue of His omnipresence, but because of His love and sympathy for those in need. He is especially nearby to hear our prayers. God is not only transcendent, above all, but He is also immanent, nearby, close at hand. Those who call on Him "fear Him" and therefore won't ask for what they know they shouldn't have. True godly fear gives direction and places limitations on our prayers. It keeps us from praying rashly for things contrary to God's will.

And how shall we respond to Him? By all means we shall meditate on Him, as verse 5 teaches us. But we also are to extol Him (verse 1), a word that literally means "to be high." God is high and we acknowledge and declare it so. To extol is to exalt above all others, to set as preeminent over every other thing. More than that, we are to bless Him (verses 1–2,10), praise Him (verse 2), declare His mighty acts (verse 4), speak of Him (verse 6), tell of His greatness (verse 6), and eagerly utter (literally, "bubble over!") His abundant goodness. We shout joyfully (verse 7) and give thanks (verse 10) and make known (verse 12) the glory of the majesty of His kingdom.

How do we do it? For starters, we do it forever and ever (verses 1-2,21; see Psalm 104:33; 146:2). Simply saying "forever" wasn't enough for David, so he added "and ever"! He permits no loopholes. One day we shall cease praying, we shall cease hoping, we shall cease watching, we shall cease waiting, but we shall never cease praising.

A heart full of thoughts about the splendor of who God is and what God does can no more conceive of an end of praise than it can conceive of an end of God! So we shall bless Him on every day (verse 2). That means on both good days and bad days. Our praise and worship are to be in proportion to their object: High and Great! Great praise for a great God. As Spurgeon put it, "No chorus is too loud, no orchestra too large, no Psalm too lofty for the lauding of the Lord of Hosts."[11] And this from generation to generation (verse 4).

Finally, to complete your biblical contemplation of meditation, take some time to read and ponder the following texts: Psalm 19:14; 46:10; 49:3; 104:34; and Philippians 4:8.

CHRISTIAN VERSUS NEW AGE MEDITATION

Many are frightened because meditation has become something of a buzzword in New Age circles. But the differences between biblically based meditation and what we find in Eastern religions and the New Age movement are profound. Here are a few of them.

1. Unlike Eastern meditation, which advocates emptying the mind, Christian meditation calls on us to fill our mind with God and His truth. I've often heard well-meaning but misguided Christians suggest that the mind is dangerous or at least inferior to the heart. We frequently hear it said that God does not want to lead us or guide us or speak to us through our minds but through our hearts, as if "mind" and "heart" in Scripture are at odds with each other. A careful examination of the use of those words in the Bible will reveal that nothing could be further from the truth. The Bible repeatedly exhorts us to be renewed and transformed in our minds (see Romans 12:1-2). Paul prayed for the Philippians that they might "abound still more and more in real knowledge and discernment" (1:9). He

prayed for the Colossians that they might "be filled with the knowledge of His will in all spiritual wisdom and understanding" (1:9).

Nowhere in the Bible is the "mind," per se, described as evil or unworthy of being the means by which God communicates with us. What the Bible does denounce is intellectual pride, but not the intellect itself. It is humility that we need, not ignorance. I stand opposed to arrogant and cynical intellectualism. But that is not the same thing as using the mind God has given us, with the help of the Holy Spirit and the instruction of Scripture, to evaluate and discern and critically assess what is happening in both the church and the world. Whereas some things that God says and does are transrational, insofar as they are mysterious and often go beyond our ability to fully comprehend, God never does things that are irrational in the sense that they might violate the fundamental laws of logic or the reasonable and rational truths of Holy Scripture.[12]

2. Unlike Eastern meditation, which advocates mental passivity, Christian meditation calls on us to actively exert our mental energy. This is nowhere better stated than by Paul in Philippians 4:8. Here he encourages us to "let our minds dwell on" whatever is "true," "honorable," "right," "pure," "lovely," and of "good repute." Those things that are "excellent" and "worthy of praise" are to be the targets of our mental aim.

It isn't enough merely to acknowledge that things and ideas of moral and mental excellence are important. Merely affirming such truths and virtues will avail little in a time of testing. We must energetically reckon, take into account, and give deliberative weight to these things. Our minds must be captivated by them in such a way that the tawdry, sleazy, fictitious, and fanciful fluff of the world loses its appeal. D. A. Carson reminds us that "this is not some escapist demand to avoid the harsh realities of our fallen world. The sad fact is that many people dwell on dirt without grasping that it is dirt. The wise Christian will see plenty of dirt in the world, but will recognize it as dirt, precisely because everything that is clean has captured his or her mind."[13]

3. Unlike Eastern meditation, which advocates detachment from the world, Christian meditation calls for attachment to God. If the believer disengages from the distractions and allurements of the world, it is in order that he or she might engage with the Father, Son, and Holy Spirit.
4. Unlike Eastern meditation, which advocates visualization in order to create one's own reality, Christian meditation calls for visualization of the reality already created by God.
5. Unlike Eastern meditation, which advocates metaphysical union with "god," Christian meditation calls for spiritual communion with God.
6. Unlike Eastern meditation, which advocates an inner journey to find the center of one's being, Christian meditation calls for an outward focus on the objective revelation of God in Scripture and creation.
7. Unlike Eastern meditation, which advocates mystical transport as the goal of one's efforts, Christian meditation calls for moral transformation as the goal of one's efforts.

SOME PRACTICAL GUIDELINES

It's not enough for us to acknowledge the value of God's Word or even to prize it among our most cherished possessions. It may be aesthetically pleasing and make for decorative beauty, but a Bible is of no practical use if it is left lying on a coffee table in the living room of your home. We must "treasure" it in our hearts. This is where many give up. They simply don't know how to meditate. They are lavish in their praise of God's Word but lost when it comes to the practical steps by which it might become a living, life-changing power in their inner selves. So here are a few suggestions to get you started.

1. *Prepare*. It helps to begin by rehearsing in one's mind the presence of God. Perhaps reading and reflecting on Psalm 139:1-10 will help. Focus your attention on the inescapable presence, the intimate nearness of God.

Issues of posture, time, and place are secondary, but not unimportant. The only rule would be: do whatever is most conducive to concentration. If a posture is uncomfortable, change it. If a particular time of day or night is inconvenient, change it. If the place you have chosen exposes you to repeated interruptions and distractions, move it. I enjoy watching football on TV as much as the next guy, but trying to engage with God's Word during the huddle is hardly an effective way to experience its power!

2. *Peruse*. By this I mean read, repeat the reading, write it out, then re-write it. Peter Toon takes this approach:

I read aloud slowly the verse(s) chosen. One method is to notice the punctuation and to slow down and breathe more slowly for the commas and even more slowly for the periods, so I read aloud softly but clearly so that I may "taste" the flavor of the Word and may also hear the gracious sound of the Word. At the same time, my eyes see the content of the Word. And I read again—gently dwelling on each word, each phrase and each sentence.[14]

We must keep in mind the difference between informative reading of the Scriptures and formative reading. The former focuses on the gathering of information, the increase of knowledge, the collection and memorization of data. The purpose of the latter is to be formed or shaped by the text, through the work of the Holy Spirit. With informative reading, I am in control of the text. With formative reading, the text controls me. With formative reading, writes Toon,

> I do not hold the Bible in my hand in order to analyze, dissect or gather information from it. Rather I hold it in order to let my Master penetrate the depths of my being with his Word and thus facilitate inner moral and spiritual transformation. I am there in utter dependence upon our God—who is the Father to whom I pray, the Son through whom I pray, and the Holy Spirit in whom I pray. [15]

3. *Picture.* Apply your imagination and senses to the truth of the text. Envision yourself personally engaged in the relationship or encounter or experience of which the text speaks. Hear the words as they are spoken. Feel the touch of Jesus on a diseased body. Taste and smell the fish and bread as they are served to the multitudes. See the truths that God has revealed by mentally recreating the scene with yourself present. There is nothing magical or mysterious in this. The purpose of the imagination is not, as some have argued, to create our own reality. Our imagination is a function of our minds whereby we experience more intimately and powerfully the reality God has created.

4. *Ponder.* Reflect on the truth of the Word; brood over the truth of the text; absorb it, soak in it, as you turn it over and over in your mind. By all means, internalize and personalize the passage.

5. *Pray.* It is difficult to know when meditation moves into prayer. It isn't really that important. But at some point, take the truth as the Holy Spirit has illumined it and pray it back to God, whether in petition, thanksgiving,

or intercession. In other words, take Scripture and turn it into dialogue with God.

6. **Personalize.** Where possible, and according to sound principles of biblical interpretation, replace proper names and personal pronouns with your own name. God never intended for His Word to float aimlessly in impersonal abstractions. He designed it for you and for me.

7. *Praise.* Worship the Lord for who He is and what He has done and how it has been revealed in Scripture. Meditation ought always to lead us into adoration and celebration of God.

8. *Practice.* Commit yourself to doing what the Word commands. The aim of meditation is moral transformation. The aim of contemplation is obedience. And in obedience is joy inexpressible and full of glory.

CHAPTER TEN

Feasting on God

Why do you worship? What is your motivation in investing so much time and making such great sacrifices to expend your energy in the praise of God? Some of you know immediately the answer to that question and it strikes you as a bit silly that I should even dare to ask it. Others of you, quite honestly, are more than a little unsure. You're confused. You don't fully understand your motives. Some of you probably worship from a sense of duty. You say to yourself: "Worshiping God is like studying the Bible and praying and witnessing. God commanded it, so here I am reporting for duty. I don't know if I really like it all that much, but being willing to obey God even when I don't feel like it is what being a Christian is all about. Right?"

Whenever I hear someone say that I immediately think of a fascinating verse in the book of Deuteronomy:

Because you did not serve the LORD your God *with joy and a glad heart,* for the abundance of all things; therefore you shall serve your enemies whom the LORD shall send against you. (28:47-48, emphasis added)

My response to that verse has always been, "Wait a minute, Lord. Isn't it enough just to serve and obey you?" "No," says God.

"It is because they didn't serve me with joy and a glad heart that I will discipline them."

This verse in Deuteronomy 28, along with scores of others in both the Old Testament and New Testament, alerts me to the fact that why we do something for God is absolutely fundamental in determining whether or not what we do is virtuous and good and pleasing and glorifying to our heavenly Father. Now let's apply this to worship.

HYMNS OF THE HUNGRY

The proposition I want to place before you is this: If you come to worship for any reason other than the joy and pleasure and satisfaction that are to be found in God, you dishonor Him. To put it in other words, worship is first and foremost a feasting on all that God is for us in Jesus. This is because God is most glorified in you when you are most satisfied in Him. Or again, you are His pleasure when He is your treasure. Which is to say that God's greatest delight is your delight in Him.

The bottom line is that you and I must come to worship hungry! We must not come with hands full of goodies and gifts, thinking that worship is fundamentally where we serve and feed God. As we saw in chapter three, God is not in need of us. We are in need of Him. Don't come to God with a cooked goose on a platter, as if God were hungry. Come with open hands and an empty belly and let Him honor Himself by filling you! We've already seen this, but it bears repeating. Consider this claim, outlandish were it not God Himself who makes it:

> For every beast of the forest is Mine, the cattle on a thousand hills. I know every bird of the mountains, and everything that moves in the field is Mine. If I were hungry, I would not tell you; for the world is Mine, and all it contains. (Psalm 50:10-12)

This sentiment was echoed by Paul in his sermon on Mars Hill:

The God who made the world and all things in it, since He is Lord of heaven and earth, does not dwell in temples made with hands; neither is He served by human hands, as though He needed anything, since He Himself gives to all life and breath and all things. (Acts 17:24-25)

Worship is a feast in which God is the host, the cook, the waiter, and the meal itself.

It's not unusual for people to voice an objection at this point: "But I thought worship was all about glorifying God. You seem to be saying it's all about my enjoyment and my pleasure and my delight and my satisfaction. There you go again, Sam, barking up that hedonistic tree!" But this is a false dichotomy. To say that worship is either about glorifying God or finding personal satisfaction is to put asunder what God has joined together. His glory and your gladness are not separate tracks moving in opposite directions. Rather His glory is in your gladness in Him.

Let's engage in a hypothetical conversation that I think will make my point somewhat clearer. Let us suppose that you and I meet at the door of a church just prior to a night dedicated to extensive worship. I initiate a dialogue with you that goes something like this:

"Excuse me. I'm curious. What did you hope to *gain* by coming to this worship service tonight?"

To which you respond, in your very best religious, self-effacing, humble tone of voice (perhaps even with a frown on your face): "Who, me? Oh, my no. You have seriously misinterpreted my motives. I didn't come to *gain* anything. That would be so self-seeking and selfish. Don't you realize: I'm a Christian! I came here tonight to *give*."

"Oh," I reply. "That's interesting. But tell me, *give what to whom?*"

"Well," you reply, somewhat indignantly, "I came to give glory to God."

"Oh, I didn't know God was lacking glory. Poor chap. How long has He been in this dreadful condition? And I certainly had no idea that you had any glory to give!"

"Oh, come on, Sam. You know what I mean."

"No, I'm not really sure I do know what you mean. Help me."

"Okay. I don't actually give God glory. But worship is about glorifying God, isn't it?"

"Well, of course it is," I reply. "But *how* do we glorify God without appearing to *contribute* or *add* to Him as if He were lacking something?"

"I don't know, Sam. You tell me."

"OKAY. I'll try. You glorify God not by coming to give Him anything. After all, how can you give to someone who has it all? Instead, you should come to gain all that He is as God and all that He offers to be for you in Jesus. When that happens, God is most gloriously glorified."

"How?" you ask. "I don't get it. How does God get glory by giving Himself to us?"

"It's easy. The psalmist says that God satisfies 'the thirsty soul' and fills 'the hungry soul' with 'what is good' (Psalm 107:9). In other words, when He overflows in love to you, when He blesses you and empowers you and forgives you and heals you and fills you with delight and satisfies the deepest needs of your soul, He is manifested and therefore honored as the only, all-sufficient supply for His people. He is revealed as the only, all-sufficient treasure in whom we find 'fullness of joy and pleasure evermore' (Psalm 16:11). That is why worship is all about glorifying God by finding or gaining personal satisfaction in Him. When you worship you glorify God through glad-hearted getting of all He gives!"

Following a conversation like this I would do well to carefully explain my statements lest I be misunderstood. Worship is not about my enjoyment. It is about my enjoyment of God. It is not about my pleasure or my delight or my satisfaction. It is about my pleasure, delight, and satisfaction in God. Worship is not simply about glorifying God. It is about glorifying God by enjoying Him forever.

The issue is not whether worship is concerned with glorifying God. Everyone agrees it is. The issue is: How does one best glorify God? Is it by coming to enrich an impoverished God with what we think we have to offer, or by becoming enriched by an all-sufficient God as He overflows in goodness to us? Are we to come in our alleged wealth intending to lavish it upon God? Or do we come in our abject spiritual poverty to the God who owns everything, asking for help and hope and happiness? Clearly, we best glorify God by enjoying Him forever, by drinking our fill of the abundance of His house and from the river of His delights (see Psalm 36:8).

Come, Poor and Needy

I had been led to believe that to come into a worship service conscious of my need and my desire for joy and my hunger for satisfaction was sinful and selfish. I was led to believe that to come to worship with the expectation and desire and hope of finding personal joy ruined or undermined the moral value and virtue of praise. "Come and focus on God, not your need," I was told (quite sternly, most often). But what if I come and focus on my need for God and exalt Him by declaring that He alone satisfies my soul and meets the need of my heart?

Let's think through this by considering David's experience as described for us in Psalm 63:1-5: "O God, Thou art my God; I shall seek Thee earnestly; My soul thirsts for Thee, my flesh yearns for Thee, in a dry and weary land where there is no water" (verse 1).

Let's stop there for just a moment. The psalmist unashamedly declares his need: seeking, thirsting, yearning. Not only is he needy, he is earnestly needy, desperately needy. Is this wrong? Should he be rebuked for self-centeredness? Is his motivation for seeking God misguided and sinful? Evidently not. There is no hint of sin in being thirsty. Nor is there a hint of sin in desiring to have one's thirst quenched. He continues, "Thus I have beheld Thee in the sanctuary, to see Thy power and Thy glory. Because Thy lovingkindness is better than life, my lips will praise Thee" (verses 2-3). Here again, David says he praises God because God's love for him fills the emptiness of his soul. God's lovingkindness soothes and satisfies the desperate ache in his heart to be loved and accepted and affirmed and securely protected. Is that wrong? Is David off base in focusing so firmly on the passion of his heart? If he were, would he have declared in Psalm 4:7, "Thou hast put gladness in my heart, more than when their grain and new wine abound"?

This same point is made in Psalm 84. The soul of the psalmist "longed" for the courts of the Lord. He "yearned" (84:2) to be found in God's dwelling place. Why? Because he found it altogether "lovely" (84:1). The beauty and sweetness of God's courts transcend the most sublime of earthly locales. The author of Psalm 84 undertook a comparative study as he prepared to worship. He looked at the best and the most and the sweetest and the highest and the happiest this world could offer and drew this profound conclusion: "A day in Thy courts [O God] is better than a thousand outside. I would rather stand at the threshold of the house of my God, than dwell in the tents of wickedness" (84:10).

All of life is inescapably competitive. Every choice we make is a decision between competing pleasures. Even if we are not immediately conscious of what is happening, such choices demand of us a comparative evaluation of rival claims. These crossroad decisions in life don't spring up *ex nihilo* (out of nothing). They aren't causeless. The psalmist declares in 84:11, "I choose God and the pleasures of life in his courts" because "the LORD God is a sun and shield." The world, on the other hand, leaves me scorched and defenseless. "The LORD gives grace and glory. The passing pleasures of sin, on the other hand, lead only to misery and despair. "No good thing does He withhold from those who walk uprightly." People, on the other hand, demand their pound of flesh. This is precisely what we see yet again in Psalm 63: "So I will bless Thee as long as I live; I will lift up my hands in Thy name. My soul is satisfied as with marrow and fatness, and my mouth offers praises with joyful lips" (verses 4-5).

But what does worship have to do with "my soul" or "your soul" being satisfied? Is it not clear that the reason David "blesses" God (verse 4) is because God is the One who satisfies his soul? Is it not because God satisfies his soul that David doesn't simply praise God, doesn't simply sing songs, but does so with "joyful lips"?

IS PRAISE A PROBLEM?

Let me pause here and address a problem that many have with worship. It is a struggle that tore at the heart of C. S. Lewis and one that perhaps many of you face. Lewis was extremely puzzled, even agitated, by the recurring demand by Christians that we all "praise God." That was bad enough. What made it even worse is that God Himself called for praise of God Himself. This was almost more than Lewis could stomach. He describes his struggle and how he worked through it in an enlightening passage from the essay, "A Word About Praising." As you read this, observe how Lewis works step-by-step to the same conclusion this chapter draws about our motivation in the worship of God. I'm going to resist the temptation to interject any explanatory comments lest you miss the cumulative force of his logic.

We all despise the man who demands continued assurance of his own virtue, intelligence or delightfulness; we despise still more the crowd of people round every dictator, every millionaire, every celebrity, who gratify that demand. Thus a picture, at once ludicrous and horrible, both of God and His

worshippers, threatened to appear in my mind. The Psalms
were especially troublesome in this way—"Praise the Lord,"
"O praise the Lord with me," "Praise Him." . . . Worse still
was the statement put into God's own mouth, "whoso
offereth me thanks and praise, he honoureth me" (50:23).
It was hideously like saying, "What I most want is to be told
that I am good and great." . . . It was extremely distressing.
It made one think what one least wanted to think. Gratitude
to God, reverence to Him, obedience to Him, I thought I
could understand; not this perpetual eulogy. . . .

[Part of my initial problem is that] I did not see that it is
in the process of being worshipped that God communicates
His presence to men. It is not of course the only way. But
for many people at many times the "fair beauty of the Lord"
is revealed chiefly or only while they worship Him together.
Even in Judaism the essence of the sacrifice was not really
that men gave bulls and goats to God, but that by their so
doing God gave Himself to men; in the central act of our
own worship of course this is far clearer—there it is mani-
festly, even physically, God who gives and we who receive.
The miserable idea that God should in any sense need, or
crave for, our worship like a vain woman wanting compliments, or a vain author presenting his new books to people
who never met or heard him, is implicitly answered by the
words, "If I be hungry I will not tell thee" (50:12). Even if
such an absurd Deity could be conceived, He would hardly
come to us, the lowest of rational creatures, to gratify His
appetite. I don't want my dog to bark approval of my books.

But the most obvious fact about praise—whether of
God or anything—strangely escaped me. I thought of it in
terms of compliment, approval, or the giving of honour. I
had never noticed that all enjoyment spontaneously overflows into praise unless . . . shyness or the fear of boring
others is deliberately brought in to check it. The world rings

with praise—lovers praising their mistresses [Romeo praising Juliet and vice versa], readers their favourite poet,
walkers praising the countryside, players praising their
favourite game—praise of weather, wines, dishes, actors,
motors, horses, colleges, countries, historical personages,
children, flowers, mountains, rare stamps, rare beetles, even
sometimes politicians or scholars. . . . Except where intoler-
ably adverse circumstances interfere, praise almost seems to
be inner health made audible. . . . I had not noticed either
that just as men spontaneously praise whatever they value,
so they spontaneously urge us to join them in praising it:
"Isn't she lovely? Wasn't it glorious? Don't you think that
magnificent?" The Psalmists in telling everyone to praise
God are doing what all men do when they speak of what
they care about. My whole, more general, difficulty about
the praise of God depended on my absurdly denying to us, as
regards the supremely Valuable, what we delight to do, what
indeed we can't help doing, about everything else we value.

I think we delight to praise what we enjoy because the
praise not merely expresses but completes the enjoyment;
it is its appointed consummation. It is not out of compliment that lovers keep on telling one another how beautiful
they are; the delight is incomplete till it is expressed. It is
frustrating to have discovered a new author and not to be
able to tell anyone how good he is; to come suddenly, at
the turn of the road, upon some mountain valley of unexpected grandeur and then to have to keep silent because
the people with you care for it no more than for a tin can
in the ditch; to hear a good joke and find no one to share
it with. . . .

If it were possible for a created soul fully . . . to
"appreciate," that is to love and delight in, the worthiest
object of all, and simultaneously at every moment to give
this delight perfect expression, then that soul would be in

supreme beatitude. . . . To see what the doctrine really means, we must suppose ourselves to be in perfect love with God—drunk with, drowned in, dissolved by, that delight which, far from remaining pent up within ourselves as incommunicable, hence hardly tolerable, bliss, flows out from us incessantly again in effortless and perfect expression, our joy is no more separable from the praise in which it liberates and utters itself than the brightness a mirror receives is separable from the brightness it sheds. The Scotch catechism says that man's chief end is "to glorify God and enjoy Him forever." But we shall then know that these are the same thing. Fully to enjoy is to glorify. In commanding us to glorify Him, God is inviting us to enjoy Him.[1]

Whew! If you can, go back and read it again. It's not the sort of statement one can fully digest at one sitting. Lewis has here forged the link that makes sense of it all.

God's pursuit of my praise of Him is not weak self-seeking but the epitome of self-giving love! If my satisfaction in Him is incomplete until expressed in praise of Him for satisfying me, then God's effort to solicit my worship is both the most loving thing He could possibly do for me and the most glorifying thing He could possibly do for Himself. For in my gladness in Him is His glory in me.

COMMUNION AS WORSHIP

I want to dwell for a moment on something else Lewis said above. He noted that part of his problem with praise was his failure to see that "it is in the process of being worshipped that God communicates His presence to men." I agree. And nothing bears this out more clearly than what we experience of God during observance of the Lord's Supper. If the notion of communion as worship strikes you as odd, I suggest that you, like countless others, have lost sight of the role of the sacraments in the life of the local church. Whereas singing may well be the most obvious way to worship, it is by no means the only way. Let me explain what I mean.

When, on the night of His betrayal, Jesus uttered the awesome words, "This is my body, this is my blood," in some sense He was providing a pledge of His abiding presence with His people that is to be recalled and experienced whenever they break bread together. In spite of His impending death, and exaltation to the Father's right hand, Jesus will yet be truly and powerfully "there" whenever His followers gather to celebrate the sacrament. The implication is that in spite of Christ's physical departure from the earth, the bread and wine of the Supper in some sense serve to mediate His spiritual presence with those who know and love Him. The elements not only point to and recall His death, they also awaken us to the fact that Christ in His saving and sanctifying power is forever in our midst.

Paul's statement in 1 Corinthians 10:16-21 is especially important in this regard. We read in verse 16, "Is not the cup of blessing which we bless a sharing in the blood of Christ? Is not the bread which we break a sharing in the body of Christ?" To partake of the elements of the Lord's table is to come under His influence and power; it is to commune and share with His abiding presence; it is to experience in a special way all those saving benefits and blessings that Christ's body and blood obtained for us.

This is simply another way of saying that the Lord's Supper is a means of grace. Don't be misled by this phrase. I am thoroughly Protestant! What I'm advocating here has nothing to do with the doctrine of transubstantiation or other related Roman Catholic concepts.

The Catholic doctrine of transubstantiation contends that a physical conversion of ordinary bread and wine into the literal body and blood of Jesus occurs at the moment the words of consecration or blessing are pronounced by the priest. The fact that after this transformation the elements still look, taste, smell, and feel like bread and wine is due to a distinction Rome makes between the substance of a thing and its accidents (that is, its external features). The bread and wine continue to appear as such, but are essentially and truly the literal body and blood of Jesus.

When I refer to the Lord's Supper as a means of grace I most certainly do not mean that the bread and wine in any way cease to be bread and wine or that they become something other than the simple physical realities that we know them to be. Furthermore, we are not saved by partaking of this or any other ordinance. We do not receive forgiveness of sins nor are we regenerated in the waters of baptism. The Lord's Supper does not "atone" for sin in any sense of the word. The ordinances do not impart eternal life to the believer, but they do confirm, strengthen, and heighten our awareness and enjoyment of that life. The bread and wine are means or instruments by which God quickens us to apprehend, understand, visualize, and experience the sanctifying influence of the Holy Spirit and His unique ministry of shining the light of illumination and glory on Jesus.

The reception and experience of spiritual blessing is often described in Scripture in terms of eating and drinking (see especially Ezekiel 47:12, in conjunction with Revelation 22:2; Matthew 4:4; 5:6; 8:11; Luke 14:15; John 4:13; 6:33,35,41,48,50-51; Revelation 2:17; 19:9; 21:6; 22:1,17). Might we not infer, then, as Charles Hodge suggests, that "as our natural food imparts life and strength to our bodies, so this sacrament is one of the divinely appointed means to strengthen the principle of life in the soul of the believer, and to confirm his faith in the promises of the gospel"?[2]

This can happen in other ways, to be sure, but they are not for that reason "means of grace" in the way that I am using that phrase here. For example, I am often deeply stirred and edified by gazing on the majesty of God's creation or by watching a young child pray or by reading of the courage of a dying saint. All such experiences may well serve to bring me closer to Christ and to motivate me to service, gratitude, and sacrifice. But they are not, strictly speaking, "means of grace." I might not be able to specify precisely in what way(s) the influence of the Spirit through the Lord's Supper differs from His influence through other "natural" phenomena. I'm not even sure I need to. The point is simply that, unlike a multitude of other activities and experiences that may well edify, the Lord's Supper is ordained by God and required by Scripture to function as a means for mediating the spiritual presence of Jesus in the hearts of God's people.

I don't think my experience is unique when I say that I invariably find participation at the table of the Lord to be a profound moment of increased spiritual blessing. It is a means, through prayerful reflection, by which the Lord manifests His glory, love, mercy, and kindness to my religious consciousness. The Spirit works profoundly at the time of communion to awaken in my mind and to impress upon my heart the eternal significance of Christ's finished work at Calvary and His love, not merely for people in general, but for me in particular.

WHAT TO DO WHEN YOU DON'T FEEL LIKE WORSHIPING

If your reason for worshiping God is merely from a sense of moral duty, God would rather you not worship Him at all. To say that God is pleased with worship that lacks passion is to say God endorses hypocrisy. How can one ever forget the stinging rebuke Jesus made of the Pharisees in this regard?

> "You hypocrites, rightly did Isaiah prophesy of you, saying, 'This people honors Me with their lips, but their heart is far away from Me. But in vain do they worship Me, teaching as doctrines the precepts of men.'" (Matthew 15:7-9)

If ever there were a scary verse in the Bible, this is it. It frightens me to think that it is possible for me to have "singing lips" and a "distant heart" at the same time. My body can be fully engaged in worship while my heart is totally disengaged.

Passion is essential to the act and experience of worship. Granted, you may be at a stage in your life where the only passion you feel is pain or brokenness or emptiness. It may be the passionate ache and yearning to be filled, feeling empty as you do. It may be the passion of desperation and need or of longing and anticipation for what you don't have but know you must have if you are going to survive. But it is, nonetheless, passion.

Put yourself in God's place. Try to see things from His point of view. Standing or kneeling before You is one of Your children whom You've redeemed by the blood of Your Son. This child, in effect, says to You:

> God, I don't really want to be here right now. I don't feel anything for You right now. I'm not moved by a spontaneous affection for You as a Person. I'm not particularly overwhelmed by your beauty. Your splendor and glory really leave me cold and lifeless. But I'm going to worship anyway. I'm going to declare Your worth anyway because You've commanded me to do so in Scripture and because You are God.

I could be wrong, but I don't think God is going to be thrilled with that.

So what should we do when we feel nothing, when we are bored and indifferent and dead on the inside, when we are downcast and can barely move our mouths to sing? What should we do when we've lost our sense of intimacy with the Lord, when we feel nothing of His presence, when there is but a haunting echo of His distance? Some of you struggle to attend church. You find little appealing in it but feel obligated to go because a friend or family member pressures you into going. Can you still glorify God in worship? Yes!

Even though you may not now feel any joy or satisfaction in

His presence, you want to. You remember days past when your heart was aflame and your spirit ablaze with passion for God and with a sense of His presence. You delighted in His goodness and praise was easy and natural and free. You want it. You are desperate for it. You cry for it. But it's not there, for now.

Perhaps you are in a place of extreme emotional brokenness. Your life is crumbling all around you. Nothing has worked out the way you hoped. All that you've strived to achieve is disintegrating before your eyes and you are helpless to stem the tide. All that you once valued is vanishing. You feel nothing. Your spirit is dry and barren and you sense an ugly anger and bitterness rising up in your heart. Can you worship in a way that honors and glorifies God? Yes. So what should you do?

Sing anyway. Worship anyway. Praise God for His matchless worth and His unexcelled beauty. "Wait a minute, Sam. That sounds like you're encouraging me to be a hypocrite. I thought I heard you moments ago denounce the very thing you now seem to endorse. I'm confused." I can appreciate that. But what I'm advocating isn't hypocrisy, because God is glorified by your longing for the joy that is to be found in Him even if you are not yet experiencing it. God is honored by what John Piper calls "the spark of anticipated gladness" that leads you to praise Him even when you don't feel like it.

In your brokenness you know that there is only One who can heal and bind up your wounds. In your spiritual weariness you know there is only One who can bring refreshment and renewal to your arid soul. In your cold-heartedness you know there is only One who can bring life-giving warmth. In your joylessness you know there is only One who can restore delight to your spirit. And it is precisely this deep and desperate desire in your spiritual desert that so profoundly honors God.

Let me try to illustrate my point. Think of God as if He were a desert oasis. As I see it, you can magnify an oasis in either of two ways. The most obvious way is by jumping into its refreshing, cool, life-giving waters and drinking to your heart's delight. But you can also honor the oasis by the painful sorrow you feel in not yet having reached it as you continue to press on in the spiritual desert. When you ache for the refreshment of the oasis, even though you're still hot and dry and thirsty, when you grieve because of the absence of its life-giving waters, you magnify the oasis even before you have opportunity to enjoy it. So too with God.

So, if you went to church last weekend feeling nothing for God, feeling that He's a million miles away, you could and should have worshiped Him anyway.

Isn't this what we see in Psalm 42:1-2? "As the deer pants for the water brooks, so my soul pants for Thee, O God. My soul thirsts for God, for the living God." What honors the water: the deer bent over drinking, after a long journey in the desert, or the deer diligently panting for the water while yet in the desert? Both! Actually drinking is the best and most satisfying way to honor the water; but until you get there, continue to thirst for it.

In the Meantime

Come to God in worship to enjoy the satisfying richness of all that He is for you in Jesus. If you are not yet enjoying Him, here are a few words of practical advice: First of all, confess the sin of joylessness. Joylessness, writes John Ortberg, "is a serious sin."[3] Acknowledge the coldness and indifference of your heart. Don't pretend that it doesn't matter how you feel. It matters, not only to you but especially to God.

Second, pray for a revelation of God's splendor and beauty and majesty and sweetness and all-satisfying, all-sufficient goodness. Ask the Holy Spirit to grant you spiritual ears that you might hear the Father rejoicing over you with loud and boisterous singing (Zephaniah 3:17). Ask the Holy Spirit to grant you spiritual eyes that you might again see the goodness of the Lord in the land of the living.

Third, begin to take those steps set forth in Scripture to renew your joy: Bible reading, prayer, participation at the Lord's Supper, remembering God's past deeds of kindness, focusing on the cross, fellowshiping with those who are enjoying God, and so on.

Fourth, think about hell! Yes, you read it right. Think about hell. Among his personal resolutions, Jonathan Edwards included the following: "Resolved, when I feel pain, to think of the pains of martyrdom, and of hell."[4] You'll be amazed at how a brief time of meditation on the agonies of hell, from which you have been so graciously delivered, will serve to increase and deepen your joy and gratitude!

Fifth, and finally, praise Him anyway. Pursue the outward dimension of your duty in prayerful hope and expectation that it will help to rekindle the inward delight. Again, the reason this is not hypocrisy is because you are doing the outward act hoping to regain the inward joy, not as a substitute for it or as a disguise to convince others you mean it when in fact you don't.

In conclusion, don't come to God in times of worship arrogantly presuming to give. Come humbly yearning to get, for God always feeds the hungry heart.

CHAPTER ELEVEN

Sex and Integrity

I'M WRITING THIS CHAPTER ON AUGUST 18, 1998, THE DAY FOL-
lowing the unprecedented testimony of President Bill Clinton before
a grand jury. It is also the day following a brief speech by the president in which he "confessed" to having misled his family and the
American people about his relationship with a twenty-one-year-
old White House intern. Regardless of your political affiliation or
your feelings about our national leader, what happened on August
17 is symptomatic of the moral sickness that pervades our entire
country, indeed the entire globe.

If that were not bad enough, one needed only to wait until
today, August 18, to hear the reaction of people around the nation.
Amazingly, the majority of people interviewed by the media didn't
seem to care that our president had engaged in sexual activity with
a young lady not much older than his own daughter. They were
even less concerned that he had lied about it to everyone on
national TV! As long as they were employed and life was relatively peaceful and basic utilities suffered no interruption, they
simply couldn't have cared less about what was happening
"behind closed doors" at the White House. Or any other house
for that matter.

Sexual purity and integrity don't seem to matter unless one is unemployed, inconvenienced, or of a different political party. Well, they matter to God no matter what the latest economic indicators may be, no matter who's sleeping in the Lincoln Bedroom. At the heart of purity is purity of heart. And at the heart of purity of heart is sexual purity and personal integrity.

I didn't select these two issues because of presidential shenanigans. I chose them because they are so conspicuously absent in our society. They are even on the wane in the church. Something must be done.

SEX

The most important thing to remember as we talk about sexual purity is this: God is for you! God wants you to win. People often view God as their adversary when it comes to sex: "He's against me. He hates sex. I'm repulsive to Him. He's ashamed of me for what I've done. And to be perfectly honest, I can't blame Him much." Misconceptions such as this only serve to convince us that our situation is hopeless and drive us farther away from the arms of Him whose love and support and affirmation are the only thing that will enable us to win this war with the flesh.

We must embrace the truth that no one wants our sexual satisfaction more than God. I know that sounds bizarre, but it's true. This being the case, you may rest assured that He has provided everything necessary for your success and for your holiness. This is important to understand because people who struggle with sexual sin feel hopelessly locked into an unbreakable cycle of failure. Their experience has convinced them there is no reasonable chance for change. Worse still, they are convinced that God is disgusted with them and that they will never be of any use in the church. Certainly God is grieved by sexual sin, but it is a grief rooted in love. The only reason God is grieved by our failure is because He loves us so much. If He didn't love you, if His heart wasn't for you, why would He care what you do?

How do I know God is on our side when it comes to sex? Paul states it clearly in 1 Thessalonians 4:3-8:

> For this is the will of God, your sanctification; that is, that you abstain from sexual immorality; that each of you know how to possess his own vessel in sanctification and honor, not in lustful passion, like the Gentiles who do not know God; and that no man transgress and defraud his brother in the matter because the Lord is the avenger in all these things, just as we also told you before and solemnly warned you. For God has not called us for the purpose of impurity, but in sanctification. Consequently, he who rejects this is not rejecting man but the God who gives His Holy Spirit to you.

The "will of God." Do you cringe when you hear it? Does it stir up images of an inflexible task master whose greatest delight is in making sure no one else has any? Try something radical. Replace the English word "will" with "want" and listen to the Father's heart for your holiness: "I want you to feel the joy and satisfaction that come from experiencing the fullness of sexual delights. I want you to revel in the physical passion I had in mind when I brought Eve to Adam. Don't squander the opportunity by twisting and perverting what I made for your enjoyment."

Most of us hear the word "will" and instinctively envision a celestial frown. The phrase "will of God" often conjures up the mental impression of an inflexible and colorless lawgiver whose sole concern is for His own reputation. But when I hear Paul speak of God's "will" for human sexuality I think of His heart's desire, His yearning, His fatherly passion for our maximum enjoyment of one of His most precious gifts. I hear God saying, "This is what I long for you to experience as a sexual being. I made you. I put those sexual impulses in your spirit and in your body. I created hormones. Trust me when I say that I know far better than you what will bring the greatest joy and optimum pleasure." The point is simply that God's "will" for you and me is always an expression of His love. So what exactly is it that God "wants" of us when it comes to our sexual behavior?

Abstinence Can Be Fun

God's desire for His people is that they abstain from "sexual immorality." The word Paul uses is *porneia*, from which comes our English term "pornography." But don't think merely in terms of visual images such as *Playboy* magazine or an NC-17 movie. This word points to any form of illicit sexual behavior, whether fornication, adultery, or homosexuality. But it especially refers to sexual relations before or outside of marriage (see 1 Corinthians 6:15-20).

Don't believe the propaganda the world is peddling. This is not God's way of robbing you of fun and pleasure. It is His passionate desire to intensify it. This prohibition exists in order to protect and preserve the beauty and joy of marital sex. Our laws against theft and murder exist because of the high value we place on personal property and human life. So, too, with this prohibition against illicit sex. The purpose is to guard, preserve, and enhance something far more exciting and fun and full of pleasure, namely, marital love.

The biblical exhortations to resist sexual sin are motivated by a recognition of how it deprives us of even greater satisfaction. The principal reason for saying No to physical immorality is that it undermines the ability of our hearts to deeply enjoy the multifaceted joys that God provides for His children. Sexual sin diminishes our capacity to feel God's delight in who we are. It drains us of His power and hardens us to the loving overtures of His Spirit.

While standing in line at the grocery store I made the mistake of scanning the covers of several rather tawdry tabloids. The headline on one of them virtually shouted at unwary customers: "The Greatest Sex You've Ever Had!" No, I resisted the urge to read the article. Because I've read the book! The Bible! God, yes God, has a prescription for great sex for His people.

Paul's way of expressing this idea sounds a little odd at first.

He speaks in 1 Thessalonians 4:4 about each of us knowing how to "possess" our "own vessel in sanctification and honor." What in the world does that mean?

The word translated "possess" in the *New American Standard Bible* means to control or to gain mastery over something. The word rendered "vessel," translated as "body" by the *New International Version Bible*, was probably a euphemism for one's sexual organs. It's a vivid image: each of us must learn how to control our sex drive; how to channel its release in that way which its Creator has fashioned; how to live each day in control of our impulses; how to submit our bodies to God for holiness and purity.

This sexual self-mastery is to be done in "sanctification" and "honor," again interesting words, but especially the latter. When we behave in sexual purity we not only "honor" God, whose "will" we embrace, but also others. Sexual immorality dishonors the other person by depriving them of the opportunity to enjoy sex as their Creator intended. God knows that really good sex is found only in a monogamous, heterosexual relationship.

This point is made again in verse 6 where Paul exhorts us not to "defraud" our brother (or sister) in "the matter." When Paul mentions "the matter" he has in mind the issue of sexual purity. His warning here is that Christians must not use their familiarity or friendship with others in the church to gain sexual favors. We must never exploit the trust that exists between fellow-believers for the sake of sexual gratification. But how does sexual immorality or impurity defraud or wrong another Christian? In 1 Corinthians 6, Paul says that the one who commits fornication sins against his own body, but here he goes further and says it also transgresses and defrauds his or her fellow Christian. How?

Consider two ways. First of all, adultery is an obvious violation of the rights of another. You are stealing what doesn't belong to you. And secondly, premarital sex defrauds the future marriage partner of the person with whom you are involved. You are robbing that person of the virginity and single-minded intimacy that ought to be brought to a marriage. Thus, sexual impurity is as much a social injustice against others as it is a personal sin against God.

Beyond this, illicit sexual conduct also dishonors oneself. We were meant for better. We besmirch our dignity as image-bearers and rob our bodies of their divinely ordained function when we step outside the bounds of God's "will" and seek for sexual satisfaction in ways He knows will only bring disaster, disrespect, and often disease.

SEX "APPEAL"

Why is sexual sin such a powerful temptation? What is it about illicit sex that makes it so appealing? Some might be quick to respond: "That's easy. Sex feels good!" But I am convinced that the energy that fuels sexual impurity is more than biochemical. In addition to physical pleasure, there are at least five components in the energy that leads to sexual immorality.

The first thing that comes to mind is woundedness, which is often fueled by self-pity. We often use our woundedness as a warrant for our sin. It's so easy for us to say: "If you only knew how badly she or he hurt me, you wouldn't be so quick to judge me for what I've done." In other words, one reason sexual sin is so powerfully appealing is that it feels reasonable. At times we can even make it a matter of personal justice: "Anyone who has been victimized as badly as I have deserves a little relief." One man sat in front of me and spewed this excuse: "No one, least of all my wife, understands the kind of pressure I'm under. She has no way of knowing how lonely I feel. I'm tired of being an example for everyone else and getting nothing in return. If I'm going to have the strength to survive I've got to get some no-strings-attached affection from someone."

Others prefer to draw on their bitterness. We are told to trust a loving God who then fails to protect us from the hard circumstances of life. Suddenly living our lives for the sake of others seems senseless and stupid. "If obeying God were the right thing to do, my life wouldn't be in such a mess. So why not sex?"

For some it's simply a matter of selfishness: "I've given so much to so many for so long that the time's come for me to do something for me." Again, that is why sin keeps so strong a hold on us: we feel justified in doing it; we feel we have a right to sin. Still others have given up on purity because of an overwhelming sense of hopelessness: "I've tried everything and nothing works. I've held on for as long as I can. I'm not going to kid myself that anything will change. So why bother?"

If none of the above provides sufficient grounds for immorality, perhaps good old-fashioned pain will do. We all feel it. We're weary, worn out, beat up, and it hurts. And sexual sin brings so much immediate relief. Part of the pain is the emotional anguish of failed relationship: "I trusted him and he betrayed me." "I opened my heart to her and she rejected me." Sexual sin is powerfully appealing and attractive because, at least in the short term, it appears to work. The lie of Satan seems to work better, at least in the short term, than the truth of God.

What are all these rationalizations based on? One lie. The most pernicious, heinous, satanic lie of all. They are based on the lie that God really isn't good after all; that God is neither able nor willing to do for our souls or bodies what they so desperately need done; that therefore God can't be trusted with our fears and doubts and hopes and hurts. Because God doesn't care and can't be trusted, we'll find satisfaction somewhere else. And so often, we do.

Sin Hurts

Make no mistake about it. God will not permit His children to sin with impunity. There are consequences for sexual impurity. But please note that God's discipline does not mean He is disgusted with you. God's recompense is not rejection. It's hard for people to conceive of a God who avenges but loves. But according to Hebrews 12:5-13 God chastises and disciplines because He loves.[1]

More important still, we should pursue purity because the purpose of our redemption is holiness, not impurity. Impurity runs counter to everything God had in mind when He created us, called us, and redeemed us in Jesus (verse 7). And remember, says Paul, that it isn't just God we reject when we indulge in sexual impurity, it is "the God who gives His Holy Spirit to you" (verse 8).

It's important you know that the verb translated "gives" in verse 8 is in the present tense, not the past tense which is Paul's normal way of referring to the gift of the Holy Spirit. The point is not so much that God "gave" us His Spirit in the past, when we first came to saving faith (although that is certainly true enough in itself), but that in the present, right now, God is committed to us as seen in the ongoing, ever-present impartation of His Spirit. In fact, He is perpetually sustaining and supporting us through the Spirit even now in the midst of our struggle over whether or not to obey His will in regard to sexual purity.

Better still is the fact that God doesn't simply give us His Spirit, He gives the Spirit "into" us. Not just "to" us, but by an act of what can only be called intimate impartation His Spirit resides within to encourage, energize, and enable. The Spirit isn't just here, He's inside.

There is tremendous hope in this truth. The God who says, "My will is for you not to submit to the temptations of the world or the passions of the flesh" is the God who also says, "I am right now giving you my Holy Spirit to help you say Yes to purity! Come to Me," He beckons. "I won't put you to shame. I'm not here to ridicule but to restore. I'll cover you. I'll cleanse you. I'll quicken your soul with divine energy to say No to illicit urges. I'll do it by setting before you the surpassing delights of trusting in My promise of superior pleasures."

There is hope! There is help! Whatever God requires, God provides. He requires holiness, so He provides the infinite power of the Holy Spirit to assist you and me to do it. Don't despair. Don't give up. Don't resign yourself to live in bondage. Even as you read these words, the power of God is being infused into your heart to break the power of sin.

So often when we tell our children, for example, to do something we believe to be their moral obligation, we expect them to pull themselves up by their bootstraps with little if any assistance from us or anyone else. Who knows why. Perhaps we're simply too busy to bother. Perhaps some, tragically, just don't care. Maybe you sincerely believe that helping them would undermine the development of their moral maturity. So, yes, we encourage them, we cajole, we plead. But often in our frustration with their failure we turn to angry threats or shame-based warnings. Not God. With every word of exhortation comes the wind of His Spirit to energize and uphold us, instruct and inspire us. If you find yourself doubting where God stands when it comes to your sexual impulses, if you fear He will abandon you when impulse turns to indulgence, recall this simple truth: He is ever-present in you, through His Spirit, to empower your Yes to sexual purity.

INTEGRITY

My favorite text on integrity has always been Psalm 15:

> O LORD, who may abide in Thy tent? Who may dwell on Thy holy hill? He who walks with integrity, and works righteousness, and speaks truth in his heart. He does not slander with his tongue, nor does evil to his neighbor, nor takes up a reproach against his friend. In whose eyes a reprobate is despised, but who honors those who fear the LORD; he swears to his own hurt, and does not change. He does not put out his money at interest, nor does he take a bribe against the innocent. He who does these things will never be shaken. (verses 1-5)

Some people have been misled by what they think David is saying in this psalm. In the first place, he is not talking about how to get saved.

Rather, he is describing what it is to be saved. These moral declarations are not conditions for acceptance with God. They are the consequence of it. Thus, David is not talking about requirements for entrance into the kingdom on the part of those outside, but about enjoyment of the King on the part of those on the inside. The question David is asking, then, is this: "Who will enjoy God's fellowship? Who will commune with God?" God cannot and will not abide in the presence of nor bless moral corruption (see Psalm 5:4-7).

When you hear that obedience and righteousness please God, is that good news that lifts you up or is it a discouraging burden that oppresses and depresses you? Do you get excited when you read Psalm 15? These moral guidelines are oppressive and legalistic only to those who still love their sin. For example, the only reason integrity should be a burden to you is if you enjoy being dishonest. Righteous deeds will be bothersome only because you prefer unrighteous ones. Speaking the truth will hurt only because it feels good to lie.

Obedience to the righteous commands of God is easy for those whose hearts have been gripped by grace and whose lives are empowered by grace. After reiterating the stringent requirements of the Mosaic Law, God declared to Israel that "this commandment which I command you today is not too difficult for you, nor is it out of reach. . . . But the word is very near you, in your mouth and in your heart, that you may observe it" (Deuteronomy 30:11,14). Jesus Himself declared that His yoke was "easy" and His load was "light" (Matthew 11:30). John the apostle couldn't have been more explicit when he said that God's commandments "are not burdensome" (1 John 5:3).

Clearly, God takes great pleasure in our obedience. But His pleasure in obedience, says Piper, "is not like the sadistic pleasure of a heartless coach who likes to see his recruits sweat and strain under impossible conditioning exercises."[2] In fact, in Luke 11:46 Jesus pronounces a curse on such moral taskmasters: "Woe to you lawyers as well! For you weigh men down with burdens hard to bear,

We should not be weighed down

while you yourselves wil not even touch the burdens with one of your fingers." But God is not like that. "With every command [like those in Psalm 15], he lifts not just his finger, but all his precious promises and all his omnipotent power and puts them at the service of his child."[3]

God takes pleasure in your obedience because everything He commands is for your good. As noted earlier, all of God's commands are like a doctor's prescription or a physician's therapy. They may not always be immediately pleasant, but they are intended and designed for your health and happiness. If occasionally there are painful side effects, it is because the disease is so bad that severe medication may be required (see Deuteronomy 6:24; 10:12-13). God, our spiritual physician, takes pleasure in our obedience to His commands because the doctor really does care whether or not we get well.

To use another analogy, the loving parent forbids snacking before dinner not because she is a heartless killjoy but because she has labored long over a feast of food beyond your wildest culinary dreams.

Your attitude toward the moral commands of Psalm 15 depends entirely on whether you pursue God's righteousness by works or by faith (see Romans 9:31-32). To obey God as though it were a matter of works is to obey out of your own strength with a view to your own merit. To obey God as though it were a matter of faith is to obey out of His own strength with a view to His glory (see 1 Peter 4:11; 2 Thessalonians 1:11-12).

But how does "faith" produce "obedience"? As Piper explains, "when you trust Christ to take care of your future ('faith is the assurance of things hoped for'), the inevitable result is that sinful strategies to gain happiness sink in the peaceful confidence that God will make a greater joy for you in his own way."[4] The reason we resist God's laws and pursue our own sinful strategies is because we believe that we can do better at securing our happiness than God can.

We earlier saw this principle at work in the experience of Moses (see Hebrews 11:24-26). His faith in what God offered produced his works. He had confidence that what Christ offered is better than the fleeting pleasures of sin. Piper tells us that "Moses looked to the reward of God's promises, he weighed that against the rewards of unrighteousness, and he rested satisfied in God."[5]

ABIDING WITH GOD

David lists ten characteristics of the person who will "abide" in God's tent and "dwell" on His holy hill.

First, this person walks with integrity (Psalm 15:2). This word translated "integrity" (NASB) is something of a summary of all that follows. Integrity here does not mean sinless, but it does describe a person who by God's grace "sins less." It refers to one who is whole, complete, sound.

I witnessed this kind of integrity at work while watching the professional golf tour. One of the more successful players voluntarily disqualified himself from a tournament upon discovering he had violated the rule against dropping his ball closer to the hole. No one had seen him do it (at least no human). No one would ever have known otherwise. Besides, other players had probably committed the same infraction and had kept their mouths shut. Why draw attention to oneself by blowing the whistle? Why run the risk of being labeled "holier than thou"? These thoughts no doubt rushed through his mind, but to no avail. By initiating this action he cost himself tens of thousands of dollars. But for some people, integrity has no price tag.

Second, this individual works righteousness (15:2). This is the person who actually does what is righteous, rather than merely talks about it. Doing what is right and lawful and good and honest is eminently pleasing to God, whether it be in private or public, in the church or in the office.

Let me get real specific about what this means. Proverbs 11:1 declares that "a false balance is an abomination to the LORD, but a just weight is His delight." The same thought is found in

Proverbs 20:10, "Differing weights and differing measures, both of them are abominable to the LORD" (compare 20:23). What is it that is so horrible that God would regard it as "abominable?"

The writer is referring to an ancient practice among unscrupulous merchants. If you wanted to purchase, let's say, five pounds of sugar, the merchant would place on one side of the balance scale a stone supposedly weighing five pounds. He would then pour sugar onto the other side until the scales weighed evenly. The stone might weigh only four pounds. The customer is thereby cheated, having paid for a pound of sugar he does not receive. If a dishonest person were himself making the purchase, he might use a six-pound stone that is labeled as five. In either case, such deceitfulness is an abomination to the Lord. One cannot easily pass it off as shrewd bargaining or rationalize it by insisting that "everyone else does it." It is, quite simply, abominable to the Lord.

Consider a few more contemporary examples. A few years ago the newspapers were filled with the story of a young boy who purchased a Nolan Ryan baseball card from an unsuspecting, naïve clerk for twelve dollars. The actual price was twelve-*hundred* dollars! (Oh, the pains of a misplaced decimal point.) The boy's father actually had the audacity to defend his son and refused to return the card. The store owner eventually took the matter to court. I don't know how it was resolved. But what would integrity demand?

Ask yourself these questions: Does integrity require that the seller of a home or a car mention to a prospective buyer those unseen but undeniable flaws in the product? What if those flaws had been quietly passed on to you by the previous owner? Does that justify your silence when it comes time for you to sell? What about people who violate copyright law by duplicating rented videotapes or computer software? Is it an abomination to the Lord when a person fails to report on his or her tax return that small income earned on the side that has no traceable records? Is it ethical to use a "fuzz-buster" to circumvent speeding laws? (Yeah, I know. I'm starting to strike close to home for some of us!)

What about the parent who passes off her twelve-year-old child as eleven in order to save two dollars on a ticket at the movies ("But he only turned twelve last week! Give me a break!")? Or what of the person who pays for only one ticket at the movies but after one show slips across the hall and views another? Have you ever rationalized keeping excess change mistakenly given to you at the grocery store by saying: "Well, they're overcharging for the tomatoes, so that makes us even"?

God is concerned with the little things no less than with the big ones. It's stunning to think that God views everything we do or think in life as either an abomination or a delight! We must ask this question: Do we regard those minor misrepresentations in business or shopping or speaking as only part of the game everyone plays, or do we regard them as an abomination to God?

Third, he speaks truth in his heart (Psalm 15:2). That is to say, there is a correspondence between what he thinks on the inside and what he says on the outside. This person does not resort to hypocrisy, feigned praise, or flattery. This doesn't mean we are to speak everything in our hearts (compare Ephesians 4:29 and numerous proverbs). It does mean that when we speak, we speak the truth.

Here's one for you to ponder. What should we think of the professional football player who pretends to have caught the ball (complete with the obnoxious and self-serving celebration), deliberately deceiving the referee, in order to gain an unfair advantage for his team. Is this straining at a gnat? Is not such behavior simply assumed in advance as part of the game? Or is the person of integrity duty-bound to observe the rules of the game irrespective of other factors?

Fourth, he does not slander with his tongue (15:3). The word "slander" literally means "to spy out," in the sense that one goes looking for things in the life of another to use against that person.

The fifth and sixth characteristics are related. He does no evil to his neighbor (15:3). Neither does he take up a reproach against his friend (15:3). Here David refers to both initiating and rejoicing in gossip. His point is that the person of integrity will neither contribute to slander nor tolerate it.

Seventh, this person is one in whose eyes a reprobate is despised but who honors those who fear the Lord (15:4). The "reprobate" is someone known for evil; someone hardened in perversity; someone unrepentant and proud of his or her sin. Whom do you admire? Whom do you praise? Try to envision what society (not to mention the church!) would be like if we all suddenly ceased to praise, honor, reward, show deference, or grant special privileges to the reprobates of our world, particularly those in Hollywood, the sports world, and politics.

Eighth, he swears to his own hurt and does not change (15:4). The *New International Version* renders this, "He keeps his oath even when it hurts!" In other words, his honor is more important than his wallet. He is willing to make material and physical sacrifices to be honest. Often, if there is no risk of loss or painful consequences, one will never know if one has integrity. One will never know if what motivates us is moral conviction or moral convenience until we are forced to suffer loss for standing our ground or keeping our word.

Ninth, he does not put out his money at interest (15:5; see Exodus 22:25; Leviticus 25:35-38; Deuteronomy 23:19-20). The primary aim of this legislation was to protect the poor. In other words, it was motivated by compassion. The purpose for making loans in today's world is to make money, to develop industry, to expand capital, and so on. But for an Israelite to charge interest on loans made to a fellow-Israelite would aggravate the crisis that had produced the need for obtaining the loan in the first place, driving him yet further into debt. It might be likened to a banker today charging usurious interest on a loan—like those 22 percent credit cards we're possibly carrying around in our wallet.

Finally, he does not take a bribe against the innocent (15:5). Often the poor were taken to court and exploited by the rich who could easily afford to pay a bribe to thwart justice (see Deuteronomy 16:19-20).

And what profit is there in integrity? David's answer is, "He who does these things will never be shaken" (15:5). Shaken from what? Most likely, the promise is that this individual will never cease to "abide" in God's "tent" (verse 1) or fail to "dwell" on God's "holy hill" (verse 1). Well, what do you know . . . honesty does pay after all!

CASE STUDIES

The best way to get a grip on the meaning of integrity is by responding to a variety of instances in which people are faced with ethical decisions. What constitutes integrity in each instance? Some of these cases are brief and easy to evaluate. Others are more complex. I'm not going to answer these for you. You be your own judge.

1. Does integrity demand that one declare all purchases made abroad when going through customs, even if the amount one would be required to pay is minimal?

2. When I enrolled at Dallas Theological Seminary, I was required as a condition for admission to sign a pledge that I would abstain from the use of alcoholic beverages for the duration of my studies there. Because this is a requirement that cannot be supported from Scripture, am I free to have a glass of wine with my dinner, if only in the summer when classes are not in session? If I should travel to France between semesters, where wine is freely imbibed, does integrity demand that I abstain even then?

3. Eric Liddell, Scottish sprinter made famous in the movie *Chariots of Fire,* refused to run in a preliminary race in the Olympics because it was scheduled on Sunday. This would have violated the Sabbath, to the observance of which he had verbally committed himself on several occasions. Bobby Fischer, former world chess champion, also refused to play a tournament game on Saturday, his Sabbath (Fischer was a member of the

Worldwide Church of God, at that time a well-known cult group). His decision cost him several years of work in his progress to compete for the world championship. Does the fact that Liddell was a Christian and Fischer a nonChristian affect the integrity of their decisions?

4. What is your opinion of the lawyer who, during cross-examination, tries to make a witness he knows is telling the truth appear to be confused or even lying in order to win his case? He is deliberately attempting to deceive the jury into disbelieving a truthful witness. On the one hand, he claims that such action is required to discharge his legal responsibility in providing his client with the best possible defense. What does integrity call for in such instances?

5. Similar to the previous case, what becomes of integrity when a lawyer vigorously defends a man he knows is guilty? If the lawyer appeals to his oath by which he swore to do his best in defending his client, as well as to the fact that everyone is entitled to a competent defense, can he retain his integrity?

6. The following case study is taken from Stephen Carter's book, *Integrity*:

A man who has been married for fifty years confesses to his wife on his deathbed that he was unfaithful thirty-five years earlier. The dishonesty was killing his spirit, he says. Now he has cleared his conscience and is able to die in peace.[6]

Was this an act of integrity? Carter analyzes his decision:

The husband has been honest—sort of. He has certainly unburdened himself. And he has probably made his wife (soon to be his widow) miserable in the process, because

even if she forgives him, she will not be able to remember
him with quite the vivid image of love and loyalty that she
had hoped for. Arranging his own emotional affairs to
ease his transition to death, he has shifted to his wife the
burden of confusion and pain, perhaps for the rest of her
life. Moreover, he has attempted his honesty at the one
time in his life when it carries no risk: and . . . acting in
accordance with what you think is right and risking no
loss in the process is a rather thin and not very admirable
form of integrity. Besides, even though the husband has
been honest in a sense, he has now been twice unfaithful
to his wife: once thirty-five years ago when he had his
affair, and now a second time as, nearing death, he
decides that his own peace of mind is more important
than hers. In trying to be honest, he has violated his marriage vow by acting toward his wife not with love but with
naked and perhaps even cruel self-interest. None of this
means that the husband's thirty-five-year-old affair is a
moral irrelevancy as he faces death. But if he treats his
marriage vow with integrity, the question he should be
asking himself is not, "Did I make full disclosure before I
died?" but rather, "Did I make up for my wrong with the
way I treated my wife for the remainder of our time
together?" If he can answer yes to the second, he should
still be able to die in relative peace.[7]

Do you agree with Carter?

7. There was a case that involved the purchase of tobacco
in New Orleans at prices that were depressed because of
the British blockade during the War of 1812. The buyer
had evidently heard that the war was over, which meant
that the price of tobacco was about to skyrocket.
Communications being what they were, the seller didn't

know, and the buyer was trying to take advantage of this momentary spread in the price. When the seller learned that the war was over, he took the tobacco back, and the buyer sued. The question is this: "Did the buyer have an obligation to tell the seller that the war was over?" This particular case went to the Supreme Court in 1817. It is known as Laidlaw vs. Organ. In whose favor do you think the court ruled? How would you rule?

The Essence of Integrity

Of what, then, does integrity consist? I've listed below what I regard as the ten foundational characteristics of a person with integrity. There may well be more than ten, but I cannot conceive of any less than ten.

1. A person of integrity fulfills his or her promises. Being true to one's word, especially when doing so is costly (in terms of money, convenience, physical welfare, and so on), is a core characteristic of integrity.
2. A person of integrity speaks the truth, is honest, and does not lie.
3. A person of integrity is a person of sincerity. That is to say, a person of integrity hates hypocrisy.
4. A person of integrity manifests a wholeness of character, including kindness, compassion, mercy, and gentleness.
5. A person of integrity is committed to the pursuit and maintenance of justice and fairness.
6. A person of integrity loves as, when, and what God loves.
7. A person of integrity is humble. He or she shuns pride and haughtiness.
8. A person of integrity is law-abiding. He or she plays by the rules, both in the Bible and the law of the land.

9. A person of integrity is fundamentally altruistic. That is to say, he is committed not simply to laws and rules but to people. Could a selfish person have much integrity? What about someone who is honest, law-abiding, and fulfills his or her promises but is self-absorbed and egocentric? Does the latter eliminate the possibility of integrity?

10. A person of integrity manifests a high degree of consistency. That is to say, he or she is not always changing the principles on the basis of which they live, unless compelled to do so by the Bible or rational persuasion.

The problems faced by our president as I write this chapter may well be resolved by the time this book is released. I hope and pray that humility and righteousness will have prevailed. Whatever turns out in his case, ours is ever before us. As we wrestle with our flesh and struggle with the forces of darkness, let us never lose sight of this glorious promise: "Blessed are the pure in heart, for they shall see God" (Matthew 5:8).

CHAPTER TWELVE

The Anatomy of Temptation

DEATH AND TAXES. IF CONVENTIONAL WISDOM IS TO BE TRUSTED, they're the only two things of which we may be certain. Well, so much for conventional wisdom. There's a third: temptation. Perhaps somewhere along the way in reading this book you got the impression that falling in love with Jesus means the end of temptation. If you got it from me, I apologize. I never intended even remotely to suggest that fascination with the splendor of God or experiencing the superior pleasures to be found in His presence would eliminate the need for spiritual vigilance.

I wish that it were otherwise. Would that we might be free of the relentless assault of the Enemy. But Satan is by nature and choice a deceiver, a seducer, who is hell-bent on devouring anyone who dares fall in love with the Son of God. On two occasions he is actually called "the tempter" (Matthew 4:3; 1 Thessalonians 3:5).

No one was more entranced by the beauty of the Father than the Son. No one was more single-minded in his spiritual focus than Jesus. Yet, notwithstanding Satan's decisive defeat in the wilderness, we read in Luke 4:13 that he only departed from Jesus "until an opportune time." If Satan's attack against our Lord was interminable, we should hardly expect less.

The focus of Satan's efforts is always the same: to deceive us into believing that the passing pleasures of sin are more satisfying than obedience. But there is great diversity and insidious ingenuity in the way he goes about this task. It behooves us to become familiar with his tactics.

Knowing Your Enemy

I am reminded of a particularly illuminating scene in the movie *Patton,* starring George C. Scott as the controversial World War II general. It's early in the war and the movie. Patton is preparing to face Field Marshall Erwin Rommel, Germany's most decorated military leader. Rommel is preparing to launch a massive assault on Allied troops in North Africa. His specialty is tank warfare. But Patton's intelligence service has intercepted a German radio transmission bearing news of the impending attack. On the morning of the battle, Patton is awakened by his aides. A book lies open on his nightstand. Its title: *The Tank in Attack,* by Erwin Rommel. As Allied forces spring their surprise, and quite successful, assault on the enemy, Patton can be seen smiling as he peers through binoculars at the carnage of battle. "Rommel," shouts Patton through smiling teeth, "you magnificent (expletive deleted). I read your book!"

How do you win a battle? You read the enemy's book. Familiarity with his tactics, knowledge of his ways, is essential in waging a successful war. It's true in military warfare. It's true in spiritual warfare as well. Patton gained an immeasurable advantage by learning in advance of being attacked where, in all likelihood, Rommel would concentrate his strike. He studied Rommel's personality, his strategy in previous battles, his philosophy of tank warfare, all with a view to anticipating and countering every conceivable move. Satan doesn't have a book. But he's in ours.

It strikes some as odd to say that Satan has a strategy. They mistakenly conclude that because our Enemy is atrociously sinful he must be equally stupid. Such reasoning has been the downfall of many in the body of Christ. He does not act haphazardly or without a goal in view. In 2 Corinthians 2:11 the apostle issues a warning so that "no advantage be taken of us by Satan; for we are not ignorant of his schemes." The word translated "take advantage of" in the *New American Standard Bible* is rendered "outwit" by the *New International Version Bible*. It means to cheat or defraud someone by deception. Satan had a clear vision, an agenda, if you will, for the situation in Corinth. To think that he acts randomly and aimlessly is precisely what he wants.

Much the same idea is found in Ephesians 6:11 where Paul again speaks of satanic "schemes." Here he uses the Greek word *methodia* from which we derive our English term "method." He has in mind cunning and wily stratagems (compare Ephesians 4:14) carefully crafted to devour unsuspecting Christians. Would it surprise you to know that Satan is operative in the formation and spread of value systems in our society, that he influences institutions, organizations, philosophical movements, political, social, and economic systems? Rest assured that Satan sets his goals and then utilizes and exploits the most effective means, while avoiding all obstacles, to reach his diabolical end.

On the flip side, the fact that Satan has plans and purposes to which he devotes his considerable and perverted prowess, must not lead us to grant him a place of co-equality with God either in terms of prominence or power. It's a simple matter of logic: Satan is an angel. All angels were created (Colossians 1:16; John 1:1-3). Therefore, Satan was created. He is, therefore, God's Devil. Satan is not the equal and opposite power of God (contra dualism). He is not eternal. His power is not infinite. He does not possess divine attributes. In sum, he is no match for God! If anything, Satan is the equal and opposite power of the archangel Michael, but not God.

FOUR TRUTHS ABOUT TEMPTATION

Let me begin by stating four fundamental truths about temptation. These principles are foundational to our battle to stay satisfied with God.

First of all, whereas God tests our faith, He never tempts it (James 1:13). The purpose of divine testing is to sanctify and strengthen. The purpose of satanic tempting is to deceive and destroy. Evil neither exists in the heart of God nor is He its author. It most assuredly exists in our hearts and we are its author. This leads directly to the second point.

Temptation almost always begins in the flesh (James 1:14). Our flesh sets fire to sin. Satan simply fans the flames. Satan is powerless until we first say Yes to sin. He exploits our sinful decisions, most often by intensifying the course of action we have already chosen.

Paul makes this point in Ephesians 4:26-27. He exhorts us, "Be angry, and yet do not sin; do not let the sun go down on your anger, and do not give the devil an opportunity." Satan is not credited with nor blamed for creating the anger in the first place. We are responsible for it. Satan's response is to use this and other such sins to gain access to our lives and to expand and intensify our chosen course of behavior.

Some might think that Luke 22:31 is an exception to this rule. Jesus tells Peter that "Satan has demanded permission to sift you like wheat." By the way, it should be noted that Satan evidently obtained permission to tempt all of the disciples. When Jesus said "you," He employed the plural form of the pronoun, thereby including the other ten as well (Judas had already departed). There is no indication that Peter had planned on denying Jesus or that his "flesh" was in any way inclined to do so. Jesus seems to attribute to the Devil what is about to happen.

Satan's intent in "sifting" Peter was obviously malicious. He wanted to destroy Peter by inciting Him to deny Jesus. But God's intent in permitting Satan to do it was altogether different. (Clearly, Satan is unable to act outside the parameters established by the will of God. He must first ask permission of God.) God's purposes with Peter were to instruct him, humble him, perhaps discipline him, and certainly to use him as an example to others of both human arrogance and the possibility of forgiveness and restoration. The point is simply that often we cannot easily say "Satan did it" or "God did it." In cases such as this, both are true (with the understanding that God's will is sovereign, supreme, and overriding), but their respective goals are clearly opposite. Sydney Page's comments concerning this incident are important:

> Luke 22:31-32 reveals that Satan can subject the loyalty of the followers of Jesus to severe tests that are designed to produce failure. So intense are the pressures to which Satan is able to subject believers that the faith of even the most courageous may be found wanting. Satan is, however, limited in what he can do by what God permits and by the intercession of Jesus on behalf of his own [compare Romans 8:34; Hebrews 7:25; 1 John 2:1]. Furthermore, those who temporarily falter can be restored and, like Peter, can even resume positions of leadership. It is implied that Satan cannot gain ultimate victory over those for whom Jesus intercedes.[1]

The third principle is that temptation, in and of itself, is not sin. This is critically important, especially for those who suffer from an overly sensitive and tender conscience. Jesus was repeatedly tempted (Hebrews 2:17-18; 4:15; Matthew 4), but He was sinless. We must resist thinking that we are subChristian or subspiritual simply because we are frequently tempted. It was the great reformer Martin Luther who first said, "You can't prevent the birds from flying over your head, but you can keep them from building a nest in your hair." His point is that a temptation only becomes a sin when you acquiesce to it, "fondle" it, and "enjoy" it.

The strength of temptation also comes from a tendency to push virtues to such an extreme that they become vices. For example, it is all too easy for the joy of eating to become gluttony, or for the blessing of rest to become sloth, or for the peace of quietness to become noncommunication, or for industriousness to become greed, or for liberty to be turned into an excuse for licentiousness. We all know what it's like for pleasure to become sensuality, or for self-care to become selfishness, or for self-respect to become conceit, or for wise caution to become cynicism and unbelief, or for righteous anger to become unrighteous rage, or for the joy of sex to become immorality, or for conscientiousness to become perfectionism. The list could go on endlessly, but I think you get the point.

The story of Ananias and Sapphira in Acts 5 is a case in point. The most instructive thing in this incident is that it wasn't through some overt and terrible act of human depravity, but through an act of religious devotion that Satan brings about the downfall of this couple. This frightening story of instantaneous execution all began with an act of generosity! As Page wrote, "It is sobering to think that the very good that God's people attempt to do can be their undoing."[2]

Another instance in which Satan seeks to exploit the otherwise good intentions of the church is described in 2 Corinthians 2:10-11. Certain people in Corinth, ostensibly to maintain the purity of the church, were reluctant to forgive and restore the wayward, but now repentant, brother. This harshness would give Satan an opportunity to crush the spirit of the repentant sinner and drive him to despair, most likely resulting in his being forever cut off from the church.

Or consider how Satan employs this tactic when it comes to sexual relations in marriage (1 Corinthians 7:5). Paul approves of the decision by married couples to refrain from sexual relations to devote themselves to prayer, but only for a season. To abstain entirely for a prolonged period of time exposes oneself to unnecessary temptation (that is, lust and the satisfaction of one's sexual desires outside the bonds of marriage). Again, we see here an example of how the enemy takes an otherwise godly intention and exploits it for his own nefarious purposes.

TACTICS OF TEMPTATION

As I said, Satan has a strategy. The following is certainly not an exhaustive list of his schemes, but it's a good start.

Satan especially likes to tempt us when our faith is fresh, that is, when the Christian is only recently converted and thus less prepared to know how to resist his seductive suggestions. This is precisely Paul's grounds for warning against the premature promotion of a new Christian in 1 Timothy 3:6. An elder, says Paul, must not be "a new convert, lest he become conceited and fall into the condemnation incurred by the devil." The latter phrase is literally, "the judgment or condemnation of the devil," most likely a reference to the judgment to which Satan himself has been subjected. This isn't to suggest that older, more mature believers are exempt, for according to 1 Timothy 3:7, Satan is able to exploit any blemish on the reputation of any Christian leader.

Satan also especially likes to tempt us when our faith feels strongest, that is, when we think we are invulnerable to sin. If we are convinced that we have it under control, we become less diligent. Earlier I alluded to one of Oswald Chambers' most insightful statements that again pertains to this very point: "An unguarded strength," said Chambers, "is a double weakness." Chambers' point here is that when we come to think we are beyond "falling" in a certain area we let our guard down; we cease to be vigilant. That makes us doubly vulnerable to Satan's temptations. One example would be a famous pastor (you'd know him, but I'll leave it anonymous) who, after the problems of Bakker and Swaggart, was heard to say, "I'm beyond that temptation. My life in God and relationship with my wife are too strong for me to be vulnerable to sexual sin." That, I contend, is dangerous.

Satan especially likes to tempt us when we are in an alien environment. Gordon MacDonald explains:

> In the environs of home life with family and friends, there
> is a schedule of routines, a set of support systems, and a

way of doing things, all of which lends encouragement to responsible living and, conversely restraint against irresponsible living. Virtually all of these external systems fall away when a person is hundreds of miles from home.[3]

Certainly our desire is that our internal resistance to the temptation of sin, nourished and sustained by our fascination and joy with the beauty of God in Christ, would be adequate in such circumstances. But when the external boundaries that often unconsciously govern our behavior are removed, or are expanded, we soon discover the depth (or shallowness) of maturity in our souls.

Satan also likes to tempt us when our faith is being tested in the fires of affliction. When we are tired, burnt-out, persecuted, feeling excluded and ignored, Satan makes his play. His most common tactic is to suggest that God isn't fair, that He is treating us unjustly, from which platform Satan then launches his seductive appeal that we need no longer obey. Physical pain, relational and financial loss, when combined with the silence of heaven, serve only to intensify the appeal of temptation. This is nowhere better seen than in the experience of Job, a story that is crucial to understanding our response to God when tempted in the midst of the worst imaginable tragedies.

We read in Job 1:9-12 that Satan was at a loss concerning Job's loyal obedience to God. Job was a complete puzzle to him. He didn't doubt that Job was obedient and upright. There was no mistaking his godliness. But the Devil just couldn't bring himself to believe that anyone would want to be holy for nothing. The only thing left is to launch an assault against Job's motives. Whereas he could hardly question Job's righteousness, he did wonder about the reason for it. His diabolical conclusion was that Job served God for what he could get out of Him. Job's piety, reasoned the Devil, must be a calculated effort to milk God of His gifts. "Take away the pay and he'll quit the job," he thought. Satan was persuaded that worship must be fundamentally selfish, that it is nothing more than a man-made device to flatter God into generosity. If God's generosity were cut off, thought Satan, Job's praise would turn to cursing.

In sum, Satan accuses God of having bought Job's loyalty with health and wealth: "Job doesn't serve You for free. Don't flatter Yourself, God! No one else does either." In effect, he says: "He doesn't love You for who You are but only for what You've given him." In other words, it isn't Job that Satan accuses, but God! The question that Job will face, the question we all face is this: "Is God worthy to be loved and deserving of our obedience for who He is, irrespective of all other considerations?" Is Job sufficiently dedicated to remain loyal if no benefits are attached? Satan says No. He accuses God of being a deceptive fraud and Job of being a selfish hypocrite.

We all know what happens next. No sooner had Job concluded his sacrifice on behalf of his children (1:5) than he hears the stunning news of their demise. He is first told of the destruction of his servants and his livestock. With hardly a moment to catch his breath, word comes that his children have been killed. But Job refuses to yield to the temptation to curse God. Indeed, "through all this Job did not sin nor did he blame God" (1:22).

If that were not enough, and according to Satan's perverted way of reasoning it obviously wasn't, his sufferings continue. The Tempter persists in his skepticism about Job's sincerity. "It really wasn't much of a test," Satan snarls. "It was superficial at best. There are still too many restrictions." Satan's argument is that the experiment, cruel though it was, has not yielded a conclusive result because the terms on which it was carried out were not rigorous enough. His accusation is stinging. His manner of addressing the Almighty is insolent: "As long as you give him health and life he remains loyal. Let me touch his body and we'll see how long he loves You!"

Satan doesn't waste a moment's time. As Job sat in sorrow, trying to cope with his indescribable loss, the Enemy strikes with vicious cruelty (2:7-10). The extent of Satan's attack on Job is revealed not only here but elsewhere in the book. Some suggest

Job suffered from leprosy. Whatever "painful sores" or "sore boils" means, you can be certain it was agonizing. The disease covered his body (2:7) and led to intolerable itching (2:8; he was probably scraping pus from the sores). His appearance was disfigured (2:12; 19:19). He suffered from loss of appetite (3:24), depression (3:24-26; 7:16), and sleeplessness (7:4). When he did sleep he had recurring nightmares (7:14). He suffered from festering sores and broken skin (7:5), scabs that blackened and peeled (30:30), high fevers (30:30), excessive weeping and burning of the eyes (16:16), putrid-smelling breath (19:17), an emaciated body (17:7; 19:20), and chronic pain (30:17). It seems only appropriate that he would take up residence on a dung heap or ash heap where dogs scavenged for food among the corpses and refuse.

All of us join in affirming both the goodness and greatness of God. But that does not mean we are able to explain everything that our good and great God either causes or permits. Whether it is a terrorist bomb that destroys innocent human life or the swindling of the elderly or the diagnosis of cancer in a single mom, much in our world is beyond our ability to understand. Author Philip Yancey put it this way:

> Unfairness is no easier for us to swallow today than it was for Job thousands of years ago. Consider the most common curse word in the English language: "God" followed by the word "damn." People say it not only in the face of great tragedy, but also when their cars won't start, when a favored sports team loses, when it rains on their picnic. That oath renders an instinctive judgment that life ought to be fair and that God should somehow "do a better job" of running his world.[4]

Yancey then goes on to make this point:

> The reason the Book of Job seems so modern is that for us, too, the facts do not add up. Job's strident message of life's unfairness seems peculiarly suited to our own pain-racked

century. Simply plug contemporary illustrations into his arguments: . . . starving children in the Third World; faithful pastors imprisoned in South Africa; Christian leaders who die in their prime; Mafia dons and spoiled entertainers who profit obscenely from flouting God's rules; the millions in Western Europe who live quiet, happy lives and never give God a thought. Far from fading away, Job's questions about this world's unfairness have only grown louder and shriller. We still expect a God of love and power to follow certain rules on earth. Why doesn't he?[5]

It is precisely this confusion about the mystery of God's ways that gives strength to the temptation to curse God and die. This is what Job faced. In our own way, so do we.

Job's three friends insisted that God does, in point of fact, follow certain rules, and that these rules admit no exception. One rule in particular is the law of retribution and reward. If you are good, so goes the rule, you will be rewarded. But if you are bad, you will suffer retribution that is proportionate to your sins. Job's friends came to him convinced that they understood God's ways perfectly. Their confidence reminds me of a story of a man who found his little boy feverishly at work drawing a picture with his many colorful crayons. "What are you drawing, son?" " God," the little boy replied, without hesitation. "But no one knows what God looks like," said his dad. "They will when I get finished!"

Job's friends were convinced they knew the character of God better than anyone and that their interpretation of why Job was suffering was the orthodox one. On the one hand, Job was fortunate to have friends who would take the time and put out the effort to comfort him in his trials. Faithful, loyal, loving friends are hard to come by. "Many a man claims to have unfailing love, but a faithful man who can find?" (Proverbs 20:6, NIV). Job's friends were indeed faithful, loyal, and loving. But unfortunately they were handicapped by a faulty theological perspective that led them to say things that proved more painful to Job than even the boils on his body. Their viewpoint simply assumed that sin and suffering are always inexorably bound together in a cause/effect relationship. Whenever and wherever there is one, there is the other. Notwithstanding what they knew to be true about Job's character, they refused to budge. They refused to allow the possibility that on occasion, as mysterious as it might seem, a righteous man might suffer greatly.

If this advice had come from his enemies, Job might not have been so bothered by it. But the fact that it came from his friends made it especially difficult to endure (compare Psalm 55:12-14). Nothing cuts so deeply as a friend, someone on whom you thought you could rely, who throws cold water on the flickering flame of hope. When that happens we feel deflated, demotivated, and discouraged.

Most people come to the concluding five chapters of Job with great anticipation. Having endured the seemingly endless cycle of repetitive speeches, the time has finally come for God to speak. Now that Job has endured indescribable suffering, now that his three friends and Elihu have had their say, what might one expect God to say? Amazingly, all the things one might think God would say are nowhere to be found. Let's begin by noting what God does not say to Job.

First of all, there is no condemnation of Job, no reversal of the divine verdict on his character that was given in chapters 1 and 2. God does not agree with the assessment of Bildad, Zophar, Eliphaz, or Elihu. He says nothing that would lead us to believe that Job's suffering was the direct result of his sin.

Second, there are no apologies. Nowhere do we read anything like: "O my dear child, Job. I'm so very sorry for what has happened. You've endured a great many trials on My behalf and I want you to know how much I appreciate it. You've hung in there and shown yourself to be a real trooper. You've resisted the temptation to curse my name. I promise I'll do my best not to let this sort of thing happen again." As Larry Crabb put it, "Job apparently expected God would listen to what he had to say, pull slowly on His beard, and reply, 'Job, thanks for sharing your perspective on things. You've got a point. Frankly, I really hadn't seen things quite the way you see them. Look, I've made a bit of an error but I'll straighten it all out right away.'"[6] Not!

Third, there are no compliments. After all that Job had endured so that God might prove His point to the Devil, one might have expected to hear something like this: "Job, bless your heart! You have no idea how proud I am of you. It really means a lot to Me that you've persevered so valiantly. You exceeded all My expectations. We really showed that Devil, didn't we!" God says nothing to Job that one might think would be appropriate for someone who had suffered so much. There are no words of encouragement or consolation; no words of how much good his experience will accomplish in the lives of others who face tragedy and the temptation it brings. There are no words of praise for his having stood his ground when the barrage of arguments came from his three friends. There are no thank-yous for having held his tongue in check from cursing God when it seemed the reasonable thing to do.

Fourth, there are no explanations. This is perhaps the most shocking omission of all. At the very least you would expect God to lay it all out in black and white before Job. But nowhere do we find something like this: "Job, let me begin by explaining to you how this whole thing came about in the first place. You see, one day Satan came to Me and insisted that the only reason you worship me is because I treat you so well. I couldn't let him get away with that. I had to prove him wrong, and, well . . . the rest is history, as they say!"

Nor does God say, "Job, I know you've been wondering how I could permit this to occur and not be guilty of injustice and hard-hearted cruelty. Well, it's like this . . ." Nor do we find: "Job, you've struggled with why the righteous suffer and the wicked prosper. Sit down and take out pen and paper. You'll undoubtedly want to take notes. There are ten reasons why you, a righteous man, suffered so horribly and faced so many countless temptations. Number one: . . ."

Amazingly, there is no discussion of the problem of evil, of divine justice, of human sin, or of any such thing. In fact, God supplies no answers at all to any of the questions raised by Job or Eliphaz or Bildad or Zophar or Elihu, or by you and me! Instead, it is God who asks the questions! It isn't God who appears on the witness stand to undergo cross-examination in order to make sense of what has occurred. It is Job, of all people, who is cross-examined. More than seventy times God asks Job an unanswerable question.

For thirty-five chapters Job has been crying out, "God, put Yourself in my place for a while!" God now responds and says, "No, Job, you put yourself in My place! Until you can offer lessons on how to make the sun rise each day or give commands to the lightning or design a peacock, don't pass judgement on how I run My world." In other words, God says, "Until you know a little more about running the physical universe, don't tell Me how to run the moral universe. How do you expect to understand the complexities of My dealings with mankind when you can't even understand the simplicity of My dealings with nature?"

Instead of dealing with the complexities of temptation and human tragedy, God loudly asserts His absolute sovereignty over all of creation. He knows and controls every square inch of the universe, whether animate or inanimate. No snowflake or drop of rain escapes His providence. Every force of nature and every living thing within it are subject to His purposes. Such being the case with God's relation to nature, it stands to reason that He cares even more for those created in His image. It now seems ludicrous that a mere creature like Job would demand explanations from God. If Job cannot comprehend or control creation, what makes him think he can comprehend God's control of mankind?

Why, then, does God often decline to provide us with answers about His dealings with us, our sufferings, and the temptations that arise from them? I'm not sure, but Yancey suggests that God may keep us ignorant "because enlightenment might not help us."[7] We ask "Why? why?" on the assumption that if we had a reasonable explanation we could handle it better, be less bitter, and respond more humbly and submissively. But would we? Perhaps God keeps us ignorant because we are incapable of comprehending the answer.

Furthermore, as Yancey notes, "Maybe God's majestic nonanswer to Job was no ploy, no clever way of dodging questions; maybe it was God's recognition of a plain fact of life. A tiny creature on a tiny planet in a remote galaxy simply could not fathom the grand design of the universe. You might as well try to describe colors to a person born blind, or a Mozart symphony to a person born deaf, or expound the theory of relativity to a person who doesn't even know about atoms."[8]

It would be like trying to pour the ocean into a thimble! God has told us: "For as the heavens are higher than the earth, so are . . . my thoughts (higher) than your thoughts" (Isaiah 55:9). And again, "as you do not know the path of the wind, or how the body is formed in a mother's womb, so you cannot understand the work of God, the Maker of all things" (Ecclesiastes 11:5, NIV).

Perhaps God keeps us ignorant because ignorance is the most fertile soil in which faith can grow. In other words, ignorance in the midst of temptation compels us to do one of two things: either abandon God altogether, or trust Him all the more fervently.

In one sense, God did answer Job's questions. If God is truly such a majestic and sovereign being who rules every molecule with magnificent precision and purpose, then what He has done or allowed in the case of Job must make perfect sense. Also, it is important to remember that there is something more important than knowing why God does what He does, namely, learning to cling to Him in faith when everything else threatens to destroy your soul.

The cynical among us might argue that in the end, when all was said and done, it was easy for Job to resist temptation and to bow faithfully beneath God's sovereign purposes. After all, God restored everything he lost, and then some (see Job 42:10-17). "No wonder he kept his mouth shut. Look at what it got him!" But these people, says Yancey, overlook one important point: "Job spoke his contrite words [40:3-5] before any of his losses had been restored. He was still sitting in a pile of rubble, naked, covered with sores, and it was in those circumstances that he learned to praise God. Only one thing had changed: God had given Job a glimpse of the big picture. I have a hunch that God could have said anything—could, in fact, have read from the Yellow Pages—and produced the same stunning effect on Job. What He said was not nearly so important as the mere fact of His appearance. God spectacularly answered Job's biggest question: Is anybody out there? Once Job caught sight of the unseen world, all his urgent questions faded away."[9]

Job's case was both unusual and exceptional. But that in no way detracts from what it tells us about Satan's tactics. He is as relentless as he is sadistic in hitting below the belt, in kicking his victim while he's down. We, too, will be sorely tempted in times of physical distress to curse God and die. Job wavered, but he didn't break. God help us!

Yet another tactic Satan employs is to tempt us immediately following both spiritual highs and spiritual lows. Periods of emotional elation and physical prosperity can sometimes lead to complacency, pride, and a false sense of security. When they do, we're easy targets for the Enemy's arrows. The same thing happens during the doldrums when we find ourselves wondering if God even cares. We become bitter and despondent and sin suddenly seems the reasonable thing to do.

Perhaps Satan's most effective tactic in tempting us is to put his thoughts into our minds and then blame us for having them. As William Gurnall commented:

> When thoughts or inclinations contrary to the will and
> ways of God creep in, many dear Christians mistake these
> miserable orphans for their own children, and take upon
> themselves the full responsibility for these carnal passions.
> So deftly does the Devil slip his own thoughts into the
> saints' bosom that by the time they begin to whimper, he is
> already out of sight. And the Christian, seeing no one but
> himself at home, supposes these misbegotten notions are
> his own. So he bears the shame himself, and Satan has
> accomplished his purpose.[10]

The title "Devil" (*diabolos*) is used thirty-five times in the Bible. It literally means "slanderer" or "accuser." In Luke 4:2,13 and Revelation 12:9,12 it is the Devil's aim to defame. He is a constant source of false and malicious reports. Sometimes he slanders and utters lies to God about you (Revelation 12:10), bent on disrupting your relationship with the Father. But to no avail, thanks to the incessant intercession of Jesus on your behalf (1 John 2:2; Romans 8:33-39).

When lying to God about you doesn't work, he lies to you about God. He does everything in his power to convince you that God isn't good, that He can't be trusted, that He's holding out on you, that He won't be there when you need Him most (Genesis 3; Matthew 4). And if that weren't enough, he lies to you about yourself (Ephesians 6:16), seducing you into believing you aren't what God says you are and that you will never be what God has promised you'll be.

A related tactic of temptation is for him to launch his accusations as if they were from the Holy Spirit. In other words, he couches his terms and chooses his opportunities in such a way that we might easily mistake his voice for that of God. So how do we distinguish between satanic accusation and divine conviction? Among other things, the former comes in the shape of condemnation that breeds feelings of hopelessness. We are told that our sin has put us beyond the hope of grace and the power of forgiveness. Satan's accusations are devoid of any reference to the sufficiency of the cross. Divine conviction for sin, on the other hand, comes with a reminder of the sufficiency and finality of Christ's shed blood, together with a promise of hope and the joy of forgiveness.

FOUR TACTICS FOR RESISTING TEMPTATION

There are numerous ways to prepare ourselves for demonic enticement, but I want to focus on four in particular.

1. *The first and perhaps most important tactic for facing temptation is to embrace and pursue the central truth of*

this book. Satan's "fiery darts" do not easily penetrate a mind whose only thought is "Oh!" When our hearts beat with perpetual fascination and our thoughts are filled with the beauty and splendor and adequacy of God, little room is left for the Devil to gain a foothold (see Philippians 4:8).

When I received a desperate phone call from a friend whose sister was taking steps to abandon her family, my advice took the following form.

"Jerry, your sister has to have a powerful reason to stay with her family. Right now, she doesn't believe she has one. She has rationalized her decision in such a way that she can live with her conscience. The impact of this decision on her kids, on her reputation, as well as her sense of moral obligation, are not sufficiently persuasive to override her hunger for adventure. Perhaps she's convinced herself that the impact will not be all that bad. Perhaps out of self-pity she's come to the point where she doesn't care. Not that she doesn't care for her kids, but when compared with her own needs and the demand she feels in her heart for fulfillment, everyone and everything else runs a distant second. I don't think she'd ever admit that. All that matters or makes sense to her right now is the hunger in her heart to experience something that neither her husband nor kids nor any amount of "religious activity" (which is how she thinks of Christianity) can give her. She's right! They can't give it to her. She's ignorant of the joy, peace, affirmation, and forgiveness that the child of God is offered. She probably has no idea what you mean when you speak of the pleasures of intimacy with Jesus. But you need to describe it for her in a way that sounds like an invitation, not a condemnation.

"That's really what her hunger is for. She just doesn't know it yet. God put in her a taste and thirst and passion for the most exquisite food and sweet wine imaginable and she's determined to settle for day-old hamburger, cold french fries, and soda with no fizz. It will taste okay. Pretty much anything other than her current life routines will taste okay. Therein lies the real danger for her. She's susceptible, in a way she doesn't feel or recognize, to pretty much any low-grade temptation that makes even the slightest promise of excitement. When you're hungry like she is, virtually anything will seem like it's what you've wanted and not been given. More than that, it will feel like it's what you deserve (that's where the self-pity fits in). She desperately needs to hear and see what you've tasted in Jesus.

"It's not that she believes God is against her. But her concept of God right now is of someone whose primary task is to demand that she do hard, unrewarding, sacrificial things simply because 'it's the right thing to do,' things that until now in her life she's been doing and finding tasteless and joyless and tedious and boring and unfulfilling. I encourage you to 'tap into her hunger.' She probably expects you to condemn or reject her or get mad at her for 'wanting.' Don't. Affirm her desires and point her in the direction of limitless refreshment and satisfaction. Point her in the direction of Him whose love for her can transform those boring and lifeless daily routines into real joy. Let the aroma of the sweet-smelling fragrance of the knowledge and love of Jesus pass under her nose. Then pray that she'll catch a 'whiff' of it and change directions."

2. ***Know yourself.*** Ask the question often: "If I were the Devil, where would I attack me?" In other words, be quick to identify your weaknesses, your vulnerable spots, areas where you've failed before, and take extraordinary steps to protect yourself in the future.

If you are susceptible to the effects of alcohol, don't toy with a casual drink. If your fantasies are easily fueled by visual images, stay away from R-rated movies.

3. ***Deal radically with sin.*** In the words of Jesus, "if your right eye makes you stumble, tear it out, and throw it from you; for it is better for you that one of the parts of your body perish, than for your whole body to be thrown into hell" (Matthew 5:29). In the next verse (30) He makes the same point about one's right hand. It's one thing to say we need to deal radically with sin, but is Jesus recommending self-mutilation as the answer? A closer look at the context will lead us to what Jesus really meant.

Jesus was primarily concerned with those who thought their moral obligation was only skin-deep. Take murder, for example. As long as they refrained from literally spilling blood, these believed they had behaved righteously. They ignored the anger and malicious hatred of the heart, which are the source of murderous deeds. The same was true of adultery. Lust was irrelevant. It was a matter of the heart over which the court of Moses had no juris-diction. Again, so long as the sexual act was avoided, the sexual attitude was irrelevant. But Jesus says otherwise. In Matthew 5:21-26 He pointed out that the prohibition of murder includes the angry thought and the insulting word. Now in 5:27-30 He extends this principle to adultery: not just the physical act but the lustful look and the covetous heart must be curbed.

His point is that we must deal drastically with sin. Donald Carson states the case bluntly: "We must not pamper it, flirt with it, enjoy nibbling a little of it around the edges. We are to hate it, crush it, dig it out."[11] In the case of adulterous lust, if your eye leads you astray, "tear it out." That He does not mean literal mutilation is evident from a simple illustration.

Consider John and his relationship with Mary, his administrative assistant. John has always been stirred by Mary's beauty, but recently his gaze has turned to lust. There is no sin in merely looking. In fact, to acknowledge and compliment natural beauty is good. But looking to lust, looking to fantasize an affair, looking to mentally gratify a sexual urge is another thing altogether.

Taking Jesus' words literally, John proceeds to cut out his right eye. Thinking that the problem is solved, he returns to work after a period of rehabilitation only to find that now his left eye has lusted as well! So he cuts it out too. He now comes to work with a seeing-eye dog. He's not as efficient at his job, but he's convinced that he's been obedient to Christ and is beyond lusting after Mary. But then he hears her voice and illicit desire rages yet again in his heart. So he lops off both his ears! He again returns to work, not a pretty sight, to say the least. Confident that it won't happen again, he walks by her desk . . . and smells her perfume! Lust rages once more. So he cuts off his nose. Not even that solves his problem, for as he gropes through the office in his self-inflicted blindness, his hands accidentally brush up against Mary's body and his flesh is stirred yet again. So he (somehow?) cuts off his hands. It is only then that John realizes he still has a mind and Mary's memory lingers vividly.

I know it's a silly story. But it makes the point. The problem is not with our body parts or our physical senses. The problem is with a corrupt and deceitful heart. Our external members are but the instruments we employ to gratify the lust that emerges from within. What our Lord was advocating, claims John R. W. Stott, "was not a literal physical self-maiming, but a ruthless moral self-denial. Not mutilation but mortification is the path of holiness he taught."[12]

How, then, are we to respond to the sexually seductive and stimulating things we encounter in the world, in the media, at work? We are to act "as if" we were blind. Says Stott:

[B]ehave as if you had actually plucked out your eyes and flung them away, and were now blind and so could not see the objects which previously caused you to sin. Again, if your hand or foot causes you to sin, because temptation comes to you through your hands (things you do) or your feet (places you visit), then cut them off. That is: Don't do it! Don't go! Behave as if you had actually cut off your hands and feet, and had flung them away, and were now crippled and so could not do the things or visit the places which previously caused you to sin.[13]

And as you do so, fix your mind on things above. Focus your heart on the promise of a superior pleasure in Christ. Ponder the joy of that river of delights that never runs dry.

4. ***Confront and conquer temptation at the beginning, not at the end.*** In other words, the best and most effective tactic against temptation is to deal with it from a position of strength, before it has an opportunity to weaken you. Better to take steps up front to eliminate temptation altogether (if possible), than to deal with it later when your defenses are down.

I've found this principle to be especially helpful when I'm on the road. In the past few years my ministry has made it necessary that I travel extensively. I'm no different from any other man, whether a pastor or lawyer or salesman or computer technician. I know what it is like to walk into a lonely hotel room, alone, away from home, devoid of the normal domestic restraints that I so easily take for granted.

So I made a deal with myself. Before I ever walk into a hotel room I insist that the desk clerk black out all adult movies that might otherwise be available on a pay-per-view basis. Why do it before I check in? Because I'm a man of flesh, just like you. It's incomparably easier to say No before I'm in a position to say Yes. Once I'm in that room and the only thing that stands between me and sin is the touch of a dial, my defenses weaken. My resolve to say

No isn't nearly as strong as it was fifteen minutes earlier. My inclination to rationalize purchasing an inappropriate movie intensifies with each passing moment. If I am to defeat temptation I must do everything I can to eliminate it before it launches its assault. I need to defuse its power when I'm in a position to do so instead of arrogantly assuming that if I feel strong now, I'll feel just as strong later.

Make no mistake. There is a Tempter whose sole design is to lure you into the embrace of fleeting pleasures and transient sins. His voice is soothing. His promises sound reasonable. But in the end it is death. It is only with Jesus that you can walk "the pathway of life" (Psalm 16:11). It is only in His presence that "fullness of joy" and "pleasures evermore" may be found. According to Edwards:

> The pleasures of loving and obeying, loving and adoring, blessing and praising the Infinite Being, the Best of Beings, the Eternal Jehovah; the pleasures of trusting in Jesus Christ, in contemplating His beauties, excellencies, and glories; in contemplating His love to mankind and to us, in contemplating His infinite goodness and astonishing loving-kindness; the pleasures of the communion of the Holy Ghost in conversing with God, the maker and governor of the world; the pleasure that results from the doing of our duty, in acting worthily and excellently. These, these are the pleasures that are worthy of so noble a creature as man is.[14]

To what is it, then, that you are invited when you are invited to resist temptation? Edwards says, "You are invited to the excellent and noble satisfactions of religion; you are invited to such a happiness as is the happiness of angels, and happiness that will be able to satisfy your desires. Be persuaded, then, to taste and see how good it is; keep no longer groveling in the dirt and feeding on husks with hogs."[15]

CHAPTER THIRTEEN

GRACE THAT IS GREATER THAN ALL OUR SIN

HOLY! INEFFABLY BEAUTIFUL! UNFATHOMABLY GLORIOUS! TRIUNE! Eternal! Omniscient! Omnipresent! Omnipotent! Immutable! What splendor! What majesty! Oh!

The God of whom these things are true is indeed a great and awesome Being. Who is like unto the Lord and with whom may we compare Him? Is there another whose knowledge and power are without limit, whose life is everlasting, whose will and ways do not change, and for whom the boundaries of the universe offer no barrier? Indeed, this God is a great God!

But to say of God that He is great is not enough. What if this awesomely great God were immoral or capricious or indifferent to the suffering of His creation? No, we must proceed further in our description of God; we must proceed from His greatness to His goodness. This God whose power and presence are illimitable, whose wisdom and will are incomparable, is a God no less abounding in love and longsuffering, mercy and grace.

But it is more than God's goodness in general that I have in mind. It is the goodness of God as seen in the lavish display of His grace toward hell-deserving sinners. Even then it is not God's grace in general, great and marvelous though it be, but the grace of God that energizes our obedience and sustains our love that requires our attention.

A book on holiness without a chapter on grace is like sitting in a new car whose fuel gauge registers "E." You might draw some degree of pleasure from the carefully crafted upholstery or the sleek lines of the car's design. Perhaps you got a great deal, below factory invoice. It might even be your favorite color. But you're going nowhere. The point is that nothing I've said till now means anything apart from the fuel of God's favor (grace) that alone energizes the human heart to say No to sin.

GRACE GAFFES

Few things are as baffling to me as the degree to which professing Christians misconceive the nature of divine grace. Contrary to the thinking of many, even within the church, grace does not contemplate sinners merely as undeserving, but as ill-deserving. So often we are inclined to think of ourselves prior to our salvation as in some sense "neutral" in the sight of God. We are willing to admit that we have done nothing to deserve His favor. Our works, regardless of their character, are unacceptable in His glorious presence. But this is entirely insufficient as a background to the understanding of divine grace. It is not simply that we do not deserve grace: we do deserve hell! Fallen and unredeemed humanity is not to be conceived as merely helpless, but as openly and vehemently hostile toward God. It is one thing to be without a God-approved righteousness. It is altogether another thing to be wholly unrighteous and thus the object of divine wrath. It is, then, against the background of having been at one time the enemies of God that divine grace is to be portrayed (Romans 5:10).

Another, no less grievous, misconception about grace is the idea that it is always unconditional. Whereas grace is certainly free, it isn't always unconditional. The grace of election is unconditional (Romans 9:11). But many of God's acts and blessings are conditional. Look, for example, at these few texts:

Grace be with all those who love our Lord Jesus Christ
with a love incorruptible. (Ephesians 6:24)

[God] gives a greater grace. . . . God is opposed to the
proud, but gives grace to the humble. (James 4:6; compare
1 Peter 5:5)

The LORD your God is gracious and compassionate, and
will not turn His face away from you if you return to Him.
(2 Chronicles 30:9)

He will surely be gracious to you at the sound of your cry;
when He hears it, He will answer you. (Isaiah 30:19)

Let Thy lovingkindness [grace], O LORD, be upon us,
according as we have hoped in Thee. (Psalm 33:22)

The lovingkindness [grace] of the LORD is from everlasting to everlasting . . . to those who keep His covenant.
(Psalm 103:17-18)

The way not to become confused by this is by remembering that
conditional grace is not earned grace. Why? Because, as Piper tells
us, "when God's grace is promised based on a condition, that condition is also a work of God's grace. . . . God's freedom is not reduced
when he makes some of his graces depend on conditions that he himself freely supplies."[1] In other words, says Piper, conditional grace
is "free and unmerited because ultimately the condition of faith is
a gift of grace. God graciously enables the conditions that he
requires."[2] Or again, "this covenant-keeping condition of future grace
does not mean we lose security or assurance, for God has pledged
himself to complete the work he began in the elect (Philippians 1:6).
He is at work within us to will and to do his good pleasure
(Philippians 2:12-13). He works in us what is pleasing in his sight

(Hebrews 13:21). He fulfills the conditions of the covenant through us (Ezekiel 36:27). Our security is as secure as God is faithful."[3]

TRIUMPHANT GRACE

One of the more amazing things about grace is the unexpected places in Scripture where it may be found. Without really looking for it, I found grace in the genealogy of Jesus. You read it right. The genealogy of Jesus in Matthew 1 contains one of the most stunning portrayals of divine grace you'll ever hope to see.

The identity and mission of Jesus are incomprehensible apart from an understanding of His roots in the Old Testament. Jesus did not appear in a historical vacuum. He entered history not merely as a man, but as a Jewish man who brings the Old Testament to its proper consummation. As Christopher Wright has said, "Jesus is . . . 'the end of the line,' as far as the Old Testament story goes. It has run its completed course in preparation for Him, and now its goal or climax has been reached."[4]

Why does Matthew begin with a genealogy? It strikes the modern reader as odd, even boring. But in ancient Jewish society genealogies were an essential way of establishing one's right to belong to the community of God's people (compare 1 Chronicles 1–9; Ezra 2, 8). Wright explains:

> [In those days] your ancestry was your identity and your
> status. Jesus, then, was not just "a man." He was a particular
> person born within a living culture. His background, ancestry
> and roots, were shaped and influenced, as all his contempo-
> raries were, by the history and fortunes of his people.[5]

Also, Matthew is especially determined to demonstrate that Jesus is the Messiah. He is the rightful, legal descendant of the royal line of King David, heir to the promises made to the fathers.

You've probably never done this before, but open your Bible

to Matthew 1 and read through the list of names (if you can pronounce them!) in the genealogy of Jesus. This revelation of grace
I mentioned above is found in four people whose names you will
see. I'm talking about Tamar (verse 3), Rahab (verse 5), Ruth (verse
5), and Bathsheba (verse 6). If Matthew had ransacked the Old
Testament for improbable candidates he could not have discovered
four more unlikely ancestors for Jesus. No Jewish family would
ever have used the stories of Tamar or Rahab or Bathsheba as role
models for their children. No self-respecting Jewish mom or dad
would ever have put their children to bed with stories about these
women (perhaps Ruth being the exception).

In the ancient world women were rarely if ever mentioned in
a genealogical record. They had no legal rights and were consigned
to a low social status. Worse still, all four of these women were
foreigners or nonJews. Tamar was a Canaanite, Rahab a native of
Jericho, Ruth a Moabite, and Bathsheba, although the daughter of
an Israelite, was considered a Hittite because of her marriage to
Uriah. Most genealogies were constructed to demonstrate precisely
that a person's line had been kept free from contamination by Gentile
blood. Yet the genealogy of Jesus is intersected again and again by
Gentiles. This Jew had Gentile blood! King David's great-great-great-
grandmother (Tamar) was a Canaanite. King David's great-great
grandmother (Rahab) was a native of Jericho. King David's great-
grandmother (Ruth) was a Moabite. And he had a Hittite wife!

Surely, though, the most remarkable fact of all is that each of
these four women was either sexually immoral or the product of
sexual immorality. Rahab (Joshua 2,5) was a prostitute and
Bathsheba an adulteress. It would appear that Matthew blushes even
to pronounce Bathsheba's name, referring to her simply as the one
"who had been the wife of Uriah" (verse 6). Although not herself
personally immoral, Ruth was a Moabite, the descendants of the
incestuous relationship between Lot and his first-born daughter
(Genesis 19:30-37; Deuteronomy 23:3; according to the latter verse,
Moabites were forever excluded from the assembly of the Lord).

DON'T BLINK, IT'S IN YOUR BIBLE!

And then there is Tamar (Genesis 38). You may not be familiar with her name, but nothing you've ever read in a grocery-store tabloid or seen on a TV soap opera can compare with the sordid story of this lady. (By the way, that is not a recommendation that you read a grocery-store tabloid or watch a TV soap opera.)

Contrary to official policy in Israel at that time, Judah, one of the twelve sons of Jacob, became infatuated with a Canaanite woman named Shua. As we're about to see, Judah wasn't one to deny himself a pleasure simply for the sake of tradition! Shua became pregnant and gave birth to a son named Er. Two more sons were soon in coming, Onan and Shelah. Wanting to prove himself a good father, Judah arranged for his first-born son, Er, to be married to a young lady, our young lady, Tamar.

Unfortunately for Tamar, Er was, to put it mildly, a jerk. So much of a jerk that God killed him. Moses put it even more bluntly: "Er, Judah's first-born, was evil in the sight of the LORD, so the LORD took his life" (Genesis 38:7). You might be interested to know that in Hebrew, Er spelled backward is evil. What did he do? How did Er err? (Sorry!) Whatever it was it must have been serious, for his execution was swift and just.

Judah then orders Onan, his second-born son and Er's younger brother, to have sex with Tamar. I know what you're thinking, but in the Old Testament the so-called "law of levirate marriage" dictated that if your brother died you were responsible for raising up children with his widow in his name. The problem is that Onan was about as evil as Er. Of course, he was only too happy to gratify his sexual desires with Tamar ("what a great law!" he no doubt said). But he had absolutely no intention of shouldering the responsibility that would come with another child. With Er dead, Onan stood to inherit everything. The last thing he wanted was a son of Er to take it from him. "So it came about that when he [Onan] went in to his brother's wife [that is, had sexual relations with Tamar], he wasted his seed on the ground, in order not to give offspring to his brother" (Genesis 38:9). I want to point out in passing that Onan's sin wasn't sexual perversion or the use of birth control (coitus interruptus). What angered God was Onan's greed and selfishness in refusing to fulfill his legal obligation to his brother's name. So God killed Onan too.

Poor Tamar is caught in the middle. Judah tells her to remain unmarried until Shelah, the last of his sons, is old enough to step in as her husband and do what Onan refused to do. What Tamar didn't know is that Judah had no intention of letting Shelah get anywhere near Tamar. Judah must have thought to himself, "This woman is cursed. Two men in bed with her. Two corpses. I don't want to lose the only son I've got left!"

In the meantime, Judah's wife died. One can't help but feel sorry for the man. He lost two sons and a wife in a short span of time. After the official period of mourning was over, Judah and his friend Hirah decided to take a trip to Timnah. Perhaps it was Hirah's idea, thinking that a change of scenery might cheer up Judah.

By this time, Tamar was growing impatient. It began to dawn on her: "Shelah's a grown man by now, but Judah has no intention of letting him come within a stone's throw of me. It's obvious I'm going to have to take matters into my own hands." When Tamar found out that Judah was going to Timnah, she put her sordid little plan into action. She figured the best way to get "justice" was to exploit this widower's loneliness and weakness. So she dressed up as a prostitute, covering her face with a veil, and took to the streets.

Judah took the bait. Not knowing it was his daughter-in-law, he began haggling with her over the price for her services.

"I'll send you a goat from my flock," said Judah.

"What kind of an idiot do you think I am? I may be immoral," said Tamar, "but I'm not stupid! You're going to have give me something as a pledge that you'll come through on your offer. If you'll leave me your seal and cord and the staff in your hand, I'll do it."[6]

"Okay."

So Judah had sex with his daughter-in-law. If it weren't for the fact that this story is in your Bible, I certainly wouldn't be telling it here.

"Hirah," said Judah, "can you keep a secret? I need your help." Judah told him what happened and asked if he'd take the goat to the harlot in exchange for his seal, cord, and staff. Although Judah had sinned, at least he kept his word. Then again, maybe Judah was just afraid she might one day show up on his doorstep demanding payment. Whatever the case, he sends Hirah off to do his dirty work.

But the "prostitute" was nowhere to be found. "Thanks anyway," said Judah. "I think I'll just let her keep my stuff. After all, at least I did the honorable thing and tried to keep my end of the bargain. It's not my fault she ran away."

Three months later Judah gets news that Tamar is pregnant. "She's been selling her body," they said. "Tamar is a harlot."

"Bring her out and let her be burned," shouted Judah in all the self-righteous indignation he could muster. "We're not going to have that kind of immorality in my family!"

That's when Tamar played her trump card. "Yes, I'm pregnant. But I know who the father is. It's the man to whom this seal and cord and staff belong." The Bible doesn't tell us about the look on Judah's face when he saw his possessions. Was it shock? Shame? Fear? Humiliation? Remorse? All of the above? Whatever the case, he came clean. "I'm the one," he confessed. "Tamar is more righteous than I am. None of this would ever have happened if I'd only honored both the law and Tamar by giving my son Shelah to her."

That's the sordid part of this story. Now for the stunning conclusion. Tamar gave birth to twin boys, whom she named Perez and Zerah. Sound familiar? They should. Remember the genealogy of Jesus in Matthew 1. Look again at verses 2-3: "To Abraham was born Isaac; and to Isaac, Jacob; and to Jacob, Judah and his brothers; and to Judah were born Perez and Zerah by Tamar. . . ."

Stop for a moment while you catch your breath. Yes, Jesus, according to His human nature, is the direct descendant of this ugly, perverted sexual encounter between a man and his daughter-in-law.

THE GLORIES OF GRACE

Before I go any further, nothing that I am about to say should be taken as minimizing the horror of their transgression. The behavior of Judah and Tamar was sordid and sinful and nothing that I'm about to say is meant to diminish the insidious nature of their evil or in any way to suggest that it is okay for us to engage in similar behavior. In Romans, the apostle Paul faced the same problem I'm facing now: "where sin increased, grace abounded all the more" (5:20). "WHAT shall we say then? Are we to continue in sin that grace might increase? May it never be! . . ." (6:1-2).

Having said that, the lessons from this about the nature of divine grace are almost too good to be true. In the first place, this genealogy reveals the gracious yet mysterious work of divine providence, that is, God's control over history. He uses the righteous and the wicked to accomplish His purpose: wicked Rehoboam was the father of wicked Abijah, who was the father of the good king Asa (Matthew 1:7). Asa was the father of the good king Jehoshaphat, who was the progenitor of the wicked king Joram (Matthew 1:8). "Good or evil," observes D. A. Carson, "they were part of Messiah's line; for though grace does not run in the blood, God's providence cannot be deceived or outmaneuvered."[7]

Second, by including Tamar and the other women in this genealogy Matthew is telling us that in Jesus the barriers between male and female are torn down (Galatians 3:28). Men and women stand equally before God. It is also his way of telling us that in Jesus the barriers between Jew and Gentile are torn down. In Jesus there is neither Jew nor Gentile.

A third point to note is that Jesus was a willing descendant of human shame! "He was not ashamed to call us brothers," wrote the author of Hebrews (2:11). Contrast Herod the Great, reigning king at Jesus' birth, who had his genealogical records destroyed out of vanity because he wanted no one to compare his background with that of others. The point is that Jesus came not only to sinners, but through sinners. He came not only for sinners, but from sinners! Bruner reminds us:

> The four model matriarchs of Jewish history were Sarah, Rebekah, Rachel, and Leah, the wives, respectively, of Abraham, Isaac, and Jacob. These four women are conspicuous by their absence here. Their husbands are all here, and so there was opportunity for Matthew to include the good wives. But Matthew gives the church four new matriarchs, and all of them preach the gospel of the deep and wide mercy of God.[8]

Martin Luther said that "it is as though God intended for the reader of this genealogy to say, 'Oh, Christ is the kind of person who is not ashamed of sinners—in fact, He even puts them in His family tree!'"[9]

By including these notoriously sinful women, Matthew is preaching the gospel of grace in a genealogy! The point is that God can overcome any and all sin and can use the most soiled of human souls to accomplish His greatest purposes in history. This is a story about the triumph of divine grace over human sin. Human sin is no obstacle to God's ultimate purpose in redemptive history nor to His very personal purpose in your life. His mercy is deep enough, and His love high enough, and His grace powerful enough to forgive any and every sin and enable us to happily embrace His will.

We look at what Judah and Tamar did and gasp in disdainful unbelief. Our reaction is to forever write them off as useless to God and the situation as hopeless. God looks at Judah and Tamar and says: "Hey, as bad as that is, I think I can redeem this situation. I think I can take this moral carnage and overrule it for their redemption and My glory!"

This story is about the triumphant power of grace in God's purpose for human history: God's grace is powerful enough to take a sinfully sordid and pernicious incident and from it orchestrate history so that the Redeemer from sinfully sordid behavior comes forth from it!

But we must now individualize and personalize the principle. Don't believe the lie that your sin is greater in its power to produce evil (chaos, confusion, destruction) than is God's grace in its power to produce good (purpose, clarity, edification). Nothing is irredeemable, irretrievable, irreparable when God is present. Some who will read this book are convinced they've failed once too often and are beyond the pale of forgiveness. All this talk of holiness is but a distant dream, indeed a nightmare, given their record of failure. They feel like hopeless hypocrites. No! Don't believe the lie that your sin forever disqualifies you from usefulness to God and His kingdom. May I remind you that Rahab was a prostitute for years, yet was redeemed, cleansed, forgiven, and inducted into God's "Hall of Faith" in Hebrews 11:31!

Try to envision the sense of shame and reproach Judah and Tamar must have felt as well as their public humiliation. But I think God would say: "Fear not, for I will turn your shame into praise, I will replace beauty for ashes, and bring forth the Redeemer of all sin, even your sin, from what you've done." The hymnwriter was right: God's grace is truly "greater than all our sin!"

GRACE AS POWER

Now I want to tie all this in with our call to holiness. I begin by noting that grace is more than an attitude or disposition in the divine nature. It is surely that, but an examination of the usage of this word in Scripture reveals that grace, if thought of only as an abstract and static principle, is deprived of its deeper implications.

The grace of God, for example, is the power of God's Spirit converting the soul. It is the activity or movement of God whereby He saves and justifies the individual through faith (see especially Romans 3:24; 5:15,17). Therefore, grace is not something in which we merely believe; it is something we experience as well.

Grace, however, is not only the divine act by which God initiates our spiritual life, but also the very power by which we are sustained, nourished, and proceed through that life. The energizing and sanctifying work of the indwelling Spirit is the grace of God. After Paul had prayed three times for God to deliver him from his thorn in the flesh, he received this answer: "My grace is sufficient for you, for power is made perfect in weakness" (2 Corinthians 12:9). Although Paul undoubtedly derived encouragement and strength to face his daily trials by reflecting on the magnificence of God's unmerited favor, in this text he appears to speak instead of an experiential reality of a more dynamic nature. It is the operative power of the indwelling Spirit to which Paul refers. That is the grace of God.

We should also consider in this regard the many references to the grace of God in Paul's opening greetings and concluding benedictions (Romans 1:7; 1 Corinthians 1:3; 2 Corinthians 1:2; Galatians 1:3; Ephesians 1:2; Philippians 1:2; Colossians 1:2; 1 Thessalonians 1:1; 2 Thessalonians 1:2; Titus 1:4; 2 Corinthians 13:14). This is no mere literary formality, but an earnest and constant wish of Paul that his converts may continue to experience grace, that they may know afresh the gracious power of God moving in their lives, that they may find in that grace the spiritual resources by which to live in a way pleasing to Him.

It is interesting to observe that without exception the blessing at the beginning of each of Paul's letters says, "Grace [be] *to* you," while the blessing at the end of each letter says, "Grace [be] *with* you." Why? Piper suggests that "at the beginning of his letters Paul has in mind that the letter is a channel of God's grace *to* the readers. Grace is about to flow 'from God' through Paul's writing *to* the Christians. So he says, 'Grace *to* you.'"[10] But what becomes of this grace after his readers are done with his letter? The answer is that grace is now to be *with* you. Or, as Piper says,

With you as you put the letter away and leave the church. *With* you as you go home to deal with a sick child and an unaffectionate spouse. *With* you as you go to work and face the temptations of anger and dishonesty and lust. *With* you as you muster courage to speak up for Christ over lunch.[11]

Thus we learn that "grace is ready to flow *to* us every time we take up the inspired Scriptures to read them. And we learn that grace will abide *with* us when we lay the Bible down and go about our daily living."[12]

Besides this usage of the word with which everyone is familiar, grace can also denote the particular acts of God whereby He grants enablement for some service or authorization for a specific duty or mission (Romans 12:3; 15:15-18; 1 Corinthians 3:10). It is not without significance that the word "grace" and its derivatives are used in the description of what we call "spiritual gifts." We read in Romans 12:6, NIV: "We have different gifts [*charismata*], according to the grace [*charin*] given us."

Getting Grace

All well and good, you say, but how do I get grace? Without wanting to sound simplistic, ask for it! The man who wrote the epistle to the Hebrews put it this way:

> Since then we have a great high priest who has passed through the heavens, Jesus the Son of God, let us hold fast our confession. For we do not have a high priest who cannot sympathize with our weaknesses, but one who has been tempted in all things as we are, yet without sin. Let us therefore draw near with confidence to the throne of grace, that we may receive mercy and may find grace to help in time of need. (4:14-16)

Three questions are answered in verse 16: where? how? what?

WHERE SHALL WE GO?

First of all, where are we to go? How many times have you cried out in desperation, "I just don't know where to turn! I don't know whom to trust! I don't have any place left to go! Where can I find the grace I need?" Here we are told: "Draw near to the throne of grace."

What comes to mind when you envision a throne? A king? A sovereign ruler? Yes, God is the great monarch of the universe, the eternal potentate, premier, and president of the cosmos all wrapped up in one. Knowing this ought to create expectancy in our hearts. As the hymnwriter put it, "Thou art coming to a king, Large petitions with thee bring!" The point is, we are not coming to a cosmic welfare agency for a meager handout or to the back door for scraps off someone's dinner plate. When we need grace for our souls we are coming to the throne of the King of kings! "In prayer," said Spurgeon, "we stand where angels bow with veiled faces; there, even there, the cherubim and seraphim adore, before that selfsame throne to which our prayers ascend."[13]

Some people, on the other hand, are more intimidated than encouraged by the idea of a throne. The regal atmosphere, the power and dignity associated with one who sits on a throne, might put hesitation in more than a few hearts — that is, until we see that this is a throne of grace. Our author could have said the throne "of God" or the throne "of heaven." Make no mistake. It is certainly a throne to which we come. But it is grace that awaits us there, the same grace that we found in the genealogy of Jesus. It is grace that sits enthroned. It is not a throne of law or of criticism or of judgment but of grace. This throne exists to dispense grace to those who seek it out. Its purposes are gracious. The utterances spoken there are gracious. The answers to prayer received there are all of grace.

This being a throne of grace means that our prayers will always be heard. Though they often seem empty and frivolous to us, perhaps poorly constructed and poorly conceived, even badly spoken, God hears us. If this were a throne of justice or a throne of grammatical precision, we might have reason to worry, but it is a throne of grace! God doesn't care much for stately etiquette or courtly manners or palacial proprieties as earthly rulers do. The latter are quick to judge for one social faux pas. God only looks for humility and desperation in those who would petition Him. So come. Ask Him for grace to love Him, to obey Him, to enjoy Him. Come falteringly, come failingly, but by all means come frequently.

What if the believer is unable to put words to his wants? Because this is a gracious throne God will read your desires without the words. Spurgeon explains that "[a] throne that was not gracious would not trouble itself to make out our petitions; but God, the infinitely gracious One, will dive into the soul of our desires, and He will read there what we cannot speak with the tongue."[14] When my daughters were young and struggled to articulate their desires and needs, I didn't berate them or denounce their feeble efforts. I would help them any way I could, even by suggesting the very words they longed to utter. Will our heavenly Father do less for us? Spurgeon put it this way:

> He [God] will put the desires, and put the expression of those desires into your spirit by His grace; He will direct your desires to the things which you ought to seek for; He will teach you your wants, though as yet you know them not; He will suggest to you His promises that you may be able to plead them; He will, in fact, be Alpha and Omega to your prayer, just as He is to your salvation; for as salvation is from first to last of grace, so the sinner's approach to the throne of grace is of grace from first to last.[15]

Because it is a throne of grace, nothing is required of you but your need. Your ticket to this throne is not works but desperation. God doesn't want sacrifice or gifts or good intentions. He wants your helplessness in order that the sufficiency of His grace, at work on your behalf, might be magnified. This is a throne for the spiritually bankrupt to come and find the wealth of God's energizing presence. "This is not the throne of majesty which supports itself by the taxation of its subjects, but a throne which glorifies itself by streaming forth like a fountain with floods of good things."[16]

How Shall We Go There?

Our author answers this second question with one word: confidence. Confidence in what? Confidence in God, of course—the confidence that comes from knowing we have a great high priest who knows our thoughts, our hurts, our worst fears, and our deepest desires.

But I want to suggest that this confidence is grounded not only in what God has done but in who we are as a result of what God has done. The psalmist said of God that "He gives to the beast its food and to the young ravens which cry" (Psalm 147:9). Could it be that this is what Jesus had in mind when He said, "Consider the ravens, for they neither sow nor reap; and they have no storeroom or barn; and yet God feeds them; how much more valuable you are than birds!" (Luke 12:24). This is marvelous logic indeed.

The raven is but a bird, whose death means little. We, on the other hand, are immortal souls. No raven, as far as I know, will ever be redeemed or resurrected. No raven will ever be raptured. How, then, could God hear its cry, and He does, but turn a deaf ear to yours? No raven was ever formed in the image of God. If you heard the cry of a hungry raven simultaneous with the cry of an abandoned and starving infant, to which would you first give aid? I know, it's a silly question. But we are not better than God, are we? If we have the good sense to first attend the one who bears the divine image, will God do less?

Be it noted that Jesus refers to a raven; not a hawk or falcon or eagle or cardinal or robin or any such bird of beauty. It is to the lowly and seemingly useless raven that He appeals. If God would provide for the needs of so insignificant a bird, will He not happily and generously provide for yours. So, come to the throne of grace with confidence.

Let's stay with this analogy for a moment. Consider the cry of the raven. It speaks no words, articulates no phrases, formulates no arguments. Its cry is purely of instinct. The raven makes no appeal to grace and knows nothing of the High Priest, Jesus. In fact, Jesus didn't die for a single raven, yet the Father graciously cares for their needs. How much more, then, shall He graciously care for yours.

Nowhere are ravens commanded to cry to God, yet we are repeatedly exhorted to do so. We have the divine warrant to come to this gracious throne. Ravens aren't told to come yet they never go away empty. You and I come as invited guests. How, then, shall we be denied by Him who has issued the invitation?

The cry of the raven is at best that of an unthinking animal. Ours is the cry of the precious Holy Spirit within us (compare Romans 8:26 and following). When the ravens cry to God they do so alone, but we cry jointly with our heavenly intercessor, the Lord Jesus Christ (Hebrews 7:25). If the mere chattering of a single bird prevails upon God, how much more shall the petitions of His blood-bought child who can clench a request with the biblical plea, "Father, do it for Jesus' sake!"

So, come to the throne of grace with confidence.

What Shall We Find There?

What would you expect to find at a throne of grace? Grace, of course! But more than that, mercy too! It's one thing to find sympathy and succor, but we need strength and sustenance. We need power and energy and sustaining strength in the inner man. The purpose of this prayer isn't primarily that we might feel better but that we might get grace that will help us in our moment of need.

This grace for which we confidently and continually ask doesn't merely show us what to do, it stimulates and sustains us in the doing. Grace doesn't merely point us in the way of holiness, it infuses power that we might actually walk in that way. Grace is more than words of exhortation or cheers of encouragement. Grace is more than reasons to obey or arguments to persevere. Grace is power. Grace is energy. Grace is God at work in us to change us. Grace changes how we think, giving plausibility and sense to ideas once believed to be false. Grace changes how we feel, bringing joy in Jesus and revulsion for sin. Grace changes how we will, creating new and deeper desires for what we once found unappealing. Grace changes how we act, equipping and energizing the soul to do what we have failed to do so many times before.

If we are to have hope for holiness, we must have the heart-changing, mind-changing, will-changing work of divine grace that is sovereignly bestowed when heart-weak, mind-weak, will-weak people ask for it from the only place it may be found: the throne of grace.

If I may, for a moment, return to Philippians 2:12-13, a passage we looked at earlier, I think you'll see what I mean. There Paul speaks of "God who is at work in you, both to will and to work for His good pleasure" (2:13). If we are to resist temptation, say No to sin, walk in sexual purity and integrity of heart, God must be at work in us. When Paul says that God works in us so that we might "will" what is right, he has in mind a volitional resolve on our part. God energizes our minds and hearts to want to work His will. This is grace! This is the Holy Spirit creating in us a desire and a love and an inclination to happily embrace whatever pleases the Father (compare Psalm 119:36). When Paul says that God works in us so that we might "work" what is right, he again has in mind divine grace that brings to effectual fruition the behavioral end toward which our will is inclined. In other words, the continuous and sustained working out on the part of the Christian is the gracious product of the continuous and sustained working in on the part of God. We not only desire, we do, by virtue of the dynamic, antecedent activity of grace in our souls.

This is the grace that constitutes the help that God so freely supplies in response to the humble prayer of those who rely on Him for holiness. God helps by imparting to our souls a new taste for spiritual things that we might relish and savor the sweetness of Christ above all rival flavors. He helps by infusing our hearts with a new disposition, a fresh way of thinking, a passion for the joy of enjoying Him. This help is grace! Without it we are hopelessly consigned to living out the impulses of the flesh that will invariably lead us to the "treasures of Egypt" and "the passing pleasures of sin."

If we are to find in Jesus the fairest of ten thousand, if we are to revel in the joy He so generously supplies, our hearts must be fed with grace. If we are to see in Him surpassing excellency and for that reason say No to the passing pleasures of sin, our hearts must be fed with grace. And if we are to be fed with grace, the grace of Matthew 1, we must come boldly to the throne on which it is seated, poised and ready to help us in our time of need, and we must ask.

CHAPTER FOURTEEN

THE BURNING GOD

As we come to the close of our study, I want to return to a question I raised in chapter four:

> "Why does God care? Why is our holiness so important to Him?" Or to put it in other terms, "What is the energy behind the agenda? What is the power behind God's purpose? What is the motivation that drives God to declare: 'Be ye holy, for I am holy'?"

The answer Scripture gives is: His passion for His glory. At the risk of being horribly misunderstood, I want to replace the word "passion" with the word . . . "jealousy."

Before you dismiss this as a moral outrage ("How dare anyone accuse God of something so petty as jealousy!"), carefully consider the following array of biblical texts. After reading them, we'll come back to any lingering concern you might feel.

> You shall not make for yourself an idol, or any likeness of what is in heaven above or on the earth beneath or in the water under the earth. You shall not worship them or serve them; for I, the LORD your God, am a jealous God, visiting the iniquity of the fathers on the children, on the third and the fourth generations of those who hate Me. (Exodus 20:4-5)

Remarkably, it isn't to His righteousness or holiness or justice or majesty or sovereignty or any other attribute that God appeals, but to His jealousy:

> For you shall not worship any other god, for the LORD, whose name is Jealous, is a jealous God. (Exodus 34:14)

Here we see that the primary reason, the preeminent ground on which one might build the case for worshiping nothing else or no one else, is the fact that God's name is Jealous! In the ancient world one's name was not merely a label or a tag, but a declaration of one's character. Thus, in the very depths of God's divine character burns the fire of jealousy. Jealousy is central to the fundamental essence of who God is. Jealousy is at the core of God's identity as God. Jealousy is that defining characteristic or personality trait that makes God God. Whatever other reasons you may find in Scripture for worshiping and serving and loving God alone, and there are many of them and they are all good, paramount among them all is the fact that our God burns with jealousy for the undivided allegiance and affection of His people:

> "Phinehas the son of Eleazar, the son of Aaron the priest, has turned away My wrath from the sons of Israel, in that he was jealous with My jealousy among them, so that I did not destroy the sons of Israel in My jealousy." (Numbers 25:11)

> For the LORD your God is a consuming fire, a jealous God. (Deuteronomy 4:24)

> You shall not follow other gods, any of the gods of the peoples who surround you, for the LORD your God in the midst of you is a jealous God; otherwise the anger of the LORD your God will be kindled against you, and He will

wipe you off the face of the earth. (Deuteronomy 6:14-15; compare 29:20)

They made Him jealous with strange gods; with abominations they provoked Him to anger. (Deuteronomy 32:16; compare 32:21)

An especially interesting text is the following passage from Ezekiel:

And He stretched out the form of a hand and caught me by a lock of my head; and the Spirit lifted me up between earth and heaven and brought me in the visions of God to Jerusalem, to the entrance of the north gate of the inner court, where the seat of the idol of jealousy, which provokes to jealousy, was located. (Ezekiel 8:3)

The Israelites had placed an idol of some sort at the entrance to the north gate of the temple. Literally, it reads, "the jealousy that provokes jealousy," a reference to the passion that this object ignites in God's heart. "Look," says the Lord, "look at that abominable statue which draws away the hearts of my people. They are loving it, not Me. They are bowing down to it, not Me. I am red hot with jealousy, for I will not stand for anything or anyone to come between Me and the devotion of my bride!"

Therefore thus says the Lord GOD, "Now I shall restore the fortunes of Jacob, and have mercy on the whole house of Israel, and I shall be jealous for My holy name." (Ezekiel 39:25)

For they provoked Him with their high places, and aroused His jealousy with their graven images. (Psalm 78:58)

Then Joshua said to the people, "You will not be able to
serve the LORD, for He is a holy God. He is a jealous
God." (Joshua 24:19)

The reason they will not be able to serve God is because they
thought they could do so while simultaneously holding on to the
idols of the Canaanites whose land they had just entered.

Or do we provoke the Lord to jealousy? We are not
stronger than He, are we? (1 Corinthians10:22)

For people to sit both at the table of demons and the table of
the Lord—that is, for people to walk in idolatry, whatever form
it might take, and then to partake of the Lord's Supper, will only
serve to stoke the fires of jealousy in God's already burning heart.

There are numerous other texts that say much the same thing
(see also 1 Kings 14:22; Ezekiel 16:38,42; 23:25; 36:5 and following; 38:19; Joel 2:18; Nahum 1:2; Zephaniah 1:18; 3:8;
Zechariah 1:14; 8:2; Psalm 79:5). But I think I've made my
point. What point is that, you ask?

PASSIONATELY JEALOUS

God is an emotional being. He experiences within the depths of
His being genuine passions, contrary to those who would affirm
the doctrine of divine impassibility. The Bible is replete with references to divine joy, mercy, love, compassion, kindness, hatred,
just to mention a few. But what of jealousy? The fact that we balk
at the suggestion that God might be truly jealous indicates that we
have a weak, insipid view of the divine nature. At the very core of
His being, in the center of His personality is an inextinguishable
blaze of immeasurable love called jealousy.

What exactly does it mean to say that God feels or experiences jealousy? Most of us have seen or felt or been on the receiving end of human jealousy that is destructive and sinful and ugly. We naturally recoil from the suggestion that God might to any degree be tainted with such a terrible flaw of character.

To say that God is jealous certainly does not mean that He is suspicious because of some insecurity in His heart. This kind of jealousy is the result of ignorance and mistrust. Such is surely not true of our all-knowing God. Nor does it mean He is wrongfully envious of the success of others. Jealousy that is sinful is most often the product of anxiety and bitterness and fear. But surely none of this could be true of our all-powerful Creator—God. Sinful jealousy is the sort that longs to possess and control what does not properly belong to oneself; it is demanding and cares little for the supposed object of its love.

But as Packer explains, "God's jealousy is not a compound of frustration, envy, and spite, as human jealousy so often is, but appears instead as a . . . praiseworthy zeal to preserve something supremely precious."[1] Divine jealousy is thus a zeal to protect a love relationship or to avenge it when it is broken. Jealousy in God is that passionate energy by which He is provoked and stirred and moved to take action against whatever or whoever stands in the way of His enjoyment of what He loves and desires. The intensity of God's anger at threats to this relationship is directly proportionate to the depths of His love.

This is no momentary or sporadic or infrequent or occasional burst of anger or minor irritation in the heart of God. This is no passing twinge in God's mind. This is the incessant, intensely persistent burning in the heart of the infinitely powerful, uncreated God. In the ancient Near East, the word for "jealousy" literally meant to become intensely red, a reference to the effects of anger on one's facial complexion. Jealousy in God is not a "green-eyed monster" but a "red-faced lover" who will brook no rivals in His relationship with His people.

FOR WHAT IS GOD JEALOUS?

First of all, God is most jealous for His own glory, fame, and honor! God desires above all else that His name be preserved and promoted, and He will act quickly and powerfully to vindicate His glory. "The jealousy of Yahweh," writes Ray Ortlund, "is his profoundly intense drive within to protect the interests of his own glory (Exodus 20:4-6; Ezekiel 39:25), for he 'will admit no derogation from his majesty.'"[2]

God is jealous for the supremacy of His name in this world, in this land, in your home, in your life, and in your church. It isn't your name that He is jealous to protect, but His own. Your reputation is not first on God's agenda. His is. "For we do not preach ourselves but Christ Jesus as Lord, and ourselves as your bond-servants for Jesus' sake" (2 Corinthians 4:5).

Consider the incredible events that unfolded in the life of Nebuchadnezzar as told in Daniel 4. To put it bluntly, he was reduced to live as a cow for seven years. Why, for heaven's sake? Because he provoked God to jealousy. He claimed glory and responsibility for what God alone had done. His judgment would last until he came to recognize that "the Most High is ruler over the realm of mankind, and bestows it on whomever He wishes" (Daniel 4:32; compare 4:37).

Worse still was the judgment that came upon Herod, although the reason for it was the same as in the case of Nebuchadnezzar. We read in Acts 12:23, "and immediately an angel of the Lord struck him because he did not give God the glory, and he was eaten by worms and died." God's jealousy for the glory of His name is so intense that He may well send worms to gnaw and consume the flesh of anyone who dares try to keep a little for himself!

JEALOUSY IN ACTION

To what lengths will God go to jealously preserve the glory of His name? What does God's jealousy impel Him to do? One answer to this question is found in 2 Corinthians 2:14 where Paul says, "But thanks be to God, who always leads us in His triumph in Christ, and manifests through us the sweet aroma of the knowledge of Him in every place." The Greek word translated "triumph" or "triumphal procession" *(thriambeuo)* is used in the New Testament only here and in Colossians 2:15. Most agree that the term refers to the Roman custom in which the victorious general leads his conquered captives in triumphal procession, most often times to their execution. However, a number of other suggestions have been made.

The *King James Version* renders this word, "causeth us to triumph." Those who embrace this view contend that Paul means that he had a share in the triumph that God was celebrating. However, as several have noted, the direct object following the verb is never the triumphing subject but always the object of the triumph.

C. K. Barrett[3] popularized the view that the image is of a victorious general leading his troops, not his conquered enemies, through the city streets in a triumphal celebration. On this view, Paul is one among many soldiers, all of whom are triumphant conquerors.

Still others have rendered this, "God triumphs over us," in the sense that all Christian converts are "conquered" by God at conversion. Paul, then, would be alluding to his encounter with God on the Damascus Road. Another acknowledges the imagery of the Roman triumphal procession but limits its application to the shame endured by those who were captured. Thus, Paul is simply identifying himself with the humiliation of those prisoners who were put on parade.

The most probable interpretation is the one which recognizes an obvious paradox in Paul's use of this metaphor. On the one hand, it is God who leads Paul (and by extension, others who likewise preach the gospel as he does) in triumph. Yet, on the other hand, to be led in triumph by someone else implies captivity and suffering. Paul Barnett provides this helpful explanation:

> There is paradox here, as implied by the metaphor "lead
> [captive] in triumph," which points at the same moment to
> the victory of a conquering general and the humiliation of

his captives marching to execution. The metaphor is at the same time triumphal and antitriumphal. It is as God leads his servants as prisoners of war in a victory parade that God spreads the knowledge of Christ everywhere through them. Whereas in such victory processions the prisoners would be dejected and embittered, from this captive's lips comes only thanksgiving to God [2 Corinthians 2:14], his captor. Here is restated the power-in-weakness theme [compare 2 Corinthians 1:3-11) that pervades the letter. . . . [Thus], to be sure, his ministry is marked by suffering, but so far from that disqualifying him as a minister, God's leading him in Christ as a suffering servant thereby legitimates his ministry. Christ's humiliation in crucifixion is reproduced in the life of his servant.[4]

Or, in the words of Ben Witherington, Paul "is not saying that he is being led around in triumph, but rather that, like the captives in a triumphal process, he is being treated rudely while in the service of God."[5] Thus Paul asserts that it is precisely in his weakness and suffering as a captive slave of Christ Jesus that God receives all the glory as the One who is triumphantly victorious. Compare this passage with 1 Corinthians 4:9, "For, I think, God has exhibited us apostles last of all, as men condemned to death; because we have become a spectacle to the world, both to angels and to men."

Yes, we participate in God's triumph, but only to the degree that we willingly embrace our weakness and suffering and reproach as the vehicle through which His victory is proclaimed! We've been invited to the party, but our ticket to get in is the stigma of brokenness, humiliation, rejection, slander, and weakness.

It was also customary for those being led in this procession to disperse incense along the way. However, the reference to "aroma" (verses 14,16) and "fragrance" (verse 15) probably also points to the Old Testament sacrifice and the odor of the smoke that ascended to heaven, in which God took unique pleasure. Thus Paul portrays his proclamation of the gospel of Christ as a strong fragrance, "unseen but yet powerful, impinging on all who encounter Paul in his sufferings as he preaches Christ wherever he goes. In the victory parade metaphor of this verse, the apostle is God's captive, whom God leads about spreading the knowledge of Christ—incense-like—by means of the proclamation of Christ." Or again, says Witherington, "as God drags Paul around as his slave, the knowledge of Christ emanates from Paul wherever he goes."[6]

Earthen Vessels

In a now-famous statement, Paul declares that "we have this treasure in earthen vessels, that the surpassing greatness of the power may be of God and not from ourselves" (2 Corinthians 4:7). The important thing to see here is the reason why God has entrusted the gospel to "earthen vessels." Philip Hughes explains:

> There could be no contrast more striking than that between the greatness of the divine glory and the frailty and unworthiness of the vessels in which it dwells and through which it is manifested to the world. Paul's calumniators had contemptuously described his bodily appearance as weak and his speech as of no account (2 Corinthians 10:10; compare 10:1; 11:6; 12:7), hoping thereby to discredit his authority. But it is one of the main purposes of this epistle to show that this immense discrepancy between the treasure and the vessel serves simply to attest that human weakness presents no barrier to the purposes of God, indeed, that God's power is made perfect in weakness (12:9), as the brilliance of a treasure is enhanced and magnified by comparison with a common container in which it is placed.[7]

Amazing! This man (or, for that matter, you and I), who proclaims such an indescribably powerful and beautiful message, is himself nothing more than a fragile "jar of clay" (2 Corinthians 4:7). Many think that because of the glory and splendor of the treasure there ought to be (must be!) a complementary power and prestige in those who are its carriers. No. The unmistakable, inescapable divine design behind this incredible contrast between the splendor of the treasure and the earthiness of the vessel is so that the surplus or excess or exceeding abundance of the power may be seen to be wholly of God and not from any one of us! According to Hughes, contrary to the beliefs and expectations of the world, which thinks only in terms of human ability and accomplishment, "it is precisely the Christian's utter frailty which lays him open to the experience of the all-sufficiency of God's grace, so that he is able even to rejoice because of his weakness."[8]

If the treasure were in a chest laden with gold and covered with precious jewels, people might focus on the container and ignore the contents. And God's jealous heart won't stand for it!

If you are looking for even more good news in this truth, it is in the fact that human weakness presents no barriers to God's purposes. Lack of oratorical skills, the absence of physical beauty or strength, inadequacies in one's education, the scarcity of human resources, whatever the shortcoming, it poses no threat to God's purposes. It often only serves to enhance His glory!

I once heard Chuck Swindoll say on the radio, "When God wants to achieve a seemingly impossible task He takes a seemingly impossible person and breaks him"—of self-sufficiency, of pride, of self-confidence, of position and power, of whatever it is that threatens to diminish the glory of God's name. Those who bring the greatest glory to God are often those who are least impressive when judged by human standards.

DIVINELY ORCHESTRATED OPPOSITION

This same principle is found yet again in 2 Corinthians 4:8-11:

> *we are* afflicted in every way, but not crushed; perplexed, but not despairing; persecuted, but not forsaken; struck

down, but not destroyed; always carrying about in the
body the dying of Jesus, that the life of Jesus may also be
manifested in our body. For we who live are constantly
being delivered over to death for Jesus' sake, that the life
of Jesus also may be manifested in our mortal flesh.

Once again, Philip Hughes articulates Paul's point:

As problems and oppositions close in on him from all
sides the Apostle is perplexed, at bay, not knowing which
way to move; but, notwithstanding this, he is never in a
state of hopeless despair. To be at the end of man's
resources is not to be at the end of God's resources; on the
contrary, it is to be precisely in the position best suited to
prove and benefit from them, and to experience the surplus
of the power of God breaking through and resolving the
human dilemma.[9]

The "dying of Jesus" that daily takes place in Paul's body is
the very affliction, perplexity, persecution, and humiliation that he
just described in verses 8-9. Likewise, says Barnett, the "life of
Jesus" is "the deliverance represented by the four 'but nots' of those
verses. . . . The former (the 'dying of Jesus') were endured precisely
in order that rescue from them (the 'life of Jesus') might be experienced."[10]

Paul does not have in mind some temporary phenomenon, from
which we live in hope of being delivered. This "dying" is constant.
This spiritual dying is as much a part of being a Christian as breathing is a part of physical living. To look at Paul was to see in process
a dying analogous to that which Jesus experienced. Each time he was
delivered, each time he overcame an obstacle, additional evidence was
given that the crucified Jesus is also the resurrected Lord! By the way,
Paul was writing this in A.D. 56, after twenty years (!) of ministry,
and he is still carrying the dying of Jesus in his body, still being led

in God's triumphal procession as a weak and vilified captive.

The increase of Christ's glory in us and the expansion of the revelation of that glory to others will not displace or diminish suffering and weakness. In fact, the latter will always be the pre-condition for the former. To the degree that you work to eliminate or minimize from your life and ministry those things which provoke suffering and disclose your weakness, you lose your voice to proclaim Christ's victory and glory. When the earthen vessel starts trying to transform itself into an exquisite vase, the treasure loses its lustre.

OFFENDED AT GOD

Some of you are offended that God is exposing you to slander and suffering and reproach and weakness. You are offended at God. You don't want to be an earthen vessel. "Why do the children of the King have to live and minister in weakness and rejection and shame? Isn't it our spiritual birthright to be wealthy and famous and strong and well-respected and successful and influential and, above all, comfortable?" No. It is our spiritual birthright to be led in God's triumphal procession, exposed to the ridicule and abuse of the world. Those are the people through whom God is dispersing the sweet fragrance of the knowledge of Christ. It is our spiritual birthright to "die daily" (1 Corinthians 15:31)! It is our spiritual birthright to daily carry about in our bodies the dying of Jesus, so that the life of Jesus might ever be seen! All this because God is zealously jealous for His glory and our love.

We must evaluate and analyze our lives as well as our ministries. We must examine carefully how we use our time, how we present ourselves to the church and world, how we spend our money, how we do ministry, how we do small groups, how we worship, how we construct our children's ministry, the way we do evangelism, Bible study, church growth, youth, all in light of the standards set forth in the texts we've noted in 2 Corinthians.

But how do I keep from losing heart? If I embrace this as a

lifestyle, I'm going to get destroyed; I'll be eaten alive; I'll get wasted and worn out and burnt-out and beat up. Sam, what you're recommending is a prescription for burnout, blowup and breakdown! Paul thought otherwise, as is evident from 2 Corinthians 4:1 ("we do not lose heart") and 4:16 ("we do not lose heart"). The mercy of God and the inner reenergizing that emanates from setting our spiritual sights on things unseen (4:18) are sufficient to keep our personal lamps alight with the fire of God. And when Paul refers to our transformation "from glory to glory" in 2 Corinthians 3:18 he does not mean from poverty to wealth or from being vilified to being praised or from hard times to comfortable times or from conflict to peace.

Why is it important to understand that the energy behind this is divine jealousy? Because suffering and weakness and reproach and the stigma of leadership threaten our faith in God's goodness. Suffering tempts us to leave the path of obedience for greener and more carefree and comfortable pastures. But when we realize that God has ordained it this way to ensure that His fame be preeminent, we find strength to willingly embrace it.

GOD IS A JEALOUS LOVER!

Earlier I said that God is most jealous for the glory of His name. But God is also jealous for the devotion and wholeheartedness and loyalty and love of His bride, His people. Just as a husband cannot be indulgent of adultery in his wife, so also God cannot and will not endure infidelity in us. What would we think of a man or woman who does not experience jealous feelings when another person approaches his or her spouse and threatens to win his or her affection? We would regard such a person as deficient in moral character and lacking in true love.

If I were to receive a phone call or letter with news that a man had been seen delivering flowers to my wife, giving her expensive gifts, or serenading her outside the bedroom window, and I did nothing, felt nothing, would this not be a reflection on my lack of character, lack of love, and lack of zeal for the welfare of my wife and my relationship with her?

This is what Jesus had in mind in Matthew 10:37 when He said, "He who loves father or mother more than Me is not worthy of Me; and he who loves sons or daughter more than Me is not worthy of Me." It is as if He said, "I don't mind your loving your father and mother and children. In fact, I insist on it! But you must not love them more than you love Me. I must be preeminent in your affections!" John Calvin explains:

> The Lord very frequently addresses us in the character of a husband . . . As He performs all the offices of a true and faithful husband, so He requires love and chastity from us; that is, that we do not prostitute our souls to Satan . . . As the purer and chaster a husband is, the more grievously he is offended when he sees his wife inclining to a rival; so the Lord, who has betrothed us to Himself in truth, declares that He burns with the hottest jealousy whenever, neglecting the purity of His holy marriage, we defile ourselves with abominable lusts, and especially when the worship of His deity, which ought to have been most carefully kept unimpaired, is transferred to another, or adulterated with some superstition; since in this way we not only violate our plighted troth, but defile the nuptial couch by giving access to adulterers.[11]

This is nowhere better seen than in James 4:5, the translation of which, unfortunately, is very much in dispute. The *New American Standard Bible* renders it: "Or do you think that the Scripture speaks to no purpose: 'He jealously desires the Spirit which He has made to dwell in us'?"

Do you think God is just kidding around when His Word talks about divine jealousy? Do you think God was just filling in space between the really important verses? How dare we not take the Word seriously? The Bible isn't just any book. There is a purpose why God speaks this way and we had better take it seriously!

What provoked this statement? According to verse 4, God's people had cultivated a close intimate friendship with the world, having embraced its values (or lack thereof!). To use James' metaphor: God's people had been committing spiritual adultery. They were "sleeping with other gods!" They took God's gifts and resources and used them to pay for worldly prostitutes (not literally, but spiritually).

In verse 5 James appeals to Scripture to support his denunciation of worldliness, hoping to call them out of spiritual adultery and into conscious allegiance to Christ. But which Scripture "speaks"? Was it an unknown apocryphal work, or perhaps an unrecorded saying of Jesus? Others suggest James is referring to a paraphrase of a particular Old Testament text (perhaps Exodus 20:5). Or, maybe it was a summarizing of truth found in several Old Testament texts.

More important than deciding that question is the proper translation of verse 5 in chapter 4. Here are the options:

- "the [human] spirit which He [God] makes to dwell in us is one of jealousy and envy"or,
- "God yearns jealously for the [human] spirit He caused to dwell in us [at creation]"or,
- "God yearns jealously for the [Holy] Spirit which He has made to dwell in us"or,
- "The [Holy] Spirit which He [God] caused to dwell in us jealously yearns [for the full devotion of our hearts]."

The last rendering is the most likely one. If so, what James is saying is that the Holy Spirit is a jealous lover who will brook no rivals for the full affection of our hearts!

IN SUMMARY

In a word, the fire of divine zeal will consume and destroy and leave in a pathetic rubble of worthless ash . . . anything, everything that we have built or worked for or given our hearts to or relied upon that in any way or to any degree detracts from the glory of His name or threatens the purity of His relationship with His bride, the church. This is why God is shaking everything that can be shaken (Hebrews 12:26-29). This is why He has sovereignly orchestrated a stigma for you and me to willingly and voluntarily and happily embrace as we go forth into life and ministry. And this is why He yearns so powerfully and passionately for our holiness.

Conclusion

I MAKE NO APOLOGIES FOR THE FACT THAT MY PERSPECTIVE ON the pursuit of holiness is unashamedly experiential. Passion, pleasure, and the yearning for happiness and joy are, I believe, woven into the very fabric of what it is to be human. More than that, they are, or at least should be, at the very core of our life in Christ. It is our passion for pleasure and our hunger for happiness that will drive us either to the tawdry, temporary delights of sin or into the eternal pleasures found only in the arms of the lover of our souls, Jesus.

Some of us are right now fighting the urge to chuck it in, to bolt. You may be struggling to find a reason, any reason, why you shouldn't just quit and pursue your fantasies. The temptation to turn your sinful dreams into satisfying realities, no matter the cost, grows more powerful with each passing day. Perhaps you are feeling an overwhelming urge to leave your husband (wife), your kids, the life you've worked so hard to build. Church routines bore you. Religious activity holds no allure. You've toed the line morally long enough. The grass really does look greener on the other side. To this point, nothing has brought you the happiness and satisfaction you hoped it would. The world never looked so good.

It's so subtle. It sort of sneaks up on us unawares. We find ourselves capable of rationalizing what we used to despise. Our reasons for staying faithful gradually erode and lose their persuasive appeal. Immorality seems so reasonable. Often it sounds something like this: "If people only knew how much I've given; how I've put myself on the line time and again. You can't begin to know how many legitimate desires I've ignored and how many goals I've set aside for the sake of God and others. If you only knew how long and hard I've carried my cross, you'd understand. You'd be a little easier on me. You wouldn't be so quick to judge." When the torrent of reasons for a little self-indulgence gather such emotional momentum, it not only makes sense to sin, it ceases to be sin. It becomes a matter of justice. It seems only fair.

Why would someone turn from what the Bible says is so much to gain what is so little? I've asked myself that question a hundred times, maybe more. The answer is always the same. For some it's an issue of numbing the pain of relational disappointments. It seems the only way to deaden one's heart to the sting of betrayal or abandonment or abuse. Others can only dream of satisfying the ache, the hunger, the ever-increasing appetite for feeling enjoyed and appreciated and acknowledged. The craving to be needed and known is so intense that eventually customary restraints that keep us "in line" fall lifeless to the ground. The traditional reasons for saying No are no match any longer for the magnetic allure of tasting new fruit.

This book is an appeal for you to say No to sin. Not because the things you've trusted for so long to bring satisfaction really can. Of course they can't. But that's not enough to convince you to do what is right. If it weren't for the fact that there is something else that can, something other than the world, better than the world, more pleasing than the world, I'd be the first to tell you to go ahead and dive head first into an affair, pornography, self-indulgence, another and more expensive car, or whatever "stuff" you're convinced will turn the trick. But you'd be forfeiting your chance for a life of indescribable joy and excitement and deeply satisfying happiness and meaning and fulfillment and pleasures evermore.

Asaph knows what you're going through. He's the man who wrote Psalm 73. He was tempted to jump ship. He felt a desperate urge to switch teams. "My feet came close to stumbling," he wrote. "My steps had almost slipped" (Psalm 73:2). The reason was what he saw in those who walked the way of the world. They were prosperous, comfortable, well-fed, insulated from danger, and they happily indulged whatever sinful fantasies they could. So why didn't he join them? Because he had found something infinitely better, immeasurably more pleasing, incomparably more exciting. Listen to his words:

> Whom have I in heaven but Thee? And besides Thee, I desire nothing on earth. My flesh and my heart may fail, but God is the strength of my heart and my portion forever. For, behold, those who are far from Thee will perish; Thou hast destroyed all those who are unfaithful to Thee. But as for me, the nearness of God is my good; I have made the Lord GOD my refuge, that I may tell of all Thy works. (Psalm 73:25-28)

There it is, the nearness of God is my good. Why? Because Asaph had discovered what David knew, what I pray that you and I now know, that only "in God's presence is fullness of joy" and "at God's right hand are pleasures evermore." So come to Christ, for they who do, in the words of Edwards, "not only come to a resting-place after they have been wandering in a wilderness, but they come to a banqueting-house where they may rest, and where they may feast. They may cease from their former troubles and toils, and they may enter upon a course of delights and spiritual joys,"[1] which even the best of sin could never hope to match. Come, fall in love with Jesus.

Notes

Chapter 1—*Falling in Love*

1. C. S. Lewis, *The Weight of Glory and Other Addresses* (Grand Rapids: Eerdmans, 1965), p. 2.
2. Jeff Imbach, *The River Within: Loving God, Living Passionately* (Colorado Springs: NavPress, 1998), p. 23.
3. See Michael Brown, *Go, And Sin No More* (Ventura, CA: Regal, 1999). In this book, Brown entitles three chapters "20 Reasons Not to Sin." Brown's book is excellent in what it says. All twenty of his reasons are valid and must be heeded. But I maintain that, alone, they are not sufficient, whether individually or collectively, to energize the human soul in the face of sin's seductive power. Something more than fear of sin's consequences is necessary to resist sin's call.
4. John Piper, *Future Grace* (Sisters, OR: Multnomah, 1995), p. 9.
5. Piper, p. 326.
6. Dallas Willard, *The Spirit of the Disciplines: Understanding How God Changes Lives* (San Francisco: Harper & Row, 1988), p. 81.
7. Jonathan Edwards, "The 'Miscellanies,'" *The Works of Jonathan Edwards,* vol. 13, edited by Thomas A. Schafer (New Haven, CT: Yale University Press, 1994), p. 200, no. 3.
8. Edwards, p. 276, no. 106.

Chapter 2—*The Power of Pleasure*

1. Blaise Pascal, *Pascal's Pensees,* translated by W. F. Trotter (New York: E. P. Dutton, 1958), p. 113, no. 425.
2. Jonathan Edwards, "Safety, Fulness, and Sweet Refreshment, To Be Found in Christ," in *Jonathan Edwards on Knowing Christ* (Edinburgh: Banner of Truth, 1990), p. 166.
3. Edwards, p. 167.
4. Jonathan Edwards, "Christian Happiness," *The Works of Jonathan Edwards: Sermons and Discourses 1720-1723,*vol. 10, edited by Wilson H. Kimnach (New Haven: Yale University Press, 1992), p. 303.
5. This helpful phrase is found in the document titled "Christian Hedonism" available from Desiring God Ministries, 720 Thirteenth Avenue South, Minneapolis, Minnesota 55415-1793.

6. Piper, *Desiring God: Meditations of a Christian Hedonist* (Sisters, OR: Multnomah, 1996), p. 83.
7. John Piper, *God's Passion for His Glory: Living the Vision of Jonathan Edwards* (Wheaton: Crossway, 1998), p. 35.
8. Harper Lee, *To Kill a Mockingbird* (New York: Harper Collins Publishers, 1995 [1960]), pp. 48-49.
9. Brent Curtis and John Eldredge, *The Sacred Romance: Drawing Closer to the Heart of God* (Nashville, TN: Thomas Nelson, 1997), p. 195.
10. C. S. Lewis, *The Screwtape Letters* (New York: Macmillan, 1982 [1962]), pp. 41-42.
11. Edwards, "Christian Happiness," p. 297.
12. John Piper, *The Pleasures of God: Meditations on God's Delight in Being God* (Portland: Multnomah, 1991), p. 17 (emphasis mine).

Chapter 3—*When Serving God Is Sinful*
1. John Piper, *The Pleasures of God: Meditations on God's Delight in Being God* (Portland: Multnomah, 1991), p. 49.
2. John Piper, *Future Grace* (Sisters, OR: Multnomah, 1995), pp. 71-72.
3. Piper, *Desiring God: Meditations of a Christian Hedonist* (Sisters, OR: Multnomah, 1996), pp. 103-104.
4. Piper, p. 104.
5. Piper, p. 248.
6. Piper, p. 146.
7. Piper, *The Pleasures of God*, pp. 215-16.
8. Sam Storms, "Prayer and Evangelism Under God's Sovereignty," in *The Grace of God, The Bondage of the Will,* vol. 1, edited by Thomas R. Schreiner and Bruce A. Ware (Grand Rapids, MI: Baker, 1995), pp. 215-231. See my in-depth treatment of this passage in the article.
9. Storms, p. 218.
10. J. I. Packer, *Keep in Step with the Spirit* (Old Tappan, N.J.: Revell, 1984), p. 156.
11. Piper, *The Pleasures of God,* pp. 192-94.
12. Jonathan Edwards, "Christian Happiness," *The Works of Jonathan Edwards: Sermons and Discourses 1720-1723,* vol. 10, edited by Wilson H. Kimnach (New Haven: Yale University Press, 1992), p. 304.
13. Edwards, p. 304.
14. Jonathan Edwards, "Extractions from his Private Diary," *Jonathan Edwards: A Profile,* edited by David Levin (New York: Hill and Wang, 1969), pp. 12-13.
15. Piper, *Desiring God*, p. 147.
16. Piper, *The Pleasures of God,* p. 9.
17. Piper, p. 23.

Chapter 4—*God's Passion for God*
1. Jonathan Edwards, *Treatise on Grace and Other Posthumously Published Writings Including Observations on the Trinity,* edited by Paul Helm (Greenwood, SC: The Attic Press, 1971), p. 49.
2. All the citations from Edwards come from his "Dissertation Concerning the End for which God Created the World" in *The Works of Jonathan Edwards: Ethical Writings,* vol. 8 (New Haven: Yale University Press, 1989), pp. 405-536. An extremely helpful introduction to and interpretation of this work by Edwards is found in Piper's book, *God's Passion for His Glory* (Wheaton: Crossway, 1998).
3. J. I. Packer, *Hot Tub Religion* (Wheaton: Tyndale House, 1987), p. 42.
4. Piper, *Desiring God: Meditations of a Christian Hedonist* (Sisters, OR: Multnomah, 1996), p. 227.

5. Edwards, *Dissertation,* p. 475.
6. Edwards, p. 476.
7. Edwards, p. 476.
8. Edwards, p. 477.
9. Edwards, p. 477.
10. Edwards, p. 482.
11. Edwards, p. 483.
12. Edwards, p. 486.
13. Edwards, p. 484.
14. Edwards, p. 493.
15. Much of what follows first appeared in an appendix to my book, *The Singing God* (Orlando, FL: Creation House, 1998), pp. 195-202. I have made slight revisions to enhance its relevance to our topic.
16. Packer, *Hot Tub Religion,* p. 38.
17. Piper, *Desiring God,* p. 34.
18. Piper, p. 36.
19. Piper, p. 37.
20. Piper, p. 37.
21. John Piper, *Future Grace* (Sisters, OR: Multnomah, 1995), p. 398.

Chapter 5—*Oh!*
1. Charles H. Spurgeon, *The Treasury of David,* vol. 1 (Peabody, MA: Hendrickson Publishers, 1997), p. 63.
2. Jonathan Edwards, "The Pleasantness of Religion," in *The Works of Jonathan Edwards: Sermons and Discourses, 1723-1729,* vol. 14, edited by Kenneth P. Minkema (New Haven: Yale University Press, 1997), p. 107.
3. Edwards, pp. 108-109.
4. These excerpts are taken from the complete text as it is found in *The Works of Jonathan Edwards,* vol. 1 (Edinburgh: The Banner of Trust, 1979 [1834]), pp. lxii-lxx.
5. Anonymous, "The War Within," *Leadership* (Fall Quarter 1992), pp. 97-112.
6. "The War Within," p. 108.
7. "The War Within," pp. 108-109.

Chapter 6—*Looking unto Jesus*
1. Paul Barnett, *The Second Epistle to the Corinthians* (Grand Rapids: Eerdmans, 1997), p. 206.
2. R.C. Sproul, *The Holiness of God* (Wheaton, IL: Tyndale House Publishers, 1985), p. 57.
3. J. Alec Motyer, *The Prophecy of Isaiah: An Introduction and Commentary* (Downers Grove, IL: InterVarsity, 1993), p. 76.
4. Motyer, p. 76.
5. Sproul, pp. 40-41.
6. Sproul, p. 43.
7. Sproul, pp. 43-44.
8. Gordon MacDonald, *Rebuilding Your Broken World* (Nashville, TN: Oliver Nelson, 1988), p. 54.
9. Sproul, p. 46.
10. Motyer, p. 78.
11. John Calvin, *Institutes of the Christian Religion,* edited by John T. McNeill and translated by Ford Lewis Battles (Philadelphia: The Westminster Press, 1975), book 1, I:2 (brackets mine).
12. Calvin, I:3.

Chapter 7—*Transformed by Beauty*

1. Jonathan Edwards, "The Excellency of Christ," in *The Works of Jonathan Edwards*, vol. 1 (Edinburgh: Banner of Truth Trust, 1979 [1834]), pp. 686-687.
2. Max Lucado, *God Came Near* (Portland, OR: Multnomah, 1987), pp. 25-26.
3. Lucado, pp. 26-27.
4. G. B. Caird, *A Commentary on the Revelation of St. John the Divine* (New York: Harper & Row, 1966), p. 25.
5. G. B. Caird, pp. 25-26 (brackets mine).
6. J. A. Seiss, *The Apocalypse: Lectures on the Book of Revelation* (Grand Rapids: Zondervan, 1975 [1900]), p. 40.
7. Seiss, p. 43.
8. Jonathan Edwards, "Extractions from His Private Diary," *Jonathan Edwards: A Profile*, edited by David Levin (New York: Hill and Wang, 1969), p. 28.
9. Edwards, p. 29.
10. Edwards, p. 29.
11. Edwards, p. 29.
12. Edwards, p. 29.
13. Edwards, p. 29.
14. Edwards, p. 30.
15. Edwards, p. 35.
16. Edwards, p. 36.
17. Jonathan Edwards, "Covenant of Redemption: Excellency of Christ," *Jonathan Edwards: Representative Selections*, edited by Clarence H. Faust and Thomas H. Johnson (New York: Hill and Wang, 1962), pp. 373-374.
18. Jonathan Edwards, "Safety, Fulness, and Sweet Refreshment, To Be Found in Christ," in *Jonathan Edwards on Knowing Christ* (Edinburgh: Banner of Truth, 1990), p. 170.
19. Edwards, p. 170.
20. Jonathan Edwards, "The Spiritual Blessings of the Gospel Represented by a Feast," *The Works of Jonathan Edwards: Sermons and Discourses, 1723-1729*, vol. 14, edited by Kenneth P. Minkema (New Haven, CT: Yale University Press, 1997), pp. 285-286.
21. Edwards, pp. 286, 291.

Chapter 8—*What to Eat When You're Fasting*

1. Kevin Springer, "Hunger for God's Kingdom," *Faith and Renewal*, March/April, 1991, p. 9.
2. Richard Foster, *Celebration of Discipline* (San Francisco, CA: Harper & Row, 1978), pp. 47-48.
3. Foster, p. 52.
4. John Piper, *A Hunger for God* (Wheaton, IL: Crossway, 1997), p. 84.
5. Foster, p. 51.
6. Foster, p. 48.
7. John Piper, "Man Shall Not Live by Bread Alone," (sermon, 15 January 1995).
8. Piper, *A Hunger for God,* p. 55.
9. Piper, *A Hunger for God,* pp. 106-108.
10. Piper, p. 107.
11. John Wesley, *The Journal of John Wesley* (London: The Epworth Press, 1938), p. 147.
12. Jonathan Edwards, *The Works of Jonathan Edwards: The Life of David Brainerd*, vol. 7, edited by Norman Pettit (New Haven, CT: Yale University Press, 1985), p. 162.
13. John Piper, "Fasting for the King's Coming," (sermon, 29 January 1995).

14. Piper, *A Hunger for God,* pp. 125-153.
15. Dallas Willard, *The Spirit of the Disciplines* (San Francisco, CA: Harper & Row, 1988), p. 166.
16. Foster, p. 56.
17. Wesley Duewel, *Touch the World Through Prayer* (Grand Rapids, MI: Zondervan, 1986), p. 97.
18. See the discussion of this text in Matthew 6 in Piper, *A Hunger for God,* pp. 63-80.
19. Piper, "Fasting for the Reward of the Father," (sermon, 5 February 1995).
20. Piper, *A Hunger for God,* p. 74.
21. Piper, p. 77.

Chapter 9—*Pleasures of the Mind*
1. John Piper, "How Dead People Do Battle with Sin," (sermon, 9 September 1998).
2. Donald S. Whitney, *Spiritual Disciplines for the Christian Life* (Colorado Springs: NavPress, 1991), p. 44.
3. Piper, "Wonderful Things from Your Word," (sermon, 11 January 1998).
4. Piper, *Desiring God: Meditations of a Christian Hedonist* (Sisters, OR: Multnomah, 1996), p. 128.
5. Piper, "Wonderful Things from Your Word."
6. Edwards, "Extractions from His Private Diary," p. 26.
7. Piper, "How Dead People Do Battle with Sin," p. 3.
8. Edwards, pp. 27-28.
9. Edwards, pp. 26-27.
10. C. H. Spurgeon, *The Treasury of David*, vol. 3 (Peabody, MA: Hendrickson Publishers, 1997), p. 380.
11. Spurgeon, p. 376.
12. If anyone reading this book doubts the crucial role of the mind in the pursuit of holiness, I strongly urge you to read J. P. Moreland, *Love Your God with All Your Mind: The Role of Reason in the Life of the Soul* (Colorado Springs: NavPress, 1997). By the way, has it ever dawned on you that you can't be reading this book *without* the vigorous use of your mind? I'm almost embarrassed even to mention something so self-evident, were it not for the fact that so many in the church today would never think to think about it!
13. D. A. Carson, *Basics for Believers: An Exposition of Philippians* (Grand Rapids, MI: Baker Book, 1996), p. 116.
14. Peter Toon, *Meditating as a Christian: Waiting upon God* (London: Collins Religious Department, part of Harper Collins Publishing, 1991), p. 61.
15. Toon, p. 59.

Chapter 10—*Feasting on God*
1. C. S. Lewis, *Reflections on the Psalms* (New York: Harcourt, Brace and World, 1958), pp. 90-98.
2. Charles Hodge, *Systematic Theology* (Grand Rapids: Eerdmans, 1970), III:647.
3. John Ortberg, *The Life You've Always Wanted* (Grand Rapids: Zondervan, 1997), p. 68.
4. Jonathan Edwards, *The Works of Jonathan Edwards: Letters and Personal Writings*, vol. 16, edited by George S. Claghorn (New Haven, CT: Yale University Press, 1998), p. 754.

Chapter 11—*Sex and Integrity*
1. See my book, *The Singing God: Discover the Joy of Being Enjoyed by God* (Orlando: Creation House, 1998), pp. 77-85.

2. John Piper, *The Pleasures of God: Meditations on God's Delight in Being God* (Portland: Multnomah, 1991), p. 250.
3. Piper, p. 250.
4. Piper, p. 253.
5. Piper, p. 255.
6. Stephen L. Carter, *Integrity* (New York: Basic Books, 1993), p. 53.
7. Carter, pp. 53-54.

Chapter 12—*The Anatomy of Temptation*
1. Sydney H. T. Page, *Powers of Evil: A Biblical Study of Satan and Demons* (Grand Rapids: Baker, 1995), p. 124.
2. Page, p. 132.
3. Gordon MacDonald, *Rebuilding Your Broken World* (Nashville, TN: Oliver Nelson, 1988), p. 100.
4. Philip Yancey, *Disappointment with God* (Grand Rapids, MI: Zondervan, 1988), p. 177.
5. Yancey, p. 178.
6. Larry Crabb, *Inside Out* (Colorado Springs: NavPress, 1988), p. 146.
7. Yancey, p. 191.
8. Yancey, p. 193.
9. Yancey, p. 240.
10. William Gurnall, *The Christian in Complete Armour,* 3 vols. (Carlisle: Banner of Truth Trust, 1991), p. 262.
11. Donald A. Carson, *The Sermon on the Mount* (Grand Rapids: Baker, 1978), p. 44.
12. John R. W. Stott, *Christian Counter-Culture: The Message of the Sermon on the Mount* (Downers Grove: InterVarsity, 1978), p. 89.
13. Stott, p. 89.
14. Jonathan Edwards, *"Christian Happiness," The Works of Jonathan Edwards: Sermons and Discourses 1720-1723,* vol. 10, edited by Wilson H. Kimnach (New Haven: Yale University Press, 1992), pp. 305-06 (Emphasis mine).
15. Edwards, p. 305.

Chapter 13—*Grace That Is Greater Than All Our Sin*
1. John Piper, *Future Grace* (Sisters, OR: Multnomah, 1995), p. 79.
2. Piper, p. 235.
3. Piper, p. 248.
4. Christopher Wright, *Knowing Jesus Through the Old Testament* (Downers Grove, IL: InterVarsity, 1992), p. 7.
5. Wright, p. 3.
6. A "seal" was a cylinder of carved quartz that hung around one's neck on a "cord." If Judah had stopped to think about it, he would have realized how incredibly stupid and dangerous this was. But his fleshly passion was stronger than his wisdom.
7. D. A. Carson, *Matthew, The Expositor's Bible Commentary* (Grand Rapids, MI: Zondervan, 1984), p. 67.
8. Frederick Dale Bruner, *The Christbook: A Historical/Theological Commentary, Matthew 1-12* (Waco, TX: Word, 1987), p. 6.
9. As quoted by Frederick Dale Bruner, *The Christbook: A Historical/Theological Commentary,* p. 8.
10. Piper, p. 66.
11. Piper, pp. 66-67.
12. Piper, p. 67.
13. Charles H. Spurgeon, "The Throne of Grace," *Spurgeon's Expository Encyclopedia,* Vol. 12 (Grand Rapids: Baker, 1996), p. 206.

14. Spurgeon, p. 210.
15. Spurgeon, p. 210.
16. Spurgeon, p. 210.

Chapter 14—*The Burning God*
1. J. I. Packer, *Knowing God* (Downers Grove, IL: InterVarsity, 1973), p. 53.
2. Raymond C. Ortlund, Jr., *Whoredom: God's Unfaithful Wife in Biblical Theology* (Grand Rapids, MI: Eerdmans, 1996), p. 29, no. 15.
3. C. K. Barnett, *A Commentary on the Second Epistle to the Corinthians* (New York: Harper & Row, 1973), p. 98.
4. Paul Barnett, *The Second Epistle to the Corinthians* (Grand Rapids: Eerdmans, 1997), p. 150.
5. Ben Witherington III, *Conflict and Community in Corinth: A Socio-Rhetorical Commentary on 1 and 2 Corinthians* (Grand Rapids, MI: Eerdmans, 1995), p. 366.
6. Witherington, p. 366.
7. Philip Edgcumbe Hughes, *Paul's Second Epistle to the Corinthians,* (Grand Rapids, MI: Eerdmans, 1962), p. 135.
8. Hughes, p. 137.
9. Hughes, pp. 138-139.
10. Barnett, p. 236.
11. John Calvin, *Institutes of the Christian Religion*, edited by John T. McNeill (Philadelphia, PA: Westminster, 1975), II.viii.18.

Conclusion
1. Jonathan Edwards, "Safety, Fulness, and Sweet Refreshment, to Be Found in Christ," p. 177.

About the Author

SAM STORMS desires to see the Word and Spirit united in the lives of all believers. He is associate pastor at Metro Christian Fellowship in Kansas City, Missouri. Sam also serves as the president of Grace Training Center, Metro Christian's Bible school. The author of numerous articles and books, he contributed to *Are Miraculous Gifts for Today? Four Views* (Zondervan). His most recent title, *The Singing God: Discover the Joy of Being Enjoyed by God* (Creation House), has also been printed in England. Sam ministers both locally and abroad through church conferences. He and his family live in Grandview, Missouri.